Drinking Careers

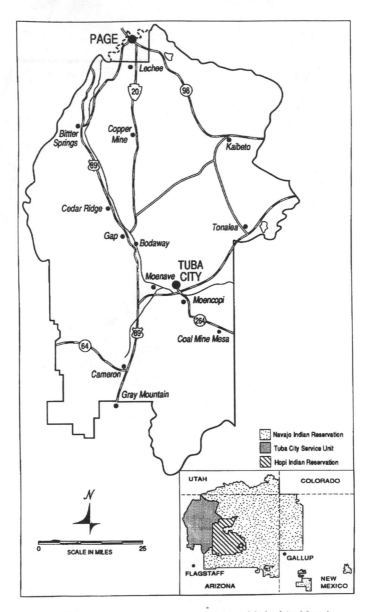

Map of Tuba City Service Unit. Originally published in *Navajo Aging: From Family to Institutional Support,* by Stephen J. Kunitz and Jerrold E. Levy, 1991, by University of Arizona Press. Reproduced by permission.

Drinking
Careers

*A Twenty-five-year
Study of Three
Navajo Populations*

Stephen J. Kunitz
and Jerrold E. Levy
*with Tracy Andrews,
Chena DuPuy,
K. Ruben Gabriel,
and Scott Russell*

YALE UNIVERSITY PRESS
NEW HAVEN AND LONDON

Published with assistance from the Mary Cady Tew Memorial Fund.

Designed by Jill Breitbarth. Printed in the United States of America by BookCrafters, Chelsea, Michigan.

Library of Congress Cataloging-in-Publication Data
Kunitz, Stephen J.
    Drinking careers : a twenty-five-year study of three Navajo populations / Stephen J. Kunitz and Jerrold E. Levy ; with Tracy Andrews . . . [et al.].
        p. cm.
    Includes bibliographical references (p.   ) and index.
    ISBN 0-300-06000-9
    1. Navajo Indians—Alcohol use—Longitudinal studies.
    2. Alcoholism—Southwest, New—Longitudinal studies. I. Levy, Jerrold E., 1930–   . II. Title.
    E99.N3K86   1994
    362.29'2'089972—dc20   92-10237

A catalogue record for this book is available from the British Library.
The paper in this book meets the guidelines for permanence and durability of the Committee on Production Guidelines for Book Longevity of the Council on Library Resources.

10 9 8 7 6 5 4 3 2 1

Contents

Acknowledgments / vii

1. Introduction / 1

2. A History of Navajo Drinking / 12

3. Longitudinal Studies of Alcohol Use / 29

4. Alcohol-related Mortality: Changing
    Period Effects / 47

5. Survival Patterns of the Original Study
    Groups / 69

6. Navajo Drinking Careers / 99

7. A Family History of Alcohol Use
    TRACY ANDREWS / 139

8. Navajo Mortality in Its Regional Context / 168

9. Alcohol Treatment and the Bureaucratization
    of Tradition / 192

10. Conclusions / 226

Appendix A   *A Retrospective Diagnosis of
    Psychoactive Substance
    Dependence according
    to* DSM-III-R *Criteria* / 241

Appendix B *Alcohol Follow-up Questionnaire* / 245

Abbreviations / 257

References / 259

Index / 275

Acknowledgments

The study that formed the basis of this book was funded by a grant from the National Institute on Alcohol Abuse and Alcoholism (5RO1 AA08153–02), "A Follow-up Study of Alcohol Abuse." We are grateful to our respondents for their patience and willingness to participate in this study, as well as to the late Amos Belone and the late Dennis Parker, who worked with us on our first study in 1966 of which this is a follow-up.

We are also grateful to the anonymous reviewer for Yale University Press, who made many helpful suggestions, and to the Navajo Area Research and Publications Committee, which has reviewed and approved the manuscript. The opinions expressed in this book are those of the authors and do not necessarily reflect the views of the Indian Health Service.

Introduction

Since the Age of Discovery Europeans have sought both to dominate and to understand the many peoples with whom they have come in contact.* One of the lubricants of domination, as well as one of the most continuously puzzling features of contact, has been beverage alcohol and the way it has been used. Europeans have recognized that they themselves

---

*A member of the Navajo Area Research and Publications Committee wrote: In their Introduction, they write about the "Age of Discovery" without realizing that they perpetuate the notion that European foreigners were first to set their feet on these "new lands" and could lay claim to lands already settled by existing populations just by virtue of their having made these "discoveries." And by their "discoveries" and laying claim to these lands, they [Europeans] feel that they automatically had the right to dominate anything and everything on those lands, including the existing populations.

Mentioning the "Age of Discovery" in this review may be considered a minor point but is, in fact, a major point to Indians because it is reflective of the authors' disrespect of Indian thought, especially in a paper about Indians.

We do not deny that other people had discovered and settled the Americas long before Europeans. We have retained the term because we are describing the attempts made by Europeans to understand and dominate the peoples who had preceded them and who they discovered when they voyaged to lands new to them, not simply in the Americas but elsewhere as well. From an Indian perspective the same period might perhaps be termed the Age of Invasion or the Age of Rediscovery.

1

have used alcohol in many ways, often with untoward consequences. Non-Europeans with no previous experience with alcoholic beverages—particularly distilled beverages with a high alcohol content—have also experienced alcohol in various ways, depending upon the situation, what they had learned from Europeans about the effects of alcohol, and their own culture and values (MacAndrew and Edgerton 1969).

Among the non-European peoples whose experience with alcohol has been especially damaging are North American Indians and Australian Aborigines. The explanations most favored have generally been either a genetically determined susceptibility or the disruptive effects of European contact, with its resulting social disorganization, deprivation, and deculturation.

This volume is a follow-up to our first book about our work among Navajo Indians (Levy and Kunitz 1974). In that book, we argued that much of the drinking behavior we observed had a different explanation. We did not think that either biological susceptibility or social disorganization was an adequate explanation—though we did believe that patterns of alcohol use among other tribes with smaller and more fragmented land bases than the Navajos' might, in fact, be explained by social disorganization and deprivation.

The research reported in this book is based on interviews conducted in 1990 with Navajo men and women (or their next of kin) whom we first interviewed about their alcohol use in 1966–67. Such a restudy allows us to look backward as well as forward, allowing us to reconsider the conclusions we reached more than two decades ago and to learn how the passage of time has shaped the lives of our informants.

The conclusions we reached in our original research were contentious; some felt we were blaming the victims for the problems that had been caused by Anglo-Americans. We had argued that there was a typical pattern of alcohol use by Navajos, especially men, which involved heavy intermittent drinking when young and which—although it looked for all the world like alcoholism as most Anglos would define it—was a normal stage of young adulthood, outgrown by the late thirties or early forties. Until it was outgrown, we agreed, heavy drinking was costly both to health and to family well-being, but it was not addictive drinking with an inevitably catastrophic outcome. If a follow-up study confirmed the trajectory of male alcohol use, then our original explanations would receive additional support.

Remarkably little is known about the course of alcohol use and abuse by adult men and women in different societies. Long-term studies have been done in European populations and among European Americans and African Americans (described in chapter 3), but virtually none, to our knowledge, has been done of American Indian populations. Suffice it to say that studying behavior across the course of adult lives in various societies is one of the few ways to comprehend the extent of heterogeneity or homogeneity in our species' encounter with beverage alcohol. Such a study is worth doing because there is a debate about whether alcohol abuse is a disease with a natural history that is everywhere the same or a far more malleable condition whose trajectory is shaped by cultural values, individual idiosyncrasies, and social institutions, which may differ from place to place and time to time. It is this latter view to which we adhere and to which we apply the term *career*. It should not be understood to imply volition, as in choosing a career, but rather—as defined in the *Random House Dictionary*—"a person's progress or general course of action through a phase of life."

Our original study was based on interviews with four groups of people, all of whom were at least twenty-one years old in 1966–67 (see chapter 5). Three of the groups represented communities on a spectrum from most traditional (the Plateau group), to transitional (the South Tuba sample), to least traditional (the Flagstaff or bordertown sample). The Plateau group comprised all the adult members of a large kin group that had been one of the wealthiest on the western part of the reservation until stock reduction in the 1930s (when the federal government forced Navajos to sell or kill their livestock to prevent overgrazing and destruction of the range). The South Tuba sample was a true random sampling of all the Navajo residents of a town in the same area of the reservation where a number of government agencies have offices and other facilities. The Flagstaff sample consisted of all the Navajos who had lived in the town for at least ten years. In addition to these populations, we included a clinical sample: the first thirty-five patients admitted to the then-new Antabuse treatment program of the Public Health Service Indian Hospital in Tuba City.

Because we had chosen the community samples as we did, we could not aggregate them and treat the sum as a random sample of the Navajo population. We did not know what proportion of the total population each represented and could not generalize our results. We subsequently became aware of other problems in our original sampling design, which we have tried to deal with in the follow-up study. Two in particular are especially important. First, subsequent work in the area from which the Plateau group came indicated not only that its members were originally from an extraordinarily wealthy family (as we already knew), but that the descendants of wealthy families, including theirs, had pursued different life careers than many of the descendants of the less wealthy or poor families (Henderson 1985). In particular, those from wealthy families were more likely to have become educated and to have made successful adaptations to a wage labor economy. Thus, the group we had treated as representative of traditional families represented traditional wealthy families but not necessarily the majority of the rural population. In chapter 7, we deal with this problem and present the contrasting history of a family of middling rank. (The history of the Plateau group is provided in chapter 6.)

The second problem was in a sense a mirror image of the first. Everyone in our bordertown sample had come from families that possessed little or no livestock even before the period of stock reduction, and their families of origin had always been disproportionately dependent on wage labor. Thus, we argued, the people we interviewed had never really been exposed to traditional Navajo life and hence had not learned to drink in the ways Navajos on the reservation had learned to drink. This interpretation was correct so far as it went, but we were looking at a small and largely self-selected segment of a large population of Navajos. Our bordertown respondents did not represent that entire poor population, as we seemed to imply, but only a small, unknown segment of the poor.

The data we collected in our original study were based on standard survey instruments, medical and police records, open-ended interviews, and participant observation (see chapters 5 and 6 for summary results). The results led us to question the then-reigning explanation of abusive drinking by Indians: that it was caused by the dislocations of acculturation and social change. We argued instead that Navajo alcohol use was learned in the nineteenth century by observing Anglo-American fron-tiermen; that the models of drunken behavior they saw were not incompatible with their own cultural values; that alcohol was consumed both at home in controlled settings by men and women and at large gatherings where young men in particular might get quite drunk; and that the effects of alcohol use were originally not disruptive, because until the 1930s alcohol was difficult to obtain—both because Navajos lived in relatively isolated areas and because most of them did not have the cash to buy it.

As the livestock economy was destroyed by the government in the 1930s and as people were paid cash for the stock they had lost, beverage alcohol became easier to purchase. Moreover, during World War II many Navajos were in the army or employed off the reservation and learned to drink in those settings. After the war, roads improved, and motor vehicles became more available. The result was that alcohol was more accessible to more Navajos. From an item of high prestige available primarily to the wealthy and their dependents, by the mid-1960s—only a generation later—alcohol had become accessible to virtually everyone. Thus, more people could drink in the highly visible groups that had been one characteristic pattern of the traditional Navajo style.

We inferred that as the drinking behavior resembled what our older respondents had described from their youth, it *was* the same and by implication would cease as people aged. Because alcohol was so much more readily available by the 1960s (particularly in agency towns like Tuba City), however, the adverse consequences of heavy drinking were especially common there. A study of the distribution of alcoholic cirrhosis on the reservation showed that it occurred at higher rates in areas near towns than it did in remote areas. We thought that this distribution of cirrhosis was caused by the high prevalence of unrestrained drinking in places like Tuba City, which put people at an increased risk of death before they reached the age when, under earlier circumstances, they would have stopped.

Although our second study has complicated our original conclusions, it has not invalidated them. It was not possible to follow the people in the bordertown sample. We limited ourselves to following the two reservation community samples and the clinical sample. To set the results of those follow-ups in context, we have also reviewed the rates of death from the same causes we first studied on a tribewide basis in the 1960s. From the 1960s to the 1970s the rates of death due to alcoholic cirrhosis, motor vehicle accidents, and suicide increased substantially and then declined—the first two substantially and the third only slightly—by the late 1980s. The homicide rate increased from the 1960s to the 1970s and has remained stable since. (See chapter 4.)

These changes, particularly in cirrhosis and motor vehicle accident deaths, suggest that the increased problems with alcohol we observed in the period before our first study persisted for another decade before declining dramatically, a surprising and welcome turn of events. Certainly for motor vehicle accidents the improvement in roads, the increasing availability of emergency medical services, and (impressionistically at least) the improvement in the quality of automobiles were important contributing factors. Beyond that, however, the changes seem to represent a major change in drinking behavior. We deal with some of the possible causes of these changes in the 1970s and 1980s. Though we cannot demonstrate it, we believe that community-based intervention programs should receive some of the credit. (See chapter 9.)

After describing the changing mortality patterns of the entire population, we deal with the mortality experience of the three reservation groups we studied. Not surprisingly, when we controlled for age and sex, survival rates were much better for the two community groups than for the clinical sample. Two findings were particularly striking in the clinical sample, however. First, there was substantial attrition in the first ten to twelve years after our initial study, but the attrition ceased about midway through the follow-up period. From then on, survival remained essentially constant. Second, the men in the clinical sample who died were significantly different from the men in the sample who survived. On average, the former were substantially younger at the time of the first study, they lived in smaller households, they were more likely to have attended school, and they tended to have had more arrests in the five years before the first interview.

These results suggest that there were at least two types of male problem drinker (defined as someone who referred himself for treatment). One was older, less well educated, and more like the people we had considered to be traditional Navajo drinkers. The others were young and troubled in some way. We do not know enough about them to say any more than that there is tenuous evidence that they may have been particularly likely to have been characterized as having an antisocial personality disorder.

We also had a few women in the clinical sample. In our earlier study we noticed that few Navajo women had difficulties with alcohol, and in fact, a high proportion of women were lifelong abstainers. When women got into difficulty with alcohol, however, it seemed to have much more serious consequences than when men did. Women were much more likely to be labeled deviant and to become victims of sexual exploitation. The follow-up study supported those early observations. Though there were too few women for the results to be statistically significant, the evidence suggests that women with a diagnosis of alcohol dependence were more likely to die in the follow-up period than men with the same diagnosis (see chapter 6).

We observed that people we diagnosed retrospectively as alcohol-dependent in 1966–67 (according to criteria identified in the DSM-III-R of the American Psychiatric Association) were at greater risk of dying in the follow-up period than people without such a diagnosis (see chapter 5). Yet a diagnosis of alcohol dependence in itself did not help us predict which ones were at the greatest risk of dying. Navajos consider solitary drinking a key indication of problem drinking. When we applied this criterion to the people we had retrospectively diagnosed as alcohol-dependent, it turned out that those described as having drunk alone did have a greater probability of dying in the follow-up period. Specifically, alcohol-dependent men who were social drinkers were more likely than solitary drinkers to have stopped drinking entirely, to have become controlled drinkers if they were still drinking, and to have survived throughout the full follow-up period. Conversely, solitary drinking is not inevitably associated with serious long-term problems: 40 percent of the men who were solitary drinkers at the time of our first interview were abstainers twenty-five years later. Social drinkers tended to be less well educated than solitary drinkers, to live in larger households, and to come from rural areas.

Of the women who had histories of drinking, those who were solitary drinkers had more arrests, more withdrawal symptoms, and were more likely to have had depressive episodes than social drinkers. Among the men there were no such differences. All the women retrospectively diagnosed as alcohol-dependent were solitary drinkers.

For both women and men, the kind of community in which they were raised seems to have strongly influenced the way they learned to drink. In chapter 6 we describe the rural area and agency town where those in our two community samples and many in our clinical sample lived. The Plateau group was a remnant of a large extended family that had controlled a vast grazing area. Alcohol use was learned in this context and was embedded in a system of mutual obligation that included co-operation in many activities associated with livestock raising. Even though drinking was heavy at times, it was markedly reduced or terminated when family responsibilities arose.

In the agency town, however, people arrived from all over the reservation to be near sources of wage labor and services. The social networks that developed comprised shifting groups of friends, neighbors, and kinspeople, and were often based on the acquisition, sale, and consumption of alcohol, which was increasingly available in the town. Behavior learned in this context was unconstrained by the responsibilities that characterized the Plateau group. In addition, the lack of knowledge of the deleterious consequences of heavy alcohol consumption was profound, with the result that within a generation several families were decimated by alcohol-related problems. In our first study we had paid insufficient attention to this phenomenon. To redress the imbalance, in chapter 7 we tell the story of one family in Tuba City that has been devastated by alcohol abuse.

The histories of the Plateau group and the family in Tuba City suggest that our initial picture of the dynamics of the changing stratification system was oversimplified. It now appears that the people we interviewed in Flagstaff represented only a small proportion of a large segment of the Navajo population that in the 1920s and 1930s had little or no livestock and thus had left the reservation. But many others of roughly the same status stayed, and many migrated to places like Tuba City, where some became involved in dysfunctional social networks. We cannot account for the choices people made, but we do suggest that the stratification system shaped the available alternatives and the options they saw for themselves and their children.

In our first book we argue that much Navajo drinking in the nineteenth century seems to have been learned from non-Indian frontiersmen (see chapter 2). In this book we pursue that line of reasoning by examining death rates from a variety of alcohol-related conditions and compare rural Navajos with rural Anglos in Arizona and New Mexico over the past several decades (see chapter 8). The striking similarities we found suggest that multiracial regional cultures continue to exist in this country that make them more similar to one another than either may be to people of the same race elsewhere in the country.

Finally, in chapter 9 we consider changes in the treatment system since our first study. It has grown enormously in size, which may have contributed to the decline of alcohol-related deaths among Navajos since the 1970s. One of the reasons for this decline seems to be that people were educated about the very real dangers of excess alcohol use—to their own health and the health of their unborn children. Our early interviews suggested that in families in which alcohol-related problems were rampant there was remarkably little discussion or knowledge of the negative consequences of heavy drinking. Whatever the effects of the treatment programs may be, the educational impact of the prevention programs seems to have been substantial.

The treatment system, however, has latent functions as well: providing jobs in a labor surplus economy and helping to preserve Navajo culture through ceremonies for the treatment of alcohol-related problems. In chapter 9 we consider these issues as well and suggest that the very process of attempting to preserve important elements of the traditional religious and healing system in a bureaucratized health care system will inevitably accelerate changes that are already under way.

We have concluded that our original work was not so much wrong as incomplete. We failed to consider sufficiently a large segment of Navajo society that had begun to use alcohol as Navajos of an earlier time had but in a different context, free of the constraints that had shaped the behavior of our rural respondents. Moreover, much unconstrained drinking behavior is based on dysfunctional social networks, a lack of knowledge of the deleterious health consequences of heavy drinking, and an exposure to a regional culture in which heavy drinking is the norm.

In respect of the trajectory of alcohol use over the course of an adult life, there are differences within Navajo society among both women and men. Some of the differences can be explained by how people learned to drink, but many remain unexplained. Among the predictors of outcome, solitary drinking is most prominent, but its origin has not been accounted for. In general, as we have already noted, there is disagreement as to whether heavy drinking is a disease with a natural history that is everywhere the same or a condition whose course is contingent upon the influence of individuals and institutions with which the drinker comes in contact. Our research suggests that there are several patterns, some with a greater likelihood of causing serious problems than others, but that none is associated with an inevitably catastrophic outcome.

A History of
Navajo Drinking

With few exceptions, the Indians of America north of Mexico had no knowledge of alcohol before contact with Europeans. In the Southwest, the Pimas, Papagos, and River Yumans made wine from the saguaro cactus in July, following the harvest of the first crops. During a saguaro ceremony everyone drank, believing that as humans saturated themselves with the wine, so the earth would be saturated with rain (Jorgensen 1980, 273). Wine made from the agave and mesquite plants was also known. The Western Apaches and Zunis are said to have known alcohol (Driver 1969, 109–10). The alcoholic content of the beverages was low, between 3 and 4 percent. Agave wine was rich in sucrose and vitamins B_1 and C and was an important and comparatively safe source of liquid in areas where drinking water was scarce or contaminated. Beer made from sprouted maize was produced in Mexico but spread north of the Rio Grande sometime during the Spanish period. Maize beer was popular among the Apaches and after with the Navajos. The informal and secular use of alcohol seems to have been relatively infrequent before the coming of the Europeans, so that none of the tribes had a well-developed "drinking ethic" to prepare them for the advent of beverages with a high alcoholic content.

The Navajos' Athabascan-speaking ancestors entered the

12

Southwest from Alaska and western Canada sometime between 1400 and 1525. By 1630, they were doing some farming and had frequent contact with the sedentary Pueblos. Other Athabascan speakers occupied areas to the south and east of what was to be known as Navajo country and over time became the distinct tribes that are today collectively called Apaches. Among these, the Western Apaches are closest to the Navajos in the development of matrilineal descent and their reliance on agriculture. Unlike the Navajos, who were pastoralists before the reservation period, which began in 1868, none of the Apaches ever became pastoralists before they were placed on reservations in the 1880s

Intensive interaction of the Navajos with various Pueblo groups began in 1690, when the Spaniards reconquered the area after the Pueblo Revolt of 1680, and lasted until about 1770. Tewa, Jemez, Keresan, and Zuni refugees lived among the Navajos during this period. According to David Brugge (1983), Navajo religion and social life became "Puebloized" at this time. Navajos adopted Pueblo architectural styles, techniques of man ufacture, religious paraphernalia, and many elements of non-material culture.

After 1770, drought, intensified Ute raiding, and a resumption of warfare with the Spaniards led to a migration of the Navajos to the south and west of their center of settlement in the upper San Juan River drainage. Their Pueblo-like settlements were abandoned, and the population dispersed. Presumably, farming declined, and Pueblo elements were diluted. By the early 1800s, stock raising had become as important as agriculture, and during the early years of the reservation period superseded agriculture for subsistence.

During the two centuries following the Spanish entry into the Southwest, wine and brandy were gradually introduced in the upper Rio Grande valley. The supply of wine, however, was so scarce that it was often difficult to fill the needs of the church. Some of the Pueblos were therefore encouraged to develop the art of viticulture. In 1786, farther to the south, the Spaniards adopted a policy of providing the warlike Apaches with brandy and mescal. Their intention was to make the Apaches dependent on the Spaniards for their supply of intoxicants (Brown 1965, 2–3). It would not only lessen their hostility and make them more amenable to Spanish direction, but it would also be profitable for the merchants. The extent to which the policy affected the various tribes is not clear, although for most Apaches, the contacts with Spaniards were degrading, and those who gathered about the Spanish settlements "not only became debauched but also to a great extent objects of scorn on the part of the Spaniards" (Spicer 1962, 243).

The policy did not affect the Navajos, the White Mountain Apaches, or the Pueblos. The Navajos did, however, participate in the Spanish slave trade, and if alcohol was available at the Taos and Pecos trade fairs during the eighteenth century, small numbers of Navajos would have had an opportunity to trade for brandy or wine (Underhill 1956, 55–56). The supply, however, was so limited that it did not play a significant role in these early experiences with other cultures.

When Mexico gained its independence from Spain in 1821, the government reversed the Spanish policy that banned trade with the United States, seeking to foster good relations and to stimulate commerce with its neighbor to the north. As Anglo-American traders and fur trappers penetrated the region there was an increase in the total amount of goods entering the area. Anglo-owned trading forts were established, and whiskey was imported. During the early 1800s the slave trade continued. Mexican merchants traded whiskey, guns, tobacco, and knives to the Navajos and Utes for horses. The horses were in turn traded to the Sevier River valley Paiutes for slaves (McNitt 1962, 17). Abiquiu, Ceboletta, Cubero, and Taos were important points of trade between Navajos and Mexicans. Navajos and other Indians traded with Pueblos at Jemez and Zuni. Zuni became a center of trade with the Western Apaches to the south as well as with Hopis and Navajos (Bailey 1964, 26, 46, 58n; McNitt 1962, 53).

The trading forts built between 1829 and 1840 were stocked with imported American whiskey for the Indian trade as well as for payment to the fur trappers. The first distillery in New Mexico was established in 1824 near Taos by four Anglo-Americans, and by 1850 "Taos lightning" was well known and highly regarded as the staple alcoholic beverage of New Mexico (Brown 1965, 5; Gregg 1954, 227). By the time New Mexico was annexed by the United States, in 1848, the supply of distilled liquor had become guaranteed, and its use in the Indian trade was ubiquitous.

After New Mexico became a territory of the United States, reports of Indian drinking escalated precipitously. It is doubtful that this was a sudden response on the part of the Indians to the disintegrating effects of a new administration. More likely it was a consequence of the American administration's attitudes toward the illicit liquor trade with the Indians and the fact that there were special agents for Indian affairs who wrote reports directly to Washington.

Mexican trading patterns continued, and Mexican traders dominated the Indian trade until the 1860s (McNitt 1962, 227). The Indian agents tried to eliminate the slave trade and the sale of liquor to Indians, and the many complaints made by the agents in Santa Fe give us an idea of the extent of the liquor trade at the time. In 1850 and 1851, agent James S. Calhoun wrote that the Rio Grande Pueblos purchased whiskey from shops within the pueblos themselves. He also found that the Pueblos became "moody" if they were not given sugar, coffee, and whiskey (Brown 1965, 6; McNitt 1962, 52). Moreover, the economy of many Mexican settlements depended on getting the Indians drunk (McNitt 1962, 23).

It is difficult for contemporary readers to visualize the drinking practices of the nation during the nineteenth century. Early drinking by Indians or frontiersmen was qualitatively different from the drinking we have grown up with in the urbanized, largely middle-class society of the late twentieth century. It was also different from drinking elsewhere in the nation in the earlier part of the century.

The consumption of alcohol in nineteenth-century America, however, was unlike anything twentieth-century Americans are ever likely to experience. Between 1790 and 1840, Americans drank more alcoholic beverages than at any other time in our history—nearly half a pint of hard liquor per man each day. The per capita consumption of pure alcohol by the drinking age population (fifteen and older) ranged from five to seven gallons a year. The most popular beverages were hard cider and whiskey. Water was usually of poor quality, milk was scarce and unsafe, and coffee, tea, and wine were imported and expensive. Moreover, Americans preferred drinks with a higher alcohol content than that of beer or wine. When they did drink wine, it was often fortified with alcohol and rarely below 20 percent alcohol (Rorabaugh 1979, 233, 113).

When the frontier moved west of the Appalachians, settlers were cut off from the East and were forced to develop their own markets. Land transportation was too expensive for the bountiful corn crops to be hauled over the mountains. Whiskey was widely produced because it was easily preserved and traded, and soon it became the medium of exchange on the frontier. By 1840 half of the nation's grain liquors were produced in southwest Ohio, southeast and southwest Pennsylvania, and in upstate New York (Rorabaugh 1979, 85).

During the colonial period, two distinct styles of drinking distilled spirits were already established. Many Americans took small amounts of alcohol daily, either alone or with the family at home. "Drams were taken upon rising, with meals, during mid-day breaks, and at bedtime." Ingesting frequent but small doses develops a tolerance to the effects of alcohol, and this style of drinking did not lead to intoxication. The other style of drinking was the communal binge, a form of public drinking to intoxication. "Practically any gathering of three or more men, from the Mardi Gras to a public hanging, provided an occasion for drinking vast quantities of liquor, until the more prudent staggered home while the remainder quarreled and fought, or passed out" (Rorabaugh 1979, 149, 150).

By 1820, routine dram drinking was dying out while binges, either communal or solitary, increased. According to William Rorabaugh (1979, 169), it was the changing patterns of drinking rather than increased consumption that alarmed many Americans and led to the organization of the temperance movement. The reformers, however, succeeded only in discouraging dram drinking and communal binges so that by 1840, the least disruptive styles of drinking had almost disappeared in the East, while the private binge remained. During the 1830s, consumption decreased rapidly, from seven gallons per person of the population fifteen years of age and older in 1830 to around two gallons by 1845.

But while consumption declined for the nation at large, binge drinking spread to the frontier areas of the late nineteenth century and became characteristic of the unrestrained drinking engaged in after long dry spells by trappers, miners, soldiers, and cowboys and associated with gambling, fighting, and whoring (Lender and Martin 1987, 48–49). Anglo-Americans, for a variety of reasons, encouraged this style of drinking among the western Indians.

After 1870, just two years after the Navajos had returned from their captivity at Fort Sumner to their newly established reservation, the westward expansion of the railways brought liquor to their doorsteps, and a new, highly visible era of Navajo drinking was born. By 1881, the Atlantic and Pacific Railroad came through Wingate, New Mexico. The railway construction camps and station towns spawned innumerable saloons that sold whiskey openly to Indians, nearby army units, construction gangs, and cowboys. Most of the towns that bordered the southern part of the Navajo reservation—Flagstaff, Gallup, Grants,

Holbrook, Thoreau, and Winslow—were railway towns. Open drunkenness was frequently observed in these towns as well as in the Mexican settlements. Drunken Navajos were a daily occurrence in Cubero, San Mateo, and other places.

It was also during this period that we find the first Navajo accounts of their own drinking in the interior of the reservation. In the area between Black Mesa and the San Juan River whiskey was being consumed at "Squaw dances" (the "Enemy Way" ceremony) between 1871 and 1888. "Lots of drunken men" were reported at "Squaw dances" near the San Juan River in 1892 (Dyk 1947, 19, 45).

By the early years of the twentieth century, bootlegging on the reservation had become a profitable business. In 1884, a bootlegger was apprehended by agency police, and according to informants, a Navajo who was becoming prominent in the 1900s built up a considerable portion of his wealth bootlegging. The practice of women bootlegging at Squaw dances is also reported before 1910 (Franciscan Fathers 1910, 217; McNitt 1962, 54).

Several of our older informants in the western portion of the reservation date their first experiences with alcohol to the period 1890–1920. According to them, riders dispatched by wealthy Navajos brought liquor to the reservation from various sources: ranches north of Flagstaff and south of Winslow, Arizona, and a still run by Mormons north of Lee's Ferry. All of them remarked on the high price of whiskey, usually a yearling calf for a gallon of whiskey. At these prices only the rich could afford to drink, a circumstance that we believe had an important influence on Navajo attitudes toward drinking.

The maize beer, called *tol'pai,* was also made at this time and was probably introduced by the Apaches. The Franciscan Fathers report that it was already less popular in the eastern portion of the reservation by 1910, although as late as 1954 its use in the Shonto area has been reported (Adams 1963, 76; Franciscan Fathers 1910, 217).

An elderly Hopi told Robert Black (pers. comm. 1969) that it was the Navajos who introduced the Hopis to alcohol. He recalled Navajos selling bootleg liquor to Hopis near Keams Canyon in 1915. In the same year, the Indian agent at the Hopi Agency at Keams Canyon said: "It must be reported that while the Hopi continues a sober tribe, absolutely opposed to the use of intoxicants, the Navajos of the reservation have been procuring more and more liquor" (Crane 1915).

By the 1900s, the eastern end of the reservation was well acquainted with alcohol. Gallup was the principal source of supply and established a reputation for illicit liquor sales and displays of public drunkenness. The reputations of the reservation bordertowns along the San Juan River and the Atlantic and Pacific Railroad differed only in degree, however. Five bootleg convictions were listed for a single week in the *McKinley County (Gallup) Republican* of 5 October 1901, and thirty cases were before the grand jury in Gallup in October 1913 (McNitt 1962, 54).

In contrast, accounts from the western end of the reservation date the appearance of noticeable drinking on the reservation to as late as the 1930s. One elderly Anglo who had lived on the reservation for many years near Tuba City maintained that she had not seen any drunken Navajos until around 1917, and even then, intoxication was so uncommon that she had to be told what was wrong with the man. A trader who had grown up on the western end of the reservation told us that drinking became more common in the 1930s as a result of stock reduction. It was not the loss of stock that drove people to drink; rather, this was the first time that many people had the cash to buy liquor.

Neither national prohibition, which lasted from 1919 to 1933, nor the Depression, which lasted from 1930 to 1940, had an appreciable effect on the steadily increasing use of alcohol. Prohibition made little difference to the Navajos, who had always been legally denied the use of liquor, and the scarcity of cash during the Depression did not have the same economic results among a people who had never lived in a cash economy. Indeed, the work projects initiated on the reservation by the New Deal gave more Navajos a cash income than ever before. The report of the Phelps Stokes Fund in 1939 attributed the growing use of intoxicants by the Navajos to the shift from a barter economy to a cash economy, the growing network of roads leading to Gallup, and the purchase of automobiles on time-payment plans. "The Navajo in the interior now has the opportunity to reach liquor sources within a few hours' time" (79–80).

Also during this period the major concern of the Navajo police force shifted from chasing Navajo stock thieves (in the nineteenth century) and bringing Navajo children to school (in the early 1900s) to cases involving alcohol. In 1937, the majority of arrests made by the Navajo police were for drunkenness or possession of alcohol (Phelps Stokes Fund 1939, 76, 79).

Since 1953, when Indian prohibition was repealed, the economic picture has changed appreciably. Now even poor Navajos have some cash, and the manufacture of cheap fortified wines has made intoxicating beverages available to all who want them at a modest price. As more roads are paved and the number of Navajos who own motor vehicles increases, there is public drinking everywhere, even at ceremonials in remote areas. By the 1960s, when we began our study, more than 80 percent of on-reservation arrests were for alcohol-related offenses (Levy and Kunitz 1974, 67).

In *Drunken Comportment* (1969), Craig MacAndrew and Robert B. Edgerton devote a considerable portion of the book to the origins of Indian drinking. Not only did Indians learn the binge style of drinking from observing those who introduced them to liquor, they also found the white person's notion that no one was responsible for actions committed while intoxicated to be consonant with their own notions of possession by supernatural agents (148–49). Western Indians, Navajos included, had as tutors some of the heaviest drinkers in the nation at the time of their most disruptive contacts with Anglo-Americans.

Most studies of American Indians attribute such deviant behaviors as alcohol abuse to social disorganization and the stress of acculturation. Edward Dozier, for instance, has listed a number of deprivations, including confinement to reservations and federal wardship, that have caused many Indians to feel inadequate. He believes that alcohol has been "the easiest and quickest way to deaden the senses and to forget the feeling of inadequacy" (Dozier 1966, 76–77). And Clyde Kluckhohn and Dorothea Leighton (1946), describing precontact Navajo culture as a "patterned mosaic," believed that under the stress of white contact, it was "becoming an ugly patchwork of meaningless and totally unrelated pieces" (237).

These interpretations accord with one of the most enduring ideas of nineteenth-century social thinkers on the transition from the rural community of feudal times to the postindustrial urban society of today. According to such authors as Henry Maine, Numa-Denys Fustel de Coulanges, Louis Henry Morgan, Emile Durkheim, Ferdinand Tönnies, Karl Marx, and Max Weber, the stability and communal cohesion of ancient society were "atomized" by the disintegrating effects of the industrial revolution. The effect of this transformation on individuals was called *anomie* and became a central concern of twentieth-century sociologists studying social deviance.

Robert Merton's (1968) structural theory of deviance, first clearly stated during the depression of the 1930s, held that deviant behavior represented a variety of responses to blocked access to the generally accepted goals of society. In his paradigm of anomie he outlined these deviant responses as innovation, rebellion, retreatism, and ritualism. Retreatism included such behaviors as alcoholism, drug addiction, and mental illness. Sioux aggression, for example, has been explained as the result of their frustration at being unable to practice their skills as warriors (MacGregor 1946, 220). Richard Jessor and associates rely much more explicitly on the anomie theory in a study of a triethnic community in southern Colorado and by Theodore Graves and associates among Navajo migrants to Denver, Colorado (Graves 1970; Jessor et al. 1968).

An early cross-cultural study by Donald Horton (1943) concluded that the primary function of alcoholic beverages in all societies is the reduction of anxiety. Anxiety, in turn, was produced by acculturation and subsistence. It was found that if acculturation were removed from consideration, societies with the most primitive economies would be the ones in which drinking was the heaviest. This was considered to be a response to subsistence anxiety and was most common in hunting and gathering societies.

The anxiety hypothesis was later recast by Peter Field (1962), who noted that the extent of drunkenness at periodic communal drinking bouts "is related to variables indicating a personal (or informal) rather than a corporate (or formal) organization, but is substantially unrelated to the level of anxiety in the society" (72). Some of the characteristics of sober societies are corporate kin groups, patrilocal postnuptial residence, and a village settlement pattern. The sober tribes, moreover, severely control aggression in their children, while the drunken tribes are relatively indulgent and permit disobedience and self-assertion. Several studies, however, are of communities that, although stable and well integrated, have normative patterns of excessive drinking (Heath 1958; Lemert 1956; Madsen and Madsen 1969; Simmons 1962). The authors of these studies explain inebriation as the consequence of the integration of drunkenness into the social order. This normative hypothesis has been more thoroughly developed by MacAndrew and Edgerton (1969, 165), who maintain that the way people behave while drunk is determined by what their society "makes of and imparts to them concerning the state of drunkenness."

We have looked at the binge style of drinking that was presented to the Navajos and other Indians by Anglo-Americans. The question remains whether Navajo drinking was a direct response to the stresses of contact or was simply an acceptance of the style of drinking presented to them and the fact that the effects of inebriation were consonant with some of the cultural values already present in the society. There is evidence for both interpretations.

The Navajos experienced two periods of intense cultural stress and disorganization during the nineteenth and twentieth centuries. The first was their defeat by the federal government in 1864 and their incarceration at Fort Sumner, New Mexico, until the signing of a treaty and their release in 1868. The dislocations were traumatic and have remained in Navajo memory as a turning point for more than a hundred years. Before this time, the Navajos' contacts with Europeans were sporadic and did not involve the majority of the population. Raiding and trading certainly led to changes, but the vast area occupied by the tribe meant that most Navajos lived without experiencing the humiliation of oppression.

The twenty years following resettlement on the reservation, as we have observed, were a time of greatly increased drinking. This period was also one of population expansion and increased livestock wealth. David F. Aberle (1966, 25–34) evaluated conditions during the early reservation years and concluded that "all in all, no picture of severe deprivation emerges." The greatest expansion of the reservation occurred between 1868 and 1886. The Navajo population had grown from about 10,000 in 1868 to 15,000 in 1880. Livestock holdings had increased from about 15,000–20,000 head of sheep and goats in 1869 to around 1 million by 1880—an increase in livestock wealth from about 2 head to between 66 and 100 head for every man, woman, and child on the reservation.

This picture of general well-being is tempered by the harsh climatic conditions of the period, which caused agricultural difficulties during the final thirty years of the century. Even as late as 1901 and 1902 rations were being issued because of bad conditions (Underhill 1956, 167), and losses to livestock were recorded for the years 1874, 1882–83, 1888, 1893, and 1895.

Perhaps the most dramatic evidence of stress in the early years of the reservation, however, was the rise of witchcraft accusations and executions, during the years 1875–90. Most scholars have attributed these events to attempts by the leading headmen of the tribe to control stock raiders and as an excuse to kill them (Bailey and Bailey 1986, 33–34). Yet a more recent analysis of Navajo testimony suggests that the witch purge represented a widespread reaction to Anglo-American domination (Blue 1988). Kluckhohn ([1944] 1962, 112–21) has suggested that witchcraft scares and purges replaced war and raiding as means of dealing with aggression and anxiety.

But if the stresses of the early reservation years were coincident with the increased use of alcohol, is there sufficient evidence to posit a causal relation? Among the earliest Navajo drinkers to be mentioned by name are two of the highest ranking chiefs of the early reservation period: Manuelito and Ganado Mucho. The fact that men of high status drank conforms to the notion that drunkenness was a desirable state. It may also indicate the despair of prominent leaders after the establishment of the reservation or—since Manuelito was one of the chiefs conducting witchcraft purges—evidence of the anxiety caused by the decline of their powers.

Ganado Mucho never became a heavy drinker. Manuelito, however, drank steadily and was a problem drinker by 1873, when he was approximately fifty years old. He was frequently arrested for drinking and died in the guardhouse, presumably from drink, in 1884 (Underhill 1956, 162–63). Ruth Underhill adopts a retreatist explanation, believing that Manuelito drank during a great period of stress and after 1873 in response to the disappointment of not being employed by the Navajo police force.

According to other sources, however, Manuelito did not die

in 1884 but was deposed as a head chief by agent Timothy
Riordan for possessing slaves and for drinking. It appears that
he died in 1893 at about age seventy-three from measles complicated by pneumonia, after treatments in the sweathouse and
perhaps too much whiskey (VanValkenburgh 1948). That Manuelito's followers were reported to have sold their sheep for
whiskey further discredits the very personal interpretation given
by Underhill and lends credence to the idea that drinking was
the proper thing to do for people who could afford it.

NAVAJO DRINKING IN THE TWENTIETH CENTURY

We gathered many statements from our elderly informants in
the early and mid-1960s concerning the positive side of alcohol
use. All emphasized the prestige status of whiskey. Only the rich
could afford to drink, and as youths they had always desired to
emulate their social betters and ultimately to achieve wealth
themselves. That alcohol facilitated conviviality in social settings
was mentioned by almost all informants. It seems likely that a
widely dispersed pastoral people, who could only infrequently
get together socially, would seek such a facilitator. Several men
mentioned that when they drank with other males, alcohol promoted a feeling of solidarity, which gave them a sense of power
and fearlessness.

A number of men said that alcohol made them better speakers
at public gatherings and that many Navajo politicians would
drink before addressing large audiences. An important quality
for a Navajo leader was that he be able to speak well and
persuasively. The Navajo word for leader, *naat'áanii,* means
speaker or exhorter, and the initiation ceremony for a leader
involved the anointment of his lips with pollen from the plants
of the four sacred mountains to enable him to make "powerful

speeches" (Wyman and Kluckhohn 1938, 5; VanValkenburgh 1948, 14).

The association of alcohol with ritual and supernatural power was never made directly. A ceremonialist once told us that he could pray and perform chants more effectively when he had something to drink. Another informant related how a ceremonialist had once asked him to drink at a healing ceremony so that he could "devote" his songs. In this context, the reference is to a facilitation of supernatural power.

Reasons for drinking that may be labeled retreatist were also mentioned frequently. Informants said that with drunkenness their troubles "fell away," they "forgot their cares," and they became less shy and constrained. The bad effects of alcohol—social, physical, and economic—were also mentioned frequently, but as generalities, and always referred to the aftereffects rather than to the intoxicated state. Thus, in the early reservation period, there is evidence of considerable stress, economic and population growth, expansion of the land base, and the rapidly increasing availability of alcohol. It is difficult, in retrospect, to assess the relative importance of each set of variables in explaining the increasing prevalence of intoxication reported, but it is clear that much of it could *not* be attributed to despair or social disorganization.

The second period of intense stress suffered by the Navajos occurred during the stock-reduction programs of the 1930s and 1940s. Although livestock holdings remained high after 1880, the population continued to grow, so that by 1930, just before the stock-reduction programs, there were approximately 39,000 Navajos and 1,370,000 sheep and goats. Per capita stock holdings had dropped from more than 65 to around 35. By the start of the depression in 1931, the reservation was overgrazed, livestock prices were low, and there were no jobs.

The aim of the reduction programs, which lasted from 1937 to 1951, was to reduce overgrazing and improve what herds were left. The per capita holdings in mature sheep and goats "declined from 20 in 1930 to 14 in 1935, when voluntary reduction was terminated, to 8 in 1940, when permits were issued, to 4 in 1951" (Aberle 1966, 72). Navajos had lost 80 percent of their per capita holdings since 1930, and as Aberle notes, a family of five with twenty mature sheep and goats could not make a living from livestock. "Reduction was sudden, cataclysmic, unrationalized, and unplanned" (1966, 62).

We have already noted that these were the years when cash had become available and levels of drinking increased. It was also during these years that many Navajos turned to the peyote religion.* It had already been practiced by the Southern Utes for some time and was known to Navajos living north of the San Juan River. It spread southward in 1936, at about the same time that stock reduction became systematic and stock permits were issued. By 1951, it had reached perhaps 14 percent of the tribe. It continues to spread, reaching new adherents in new and old areas. In his detailed analysis of the reasons for this conversion, Aberle concludes: "Although it cannot be proved that the initial spread of peyotism was promoted by the profound dislocation that resulted from livestock reduction and control, such an interpretation is supported by the lack of similar movements during the previous 65 years and by the minor religious innovations concurrently in the northern Navajo country in the late 1930s and 1940s" (1966, 353).

Peyotism differed from Navajo traditionalism in its emphasis on peyote inspiration—rather than formula and ritual—as the source of power and in its belief in a transcendental God. It was also preached that the individual was responsible for her or his own moral actions, as opposed to the traditional Navajo reliance on the "lateral sanctions on misconduct within a diffuse web of mutual interdependence, now shattered by economic changes" (Aberle 1966, 353).

*For descriptions of the history and the nature of the peyote religion see Weston La Barre (1964), Vittorio Lanternari (1963), and James Slotkin (1956).

Even though both alcohol and peyote are psychoactive substances, peyote is considered to be constructive and a medicine, whereas alcohol is said to have only illusory benefits and cannot heal the body. The opposition between the two suggests the need to deny alcohol a ceremonial status. In fact, the peyote religion has been used as a specific antidote to alcoholism by all the tribes that have adopted it.

The spread of the peyote religion has continued to this day. Whether this is because of continued acculturative stress is not easily answered. Membership in what is now known as the Native American Church (NAC) waxes and wanes in various communities. The more traditional Navajos of the Kaibito Plateau were rapidly converting to peyotism during the 1960s. Since that time, however, membership in Christian fundamentalist churches has grown at the expense of the Native American Church. Both religions preach against alcohol abuse, yet there seems to be no great abatement in drinking levels.

The causes of the phenomena we have considered in this chapter may be interpreted according to one's own theoretical taste. Increased drinking occurred during times of great acculturational stress, as did the adoption of peyotism, and both may be seen as retreatist responses. At the same time, however, a normative explanation is consonant with both the positive value placed on intoxication by many and the fact that drinking increased as alcohol became more available and affordable. It seems likely that some individuals drink to alleviate anxiety and depression, while others drink to conform to social expectations, or simply because they enjoy the experience and its effects.

3

Longitudinal Studies
of Alcohol Use

Alcohol studies are not unique in the high level of disagreement and even conflict that characterizes them, but on any scale of severity they are surely near the extreme end. The disagreements are about several often related issues that may be organized in the categories of definition, cause, and course.

By *definition* we mean whether the use of alcohol is conceived as a disease, a sin, or a crime. By *course* we mean the trajectory of alcohol use over the lifetime of an individual or a group. We include here such matters as: the ages at which drinking starts; its intensity at various points in the life cycle; whether people who have once had difficulty controlling their use of alcohol can at some later time drink in a more restrained fashion; and the differences in patterns of alcohol use among cohorts within and across societies. Such questions speak to at least two sources of disagreement in alcohol research: (1) whether alcoholism is a unitary or diverse phenomenon, and (2) whether "once an alcoholic always one" is true. Each of these positions has important implications for treatment. If alcohol abuse is a heterogeneous phenomenon, then no single treatment method is likely to be appropriate for everyone. If controlled drinking is possible for some formerly uncontrolled drinkers, then total abstinence

29

may not be an appropriate goal for everyone who has problems with alcohol.

By *cause* we mean the determinants of alcohol abuse. In contemporary debates the positions on causality are biological, psychological, sociological, and spiritual or existential. These positions are clearly related to the issue of whether alcoholism is a disease and to the course of alcohol use among and within societies. For example, the biological explanation tends to be associated with the notion of alcoholism as a disease, with perhaps several subtypes, and a more or less predictable natural history. The sociological position is more likely to take the definition of alcoholism as problematic, the phenomenon of alcohol abuse as heterogeneous, and the course of the condition as a manifestation of the career of the alcohol abuser rather than of the natural history of the condition.

Where the biological and psychological approaches tend to be realist in the philosophical sense of the term, the contemporary sociological approach tends to be nominalist (Room 1983). In applying these notions to medicine, F. G. Crookshank wrote:

> The usual medical Realist is he who, transgressing even the idealism of Plato, assigns material value in his mind to the "type" and so ultimately regards "a" disease as an object in nature, an *entity,* that attacks a patient or invades his body, and is to be recognized by its natural characters. The medical Nominalist, on the other hand, concerns himself primarily with the state of his patient and the signs and symptoms that he observes in him, and scoffingly refers to formal diagnosis—not for what it is, the identification of a particular with a generalized "type"—but as the mere sticking on of a label signifying nothing save *flatus vocis.* (Crookshank 1926, xxv–xxvi)

Longitudinal studies of alcohol use may help us to sort through some of these disputes, though not all of them are entirely susceptible to this kind of analysis. Here we consider studies of cause and course.

CAUSE AND COURSE

Longitudinal studies of nonclinical and clinical populations have different but overlapping purposes. In studies of nonclinical community populations, the concern is primarily with describing incidence (the rate at which new cases occur) and etiology, because one actually watches the condition of interest develop in some members of a previously disease-free population. Of course, since an initial survey is usually done that screens the population to determine who is already afflicted, such studies usually also provide measures of prevalence (the proportion of cases existing in a population at any time). If the population is large enough and if enough cases are discovered and followed long enough, one may also be able to say something about the course of the condition of interest. Rarely, however, are all these conditions met.

Thus the trajectory of any particular disease condition is usually the focus of studies of clinical populations. In such studies one is usually interested not so much in etiology as in course, in predictors of outcome (prognosis), and in determining the effectiveness of various therapeutic regimens, regardless of cause. Although studies of clinical populations (that is, populations that are already afflicted) are more efficient for these purposes than studies of nonclinical populations—because one must await the development of the condition—they are also subject to many forms of bias, since they primarily involve the ways by which people are selected (or select themselves) into particular groups.

LONGITUDINAL STUDIES
IN NONCLINICAL POPULATIONS

Studies of incidence may be chiefly descriptive or comparative. Implicitly or explicitly, however, their purpose is to shed light on etiology. But just how much light can be shed on etiology by such research? This question has to do with the changing nature of an adequate causal explanation in medicine and underlies some of the most rancorous debates in alcohol research.

The late nineteenth century saw a remarkable change in ideas of causal attribution in medicine. Until Robert Koch's enunciation of the germ theory and the postulates that bear his name, the dominant explanation of diseases stressed multiple weakly sufficient causes, that is, a disease could result from any of several causes. Common effects were not necessarily produced by common causes. Each patient was different, and the physician had to attend to the facts of local climate, topography, and customs as well as the characteristics of the individual patient (Carter 1985; Kunitz 1987; Rosenberg 1979; Warner 1986).

The research by Koch and other microbiologists worked a major change, for they introduced in medicine the idea of causal necessity. A necessary cause is one without which a particular effect cannot occur. Tuberculosis, for example, cannot occur without the tubercle bacillus. Thus the germ theory made possible the idea of disease specificity: thereafter common effects were understood to have common causes. This implied "a new standard for theoretical understanding of disease" (Carter 1977, 136; Maulitz 1979). No longer was it adequate to say that diseases were caused by such things as miasms, unrequited love, or crowding. Real understanding required a much deeper knowledge of biological mechanisms.

That like effects had like causes also meant that the same disease had the same causes wherever in the world it was found. Unlike the medical theories of the nineteenth century, which were based on knowledge of local conditions, the medical theories of the twentieth century are based on knowledge of causes and processes that are everywhere the same (Kunitz 1988). This was a potentially revolutionary and deeply democratic conception, for it meant that the same medicine could help rich and poor, nonwhite and white.

The new views did not, however, replace older views, which persist in ideas of multicausality and the importance of life-style and risk factors, which are simply other ways of describing multiple weakly sufficient causes. It is to the study of risk factors that longitudinal population studies are particularly suited. Such studies are of crucial importance for several reasons. First, in the absence of such definitive preventive measures as vaccines, a knowledge of risk factors is one of the few available means of prevention. For example, encouraging people to stop smoking and to reduce lung cancer does not require that one understand the etiology of lung cancer at a deep biological level.

Second, longitudinal studies give useful clues of where to look for necessary causes and underlying mechanisms. The classic investigations of pellagra by Joseph Goldberger and his colleagues is an example (Kunitz 1988). From careful observations and interviews, they concluded that the disease was the result of a dietary deficiency, not an infectious agent, but different methods were required to isolate the missing factor.

Third, and most contentious, if there turn out not to be underlying biological mechanisms that cause a variety of conditions, then it may be that our nineteenth-century predecessors' views of causality were correct, at least for some conditions. If so, longitudinal studies of the onset of such conditions in different populations will be among the few ways of identifying their causes. Motor vehicle accidents, homicide, and suicide are possible examples, though many people would question whether they are diseases at all. We may find that several psychiatric and substance-abuse problems do not have important biological causes. Indeed, it is precisely over this issue that there has been such deep disagreement in alcohol studies (Fingarette 1988; NIAAA 1985). Some investigators assume that alcohol abuse is the result of problems in private and social life, whereas others lean much more toward a biological explanation—though neither side entirely dismisses the other. Whatever the cause or causes of alcohol abuse, therefore, longitudinal studies of nonclinical populations have an important role. To date, however, insufficient advantage has been taken of this study design. Kaye Fillmore (1988) has reviewed virtually all the longitudinal studies of alcohol use in nonclinical populations. We summarize some of her results here.

First, the incidence of "unwanted drinking behaviors" is highest in young adulthood (the twenties) among men and in midlife (the forties) for women and is higher for men than women.*

Second, there is a high rate of remission of unwanted drinking behaviors. Among men the rate of remission is lowest in middle age (forties and fifties) and highest in younger and older groups. Among women the rate of remission is lowest in the forties. Thus, unwanted drinking among women begins later, ends earlier, and has a lower incidence than among men.

Third, adolescent behaviors and psychological measures that predict alcohol abuse in adulthood vary across social classes and as yet do not show consistent patterns. Among lower-class youth there is evidence that those exhibiting antisocial behavior are more likely to abuse alcohol as adults; other studies fail to find such a relation. And although some find it among the middle class, not all studies confirm such a correlation (pp. 68–74). It is far from clear whether the discrepant findings can be explained by definitional and other methodological differences or reflect real differences between and within populations.

Fourth, the search for biological predictors has not yet been successful, though there is widespread agreement that a biological causal mechanism is likely to be involved in at least some cases (see Merikangas 1990; Peele 1986; Searles 1988; Tabakoff and Hoffman 1988). For example, George Vaillant (1988, 80) has argued that heavy genetic loading for alcoholism (many alcoholic relatives) is a good predictor of whether someone will

---

*The phrase *unwanted drinking behaviors* is K. M. Fillmore's (1988) and refers to behaviors regarded as deviant in the society of the studies being reviewed.

develop alcoholism, but an unstable childhood social environment is a good predictor of whether someone will lose "control of alcohol at an early age and [have] multiple symptoms." Alcoholic family members and an unstable social environment often occur together, so disentangling causal relations requires large samples and careful fieldwork. So far Vaillant's suggestion has not been confirmed in other studies.

Fifth, longitudinal studies have examined the impact on measures of alcohol use of such social changes as increases in the price of alcoholic beverages, various pieces of legislation and modes of enforcement, and the changing availability of alcohol. Though the studies all suffer from methodological problems, such as the absence of comparison groups, the results seem to demonstrate at least measurable short-term changes in patterns of alcohol consumption.

Sixth, a subset of longitudinal studies shows that heavy alcohol use is associated with an increased risk of death from various causes. Some are evidently smoking-related, since tobacco and alcohol use tend to occur together, but there is also evidence that alcohol exerts an independent effect. On the other hand, the moderate use of alcohol is related to a reduced risk of death from coronary heart disease. (See Boffetta and Garfinkel 1990 for a recent study and literature review.)

Finally, most longitudinal community studies have been done among Caucasians of European origin, but some studies have included lower-class black Americans. These studies have come to conflicting conclusions about the value of adolescent antisocial behavior as a predictor of later alcohol-related problems (Fillmore 1988, 73). A study of a random sample of "Coloured" adults in South Africa showed that "addictive drinkers" found at the first interview were very likely to be found at the followup six years later to have remained addictive drinkers, in contrast to the high rates of remission reported in American studies. The suggestion is, therefore, that culture is a powerful determinant of the onset and course of alcohol abuse (ibid., 1988,

30–31). There have been no longitudinal studies of alcohol use in American Indian samples, except for references to the expected change in drinking behavior over the life cycle of males, said to occur among the Sioux as well as among Navajos and Western Apaches (Hill 1974; Levy and Kunitz 1974).

Longitudinal studies of nonclinical populations are thus consistent in demonstrating differences between men and women, the increased risk of death among heavy drinkers, and the short duration of unwanted drinking behaviors in some groups. So far these studies have not been especially productive in demonstrating or explaining differences in the incidence of alcohol problems cross-culturally or between historically different cohorts in the same culture. Nor have they established a consistent significance of risk factors for alcohol abuse.

LONGITUDINAL STUDIES IN CLINICAL POPULATIONS

The clinical populations are not necessarily populations of treated patients. The phrase may also refer to individuals chosen for study because they manifest a particular condition, whether or not treated. The purpose of studying such populations longitudinally is generally to assess the efficacy and effectiveness of various therapies, to describe the course of the condition, and to improve prognostic ability.

To accomplish these goals it is necessary to be able to differentiate between (or classify) afflicted individuals. There are at least two ways to do this, ways that are not mutually exclusive. One is to "stage" the severity of the condition, as is done with carcinoma of the colon and Hodgkin's disease. The other is to classify the condition on a nominal scale—not on an ordinal scale of severity. For example, a patient with pneumonia would be classified according to whether the pneumonia is viral or bacterial, by bacteria type, and so on. At one level it is enough to know that the patient has pneumonia; at another level, it is clearly important for both prognosis and therapy to be able to classify by type as well as severity.

One of the most profound consequences of the germ theory was that for the first time certain conditions could be classified by cause. Thereafter patients did not simply have pneumonia, meningitis, or peritonitis. One could say what kind of pneumonia, meningitis, or peritonitis the patient had. Clearly, classifying by severity makes most sense when the condition is homogeneous: a seriously angry mouse is less dangerous than a moderately angry lion. Until various kinds of microorganisms were described, pneumonia was a homogeneous category, and prognosis was assessed by the clinical staging of severity. Once bacteriological diagnoses could be made, "pneumonia" could be disaggregated by cause into various homogeneous types.

Only the infectious diseases can be classified by cause. For other conditions it is possible to classify by other criteria, such as the type of malignant cell in lung cancer or leukemia. Knowledge of such cell types has considerable therapeutic and prognostic significance, even in the absence of knowledge of cause. In behavioral conditions where neither causal nor anatomical classification is possible, behavior (signs) and reported symptoms are used for classification. The problem is that it is not clear whether one is measuring severity or distinguishing between truly distinct entities. For example, if the survival of a person with stage 1 adenocarcinoma of the colon is compared to that of someone with stage 4, the former will almost certainly be alive at the end of five years, and the latter will almost certainly be dead. The disease is the same; the stage of severity was different.

Now consider two people who consume excessive amounts of alcohol. One is young and has had many arrests; the other is middle-aged and has had no arrests. Do the two suffer from different levels of severity of the same condition or from different conditions?

Classification is a contentious matter among people who study psychiatric and behavioral problems precisely because there are few shared principles for gathering reliably replicable observations on which to build a taxonomy. Most of the schemes that have been developed are based on observed and reported behavior and symptoms. Because these factors are likely to be shaped by culture and social institutions (such as the greater propensity of the police to arrest young, poor Indian men than middle-aged, middle-class white men), building a stable taxonomy that is valid cross-culturally is especially problematic.

Attempts have been made to codify criteria for various psychiatric conditions. One of the most often cited is by J. P. Feighner and colleagues (1972; see also Kendell 1989). They suggest that diagnostic validity should include consideration of the following: (1) clinical description, (2) laboratory studies, (3) delimitation from other disorders, (4) follow-up study, and (5) family study. For present purposes the fourth point is especially relevant. Feighner and co-workers (1972, 57) wrote:

> The purpose of the follow-up study is to determine whether or not the original patients are suffering from some other defined disorder that could account for the original clinical picture. If they are suffering from another such illness, this finding suggests that the original patients did not comprise a homogeneous group and that it is necessary to modify the diagnostic criteria. In the absence of known etiology or pathogenesis, which is true of the more common psychiatric disorders, marked differences in outcome, such as between complete recovery and chronic illness, suggest that the group is not homogeneous. This latter point is not as compelling in suggesting diagnostic heterogeneity as is the finding of a change in diagnosis. The same illness may have a variable prognosis, but until we know more about the fundamental nature of the common psychiatric illnesses, marked differences in outcome should be regarded as a challenge to the validity of the original diagnosis.

Predictive validity is the most frequently emphasized feature of an adequate typology (for example, Babor and Dolinsky

1988, 262). It is problematic, however, not simply because one may be dealing with different disease entities, as Feighner and colleagues suggest, but because the course of the disease may differ even when initial conditions appear to be the same. Why might this be so?

Natural History and Career

In an essay on the longitudinal studies of alcohol abuse, Griffith Edwards called attention to the two models that investigators use to explain the patterns they observed: the natural history of alcoholism, and the career of the alcoholic. He defined *natural history* as "the sequential development of designated biological processes within the individual," and *career* as "an individual's sequential behaviour within a designated role" (1984, 175–83). According to the natural history conception, the disease has a life and course of its own, largely independent of the characteristics of the patient, whereas in the career conception the course of the condition is bound to and contingent upon all those individuals and institutions with whom the diseased person in teracts.

The natural history tradition is central to clinical medicine in the West. It implies observation, description, classification, and prognosis. It means that, left to run its natural course untreated, any disease will follow a predictable trajectory with a high degree of probability. It implies, further, that diseases are entities that can be classified, just as natural historians classify the wildlife they observe.

Lung cancer may be taken as an example of a condition in which neither patient nor treatment characteristics alter the course of the disease. Patients with lung cancer may receive different levels of therapy, depending on whether they are insured, but this is not predictive of survival (Greenberg et al. 1988). Nor does whether lung-cancer patients receive alternative or conventional types of therapy influence survival (Cassileth et al. 1991). The point is that the disease seems to run a highly predictable course that is independent of patient or treatment characteristics. The disease may be viewed as having an existence that is determined only by its own characteristics.

The concept of career is far more sociological. Patients are thought of as embedded in a social context that shapes both the definition and treatment (in formal and informal institutions) of their condition, how they will think of themselves, and—most important for our present purposes—how the course of the condition is influenced by interactions between patients and the world around them. In one respect, however, the concept of career has much in common with that of natural history. In the essay "The Moral Career of the Mental Patient," Erving Goffman wrote that "the perspective of natural history is taken; unique outcomes are neglected in favor of such changes over time as are basic and common to the members of a social category, although occurring independently to each of them" (1961, 127). This is to say, the careers of patients with the same condition within the same social institutions are similar—not singular—and their stages may be observed, described, and classified.

There are, however, profound epistemological differences. The natural history approach tends to be essentialist (or realist). It is assumed that a disease may be treated as a specie with an existence and course largely independent of the characteristics of the individual who suffers from it. Those who write about patient (or deviant) careers tend to take a more nominalist view. They do not necessarily deny the reality of harmful biological processes, but they argue that these do not exist as diseases until they have been defined as diseases. Moreover, so the argument goes, the very process of defining or labeling a condition as a disease rather than, say, a sin has profound implications for the person experiencing the condition and for the outcome of the condition. We may illustrate with two examples taken from our own work among American Indians.

In a long-term study of Southwestern American Indians with

grand mal epilepsy, Jerrold Levy and his co-workers (1987) observed that the incidence and prevalence of the disease were the same among Navajos and several Pueblo tribes. Yet a significantly higher proportion of Navajo than of Pueblo epileptics developed severe social and emotional problems, and when Pueblo Indians did develop such difficulties, they occurred later in life and tended to be not as severe as among Navajos.

The researchers explained their results (85): "The characteristic reaction of Navajo parents to the epileptic child was withdrawal," even in some extreme instances to the point of fleeing when the child had a seizure. "In contrast, Pueblo parents tried to treat the epileptic child as normally as possible." This "masked a tendency to deny the serious and chronic nature of the disease. . . . By treating the child as normal, Pueblo parents avoided dealing with the medical and social problems posed by the disease. By not speaking about the disorder and not answering his questions, Pueblo parents provided the child with few means of coping as he became more independent in the adolescent period."

These distinct responses to epileptics were traced to different cultural beliefs about the causes of seizures, an issue that goes beyond the scope of this chapter. What is significant is that the way each society dealt with its epileptics made a measurable and consistent difference in the way the epileptics coped with their condition, and in their life chances. The careers of epileptics differed depending upon the tribe into which they were born. This is not natural history. If anything, it is unnatural, or social, history.

A second example from the same populations concerns the differences in alcoholic cirrhosis between Navajos and the Hopis, who live as neighbors to the Navajos (Kunitz et al. 1971; Levy and Kunitz 1974). When the studies were done, in the 1960s, it was not uncommon for young and middle-aged Navajo men to drink in groups, to consume fortified wine in binges, and to go for weeks or even months without drinking at all.

Alcohol consumption was visible, commented upon widely, and accepted as a regrettable but relatively normal activity. Drinkers were not shunned by their families or their communities.

Among Hopis living in densely settled agricultural villages, alcohol use was frowned upon, and drinkers thus consumed their beverages in private. If the family and community could not control an individual's drinking, and if he or she lived in a village where traditional institutions of social control still existed, drinkers would be ejected from the community and forced to move to an off-reservation town, where their drinking then proceeded without interference.

The study results were that Hopis had much higher death rates from alcoholic cirrhosis than Navajos, and Hopi case-fatality rates (the proportion of people with the disease who died from it) were also much higher. That is, the way each community responded to its heavy drinkers shaped the course of cirrhosis. Once again we see that it is the social rather than natural history of the disease that is most helpful in understanding its trajectory.

These examples suggest not that one way of understanding the course of a disease is intrinsically better than another, but that each may be especially useful in different circumstances. For conditions like lung cancer, which run a course that seems largely independent of all we are able to measure about treatment and patient characteristics, the notion of natural history is especially useful because there are predictors (cell types, stage of severity) that may help to improve our prognostic ability. For other conditions, especially those with a chronic course and a large psychosocial component, patient and environmental characteristics may be so overwhelmingly important that prognosis early in the course of the condition may be close to impossible. Of course, the boundaries between these kinds of conditions are likely to be unstable. We may one day learn enough about various psychiatric and substance-abuse conditions to make prognoses based on as yet undiscovered biological markers. So far, however, this has not occurred.

Longitudinal Studies of Clinical Populations

Considering the problems of distinguishing between severity and type of alcohol abuse, and between natural history and career, it should come as no surprise that efforts to establish typologies based upon predictive validity have not been successful (Babor and Dolinsky 1988). It is a small wonder that in concluding their evaluation of eight alcoholism treatment centers, J. Michael Polich, D. J. Armor, and H. B. Braiker (1981, 201) wrote that "alcoholism is a multifaceted and highly variable disorder. The result of this study makes it clear that the *course* of alcoholism over time is equally variable" (emphasis in original). Studies of clinical populations do suggest several points, however.

First, clinical populations have higher mortality than do appropriate control populations (such as Finney and Moos 1991; Polich, Armor, and Braiker 1981).

Second, remission and controlled drinking are not unknown. One of the first studies of treated populations to show this was Leslie Drew's (1968) report of the prevalence of alcoholics in treatment in the state of Victoria, Australia. He showed that the expected number at older ages was much higher than what was observed and that the difference could not be accounted for by excess mortality.

Third, the effects of treatment are modest at best. Randomized, controlled trials show no differences between types of programs. Self-selected patients who stay with a program tend to do better. Clearly, under these circumstances program effectiveness cannot be said to have caused the improvement (Westermeyer 1989), although findings such as these have suggested to some that patients should be matched to specific therapies in order to improve treatment results. Nonetheless, some observers argue that the effects of treatment, though modest, are discernible (Longabaugh 1988, 268; IOM 1990, appendix B). Others say that no treatment is effective.

Richard Longabaugh (1988, 268) has summarized the results of treatment programs this way: "Within a year after treatment, 25 percent to 35 percent of treated patients will have returned to an alcohol program for further treatment. . . . Twenty to 50 percent of treated patients will have remained abstinent only one year after treatment. If the criterion is simply improvement in drinking [behavior], the percentage of improved patients remains at about 67 percent."

Fourth, posttreatment phenomena, classified as stressors, coping responses, and family environment, interact with one another and with social backgrounds, intake symptoms, and treatment to produce distinct changes, according to the outcome being measured (such as occupational functioning, abstinence from alcohol, or depression) (Cronkite and Moos 1980). Neither treatment nor patient characteristics alone predict outcome with great accuracy. Posttreatment events play a profound role in shaping the course of alcohol use.

Fifth, there are no classifications or measures of the severity of alcoholism that predict improvement, save for the obvious: if a patient is experiencing liver failure and massive gastrointestinal bleeding, someone predicting his imminent demise is probably right.

Sixth, unlike studies of nonclinical populations, there have been several studies of Indian clinical populations. For example, Robert Savard (1968) reported that of thirty Navajo patients in an Antabuse treatment program followed for an average of nine months, 75 percent showed "definite improvement." Frances Ferguson (1968, 1970) described 115 Navajo patients followed for six months after an eighteen-month Antabuse treatment period and reported a significant diminution in arrests; 23 percent continued to be uninvolved in problem drinking at the end of the twenty-four-month period. People judged as successfully treated were older and less well educated than the failures.

Moreover, the successes tended to show improvement early in the course of treatment, whereas the failures did not.

Lawrence Wilson and James Shore (1975) evaluated the treatment success of eighty-three alcoholics from five Northwest Coast tribes followed for an average of eighteen months and found that 44 percent had experienced significant improvement in their alcohol-related problems. Daniel Kivlahan and associates (1985) followed fifty people of full or partial Indian ancestry from twenty-seven different tribes who underwent detoxification in Seattle. In a two-year follow-up, 86 percent underwent detoxification again, a high rate of recidivism.

The only study in which the follow-up lasted more than twenty-four months and that was not concerned primarily with program evaluation was by Joseph Westermeyer and E. Peake (1983) and Westermeyer and J. Neider (1986). Forty-five Indians admitted to an urban university hospital for treatment of acute medical and surgical problems resulting from alcohol abuse were evaluated, referred to various treatment settings, and then followed ten years later. Three could not be located, and nine had died, all from alcohol-related causes. Nineteen were doing worse, seven were unchanged, and seven were doing better (that is, were abstinent). The low improvement rate was attributed to low job skills, unemployment, and the lack of a spouse or a stable family relationship. "Cultural factors" were said to be insignificant. Yet it was also observed that level of involvement in Indian culture was a predictor of a good outcome. Paradoxically, improvement seemed associated with becoming relatively less involved in Indian society, suggesting that forming new associations and attachments (in several instances by marrying non-Indian spouses) may have been important in becoming an abstainer.

There are often inconsistencies between these studies of Indian clinical populations and conflicting reports of the association between involvement in Indian society and the diminution of drinking problems. Such variability is no doubt partly the result of methodological differences between studies. We think, however, that there is something more at work. It seems likely that different classes and cultures (including different Indian cultures) not only socialize people differently but also exert different pressures to start and stop using alcohol in harmful ways. Moreover, there are likely to be differences in the experiences of different cohorts as historical changes influence successive generations within the same society. If so, it is important to examine the particular sociocultural setting in detail to understand better the ways they do this. This means that for conditions such as alcohol abuse—conditions with a chronic course, a highly variable outcome, and a large psychosocial component—a career, rather than natural history, approach is most appropriate, though within each society or social class there may be enough similarities to make the career more or less consistent. It also means that it is important that longitudinal studies be done in different societies, and with different generational cohorts within the same society. Comparative studies represent one of the best ways to begin to determine which of the two approaches that have been termed *natural history* and *career* are most appropriate to help us understand the trajectory of alcohol use.

4

Alcohol-related Mortality
Changing Period Effects

In our original study we used the occurrence rates of several conditions often said to be alcohol-related to assess the extent of alcohol abuse among Navajos and its rela tion (or lack of relation) to various so-called social pathologies. The conditions that concerned us were cirrhosis, homicide, and suicide. The occurrence rates had the additional advantage of being comparable to data available from other populations, such as other Indians, adjacent non-Indians, and the entire U.S. population. In this chapter, however, we deal only with patterns of the Navajo population, reserving for chapter 8 a discussion of comparisons with non-Indian populations. Moreover, we have added motor vehicle accidents as a fourth condition to the original three. The changing incidence of these phenomena reflects changes in behavior, much of which is directly related to changes in the way alcohol is used by various segments of the Navajo population. We therefore summarize the limited data on drinking patterns since the time of our first study.

The data are presented as three snapshots of the Navajo population, taken in the 1960s, the 1970s, and the 1980s. In certain circumstances the same data may be reworked to examine cohort effects. One can often show that people in one birth cohort—for example, those born in the 1930s—have very different cause- and age-specific rates of death than people born

47

in an adjacent cohort. It is then possible to make inferences about the influences at work in different historical periods that have shaped the behavior and disease patterns of people at various ages. We attempt to convert our cross-sectional period analyses into longitudinal cohort analyses, but the availability of age-specific data only from the 1970s and 1980s together with problems of census enumeration and estimation are severely limiting.

SOURCES OF DATA

The calculation of death rates from various causes depends on having adequate numerator (number of deaths due to each cause) and denominator (population) data. Neither is free of errors in the Navajo, or for that matter, in any population. Enumerations of the Navajo population have been particularly troublesome, and it is generally thought that the decennial census was significantly undercounted. For example, in our recent study of elderly Navajos on the western end of the reservation (Kunitz and Levy 1991), we estimated that the 1980 census had undercounted the population aged sixty-five and older by about 15 percent. As a result, we have made it a practice to give ranges of rates based upon high and low population estimates, and we continue to do so here.

Because enumeration of the population is incomplete, complete confidence in the numbers of people reported and estimated in each age group is not possible. Demographers have developed ways of estimating the population structure from incomplete data. The difficulty is that there is a great deal of migration and emigration to and from the reservation, and estimating the likely population structure requires the assumption that the population is closed rather than open. Thus, estimates of age- and sex-specific mortality rates need to be viewed with skepticism, and the validity of the differences in mortality experience of different age cohorts is not absolute. As we indicate in this book, we think that some, but not many, inferences are possible.

Mortality data generally come from state health departments. The fact of death seems to have been accurately reported at least since the 1960s. The cause of death and the race of the deceased are more problematic. Although there is always a place on death certificates to record the race of the deceased, it is not always accurate. In our study, however, for all the people we knew had died their race was accurately recorded. Race is most likely to be reported correctly when the death occurs on the reservation and the death certificate is signed by someone who commonly deals with Indians—either physicians in the Indian Health Service (IHS) or other reservation hospitals, or investigators for the Navajo Police Department.

Even when the correct race is recorded, tribal affiliation may not be. In any event, when deaths are aggregated for reporting purposes, the tribe name is not included. Tribal membership is inferred when an Indian dies whose place of residence is considered to be part of a particular "service area." Thus, an Indian whose residence is given as a community on the Navajo reservation is assumed to be a Navajo. Any non-Navajo Indian who dies while residing on the reservation or in an adjacent community considered part of the Navajo Service Area is thus reported as a Navajo death. This is more likely to be a problem in bordertowns than on the Navajo reservation, but it represents a potential bias, especially when considering numerically rare events.

Moreover, the population for which rates are calculated has changed. Until 1972 any Indian death in Coconino, Apache, and Navajo counties, Arizona, McKinley and San Juan counties, New Mexico, and San Juan County, Utah, were considered to be Navajos. This population included both Hopi and Zuni Indians within the Navajo population. In 1972 the system changed, and Indian deaths were tabulated by community of residence, which allowed a much more precise designation of the residence as being on the Navajo or on another reservation. The bordertowns of Flagstaff, Winslow, and Holbrook, Arizona, and Gallup and Farmington, New Mexico, continued to be included within the Navajo Area. Because the Hopi and Zuni populations are so small compared to the Navajo population, it seems unlikely that this change could cause a major change in the estimated death rates from a variety of causes.*

There is, finally, the question of diagnostic adequacy. There are two issues here. One has to do with the validity of the diagnosis recorded on the death certificate. In our study of elderly people, 30 percent died at home, and the deaths were investigated by a police coroner. It was not always clear that the cause assigned by the coroner was valid (Kunitz and Levy 1991, 106). The second issue has to do with the number of causes tabulated. Generally people with chronic diseases die of multiple causes, but for reporting purposes only the primary cause may be used. These problems are generic—no worse for Navajos than for other people in the United States—and we have accepted the reported diagnoses without attempting to correct them. There are also problems specific to particular conditions, which we deal with when we discuss those conditions. In Table 4.1 we give the estimates of death rates in the 1960s, 1970s, and 1980s for four conditions commonly considered to be alcohol-related.† We discuss each in turn, paying attention to the problems of estimation.

*The change in definition of the Navajo Area that occurred in 1972 is concurrent with increases in mortality from several causes that we discuss in this chapter. Not all causes of mortality increased, however: crude infant and maternal mortality rates declined steadily through the 1950s, 1960s, and 1970s, suggesting that the change in boundaries of the Navajo Area was not associated with an overall increase in mortality that would have been accounted for by changes in the record-keeping system itself.

†The rates are all crude rather than age-adjusted since we are concerned here with comparisons of trends within the Navajo population. The age structure of the Navajo population is not well known but is not thought to have changed dramatically from the 1960s through the 1980s.

ALCOHOLIC CIRRHOSIS

Alcoholic cirrhosis is a widely used but very imperfect measure of alcohol consumption. It is an indicator of steady drinking rather than of binges separated by weeks or months of absti-

Table 4.1 Mortality Rates per 100,000 owing to Various Causes, Navajo Indians, 1960s–1980s

Cause	1960s	1970s	1980s
Alcoholic cirrhosis	[1] (a)6.2–7.1 (b) 14.1 (c) 15.1–17.3	[2] 18.1–20.6	[3] 9.7–11.0
Motor vehicle accidents	[4] (a) 54.6–62.8 (b) 66.0–75.5	[5] 114.8–130.6	[6] 77.3–88.0
Homicide	[7] (a) 10.6 (b) 8.0–9.2 (c) 4.5–5.3	[8] 15.6–17.9	[9] 17.3–19.7
Suicide	[10] (a) 8.3 (b) 9.4 (c) 2.7–3	[11] 14.4–16.6	[12] 11.6–13.2

[1] (a) Kunitz, Levy, and Everett, 1969, years 1965–67; (b) IHS 1971, years 1965–67; (c) IHS 1970, year 1968
[2] Kunitz 1983, 104. Average annual rates, 1972–78
[3] NAIHS (unpublished data provided by Michael Everett). Average annual rate, 1985–88. These figures are for alcoholic liver disease (ICDA-9 codes 571.0–571.3). If codes 571.5 (cirrhosis without mention of alcohol) and 571.6 (biliary cirrhosis) are included, the rate increases to 11.9–13.6.
[4] (a) Brown et al. 1970, for single year 1968; (b) IHS 1970, for 1968
[5] Kunitz 1983, 101–2. Average annual rate, 1972–78, recalculated using IHS population figures (NAIHS 1989)
[6] NAIHS (unpublished data). Average annual rates, 1985–88
[7] (a) IHS 1971, 28. Average annual rate, 1965–67; (b) IHS 1970, 30, rate for single year 1968; (c) Levy, Kunitz, and Everett 1969, average annual criminal homicide rate, 1956–65
[8] Kunitz 1983, 107, average annual rate, 1972–78
[9] NAIHS 1990, average annual rate, 1985–87
[10] (a) Levy 1965, average annual rate, 1954–63; (b) IHS 1971, 28, average annual rate, 1965–67; (c) IHS 1970, 39, rate for single year 1968
[11] Kunitz 1983, 109, average annual rate 1972–78
[12] NAIHS 1990, average annual rate, 1985–87

nence and an adequate diet. In our first study, we were surprised that the death rate from cirrhosis was lower than both the national rate and the rate of the neighboring Hopis (Kunitz, Levy, and Everett 1969). The data for that study were collected from hospital records, not death certificates, and considerable ascertainment bias may have resulted. That is, not everyone with cirrhosis may have been known to the hospital system. Two Indian Health Service reports based on analyses of death certificates did indeed produce higher estimates (see table 4.1): an average annual rate of 14.1 per 100,000 in 1965–67, and 15.1–17.3 in 1968.‡ On the other hand, the Indian Health Service estimates include Hopis and Zunis in the years before 1972, so those rates may be inflated. It is probably safest to assume that the true rate lies somewhere between 7 and 14 per 100,000 per year.

Using the hospital data for fatal and nonfatal cases, we observed that cirrhotics were found in greater than expected numbers in the area around Gallup, New Mexico, as well as in other border areas, and in smaller than expected numbers in more remote areas. The 1968 mortality data display the same pattern (IHS 1970).§

As table 4.1 indicates, no matter what source of data one uses, death rates from cirrhosis increased from the 1960s to the 1970s. Age-specific rates in the 1970s showed a pattern for both males and females that was very different from the one observed

‡The rate from 1965–67 (IHS 1971) is based on the census estimate of population, which (as we have said) is generally regarded as too low. Thus, the rate may have been inflated slightly. We estimate it to have been between 12.0 and 14.1 per 100,000. On the other hand, the comparisons we made with the Hopi and White Mountain Apache tribes, in which the data were also collected from hospital discharge sheets, are still valid. That is to say, even using these new sources of data, the Navajo rate remains lower than the rates we originally reported for Hopis and White Mountain Apaches (Kunitz et al. 1971).

§The 1965–67 data cannot be used for such an analysis since only the rate for the entire population was presented, not the number of cases and their places of residence.

among Anglo-Americans. Navajo deaths peaked in the thirties, whereas Anglo deaths peaked in the fifties. The age groups that accounted for the great elevation in the 1970s were men 25–44 and women 25–54 (Kunitz 1983, 104). These patterns changed in the late 1980s, as table 4.2 indicates.

Considering the uncertainty of the population estimates and the small size of the oldest age groups, we are not confident about the precise rates we have reported. What we do think is substantively important, however, is the sizable drop in the rates for both women and men in the age group 35–44. In our previous work we were impressed that the very high age specific rates of violent and alcohol-related deaths declined in the early forties as though men in particular had passed a crisis point and entered a new phase of their lives. We were writing of people born no later than 1945. The people aged 35–44 in 1985–88 were born between the late 1930s and early 1950s, and one

Table 4.2 Average Annual Navajo Death Rates per 100,000 from Alcoholic Cirrhosis, by Age and Sex, 1972–78 and 1985–88

Age Group	Males		Females	
	1972–78[a]	1985–88[b]	1972–78[a]	1985–88[b]
25–34	62	49.7	28	27.9
35–44	103	50.2	58	20.7
45–54	46	55	47	35
55–64	52	0	31	33.3
>65	23	13.2	33	0

[a] Kunitz 1983, 104. These rates are based on what we believe to be high population estimates. The rates might therefore be as much as 15% higher.

[b] Calculated from unpublished data from the Navajo Area Indian Health Service. The population estimates are likely to be low. Higher population estimates would produce rates as much as 15% lower. Cirrhosis includes alcoholic fatty liver, alcoholic hepatitis, alcoholic cirrhosis, and alcoholic liver damage but excludes nonalcoholic cirrhosis (11 male and 6 female deaths; the youngest died in their early forties, the majority in their fifties and sixties).

wonders what in the historical experience of this cohort would have caused a change of such magnitude. As we describe in chapter 9, the period from the 1970s to the 1980s saw a great expansion of community-based prevention and treatment programs, and although temporal association does not prove causality, we think the association is not coincidental.

In general, the evidence suggests that by the 1980s mortality from cirrhosis had declined precipitously, roughly parallel to national trends (Grant, Zobeck, and Pickering 1990). Moreover, it was especially dramatic among men. We estimated the average annual rates for men and women in 1972–78 as 21.8 and 14.7, respectively, based upon high population estimates (Kunitz 1983, 104). The comparable figures in 1985–88 are 11 and 8.5, a decrease of 50 percent among men and 42 percent among women.**

MOTOR VEHICLE ACCIDENTS

Accidents are the leading cause of death among Navajos. Of these, motor vehicle accidents constitute the single largest proportion, and it is said that many (if not most) of them are alcohol-related. We did not collect data on accidents in our first study, but fortunately a study done at about the same time did (Brown et al. 1970). It was based upon data collected from hospital emergency rooms and clinics, discharges from in-patient stays, and free-standing clinics from 1 November 1966 through 31 October 1967. Pedestrian-motor vehicle accidents accounted for the greatest number of fatalities ($N = 55$). Collisions of other types accounted for four additional deaths. There was no information about alcohol involvement. The age-specific rates

---

**The cirrhosis rates in 1985–88 are calculated for the International Classification of Diseases Adopted (ICDA)–9 codes 571.0, 571.1, 571.2, and 571.3, all alcohol-related. If codes 571.5 and 571.6 are added, the rates for men are 13.9–15.8, and for women 10.0–11.4.

of death for all accidents formed a broad plateau in the age groups 25–54 for men and a sharp peak in the 35–44 age group among women. Men had about three times as high a rate as women (again, from all causes). The crude rate of death from motor vehicle accidents ($N = 59$) was between 54.6 and 62.8 per 100,000 for both sexes combined and constituted almost 50 percent of all accidental deaths.

An analysis of the vital statistics of Indians in the Navajo Area in calendar year 1968 (IHS 1970), based on death certificates, reported 156 deaths from accidents of all types, including 74 from motor vehicle accidents (47 percent). The estimated rate was thus between 66 and 75.5 per 100,000 (see table 4.1). As in the case of cirrhosis, there appears to have been underreporting when hospital records only were used, but the proportion of all accidental deaths due to motor vehicles was essentially the same (about 50 percent), as were the peak ages of mortality—the twenties and thirties.

Yet another Indian Health Service publication estimated the 1965–67 average annual mortality rate from accidents of all types to be 175.1 per 100,000 (IHS 1971, 28). If 50 percent were the result of motor vehicle accidents, then the rate owing to this cause was about 66 per 100,000.

The data from the 1960s stand in stark contrast to those from the following decade, when the annual average number of motor vehicle accident deaths was 151 (from 1972 through 1978) and the average annual rate per 100,000 was between 114.8 and 130.6. Again, as in the case of cirrhosis, this appears to represent a real increase, not simply a result of deficient case ascertainment in the 1960s. The rates were three times higher for men than women. They were highest for men in the 25–34 age group, but in fact they were remarkably high starting from the late teens right through to the sixties. Multiple-regression analyses of both the mortality rates and the hospitalization rates suggested that they were highest in the most densely settled areas of the reservation (Kunitz 1983, 101–2).

As in the case of cirrhosis, there was a dramatic decline of about one-third in deaths from this cause from the 1970s to the 1980s. The sex ratio remained unchanged, however: about three times as many men as women died in motor vehicle accidents (men, 119.6–136.2; women, 36.7–41.8 per 100,000 were the average annual rates for 1985–88). This pattern of decreasing rates of death since the 1970s parallels the national pattern, just as cirrhosis deaths do (Zobeck et al. 1991).

Unlike cirrhosis deaths, however, which showed a particularly dramatic decline in the 35–44 age group, there was a general decline of motor vehicle accident deaths in virtually all age categories (see table 4.3). This is not surprising considering that not all fatal accidents are alcohol-related, and that when an accident does occur, people of all ages and levels of sobriety may be involved, whether or not the driver was drunk.

The assumption underlying discussions of motor vehicle accidents is that they are caused primarily by drunken drivers.

Table 4.3 Average Annual Navajo Motor Vehicle Accident Death Rates per 100,000 by Age and Sex, 1972–78 and 1985–88

Age	Males		Females	
	1972–78[a]	1985–88[b]	1972–78[a]	1985–88[b]
<10	31.9	30	29	18
10–14	32.3	19	11	5.4
15–24	287	233	78	50
25–34	392	337	93	86
35–44	225	251	88	62
45–54	202	100	72	42
55–64	249	147	31	50
>65	201	152	53	82

[a] Kunitz 1983, 102. Based on high population estimates. The use of low estimates results in rates as much as 15% higher than those in the table.

[b] Based on unpublished data from the Navajo Area Indian Health Service. The population estimates may be low; higher population estimates would produce rates as much as 15% lower.

Only one study has attempted a careful analysis of the association, however. Philip Katz and Philip May (1979) analyzed police reports of motor vehicle accidents on the Navajo reservation for the years 1973–75. Even these data are subject to a potential downward bias because blood-alcohol levels were not known. Instead the investigating officer checked a box stating that the subject had been drinking, or left it blank if the subject had not been drinking. Katz and May (1979, 65) concluded, "For Indian cases the proportion of alcohol involvement for single-vehicle, multiple-vehicle, and single-vehicle/pedestrian accidents is 41 percent, 46 percent, and 44 percent respectively." They went on to point out that studies in other populations had reported higher rates of alcohol involvement in fatal motor vehicle accidents, but that those studies had used blood-alcohol levels—not simply the investigating officer's impressions—which may well have missed subtle signs of intoxication. Nonetheless, if even half the accidents were associated with drunken driving, the carnage due to alcohol use is substantial because the total rate was so high.†† It should be clear, however, that many other forces are at work to produce high accident rates, including poorly engineered roads, poorly maintained vehicles, inadequate driver training, and the great distances many people must drive for work, shopping, and medical care, not to mention for alcohol. Thus, to invoke alcohol abuse as the major determinant not only oversimplifies the problem but has the effect of blaming the victim for what may often be environmental conditions beyond his or her control.

It is unfortunate that as yet there has been no repeat of the study by Katz and May. In light of the decline in alcoholic cirrhosis and the parallel decline in motor vehicle fatalities, it would be important to know whether changes in alcohol-con-

††The Indian Health Service assumes that 60 percent of motor vehicle accident deaths are alcohol-related (NAIHS 1990).

sumption patterns are responsible for the reduction in accidents, as they must be for alcoholic cirrhosis.

HOMICIDE AND SUICIDE

Like motor vehicle accidents, homicide and suicide are often assumed to be causally associated with alcohol use. We discuss them together because in earlier studies we have considered them to be very much interrelated (Levy 1965; Levy, Kunitz, and Everett 1969). In the 1950s and 1960s criminal homicides and suicides were most common among men in their late twenties and thirties, and a characteristic Navajo pattern was for a man to kill his wife or lover and then to kill himself. We were not convinced that alcohol was causally associated with these acts, although alcohol was present in 47 percent of the suicides and 70 percent of the homicides. The motives that underlay each— most commonly domestic quarrels and sexual jealousy—were the same as had been reported from the early reservation period when the rates of both events were about the same as in the more recent period and the availability of alcohol was much less.

There is a potential problem with the homicide data, however, for those early studies were based upon police records rather than death certificates and included only criminal, not noncriminal, events; that is, accidental and justifiable homicide and involuntary manslaughter were excluded. The differences in homicide rates for the 1960s (see table 4.1) suggest that there is a difference depending upon the source of information. The lowest rate is derived from a review of ten years of police records and includes only Navajo victims of criminal homicide, twenty-four females and twenty-four males. Adding to that number the cases of justifiable homicide, involuntary manslaughter, and accidental deaths collected from the police records at the same time brings the total to 57: 27 females and 30 males. This accounting brings the ten-year average annual rate to 5.3–6.3

per 100,000, still lower than the average annual rate in 1965–
67 of 10.6, as calculated by the Indian Health Service from
death certificates for the six counties that constituted the Navajo
Area before 1972. It suggests that perhaps four or five homicides
a year were not included in the police records. Over a ten-year
period this means that 40–50 homicide victims were not included in the Navajo Police Department files, either because the
event occurred in another jurisdiction, the victims were members
of another tribe, or the records were simply incomplete. In the
unlikely event that all the cases were males, the ratio of male to
female victims would have been at most three to one. In the
1970s and 1980s the ratio was about four to one.

Recall that in 1972 the record-keeping system was changed
to include a redefined Navajo Area. Thus, neither the homicide
rates calculated from police records nor those calculated from
death certificates are directly comparable to the rates calculated
after 1971. To determine whether the change in rates and sex
ratios reflects a real change in patterns or a difference in data-
collection systems, we have attempted to get the death certificates of Indians from the Navajo Area counties before 1972. In
those years, the data were hand-tabulated, and the only work
sheets that have been located by the Indian Health Service are
from 1969.[++] There were five male and three female Indian
victims in the six counties in that year. Because there was a
substantial increase in the homicide rates from the 1960s to the
1970s, no matter what the source of data in the 1960s—and
because it is implausible that all the missing cases in the 1960s
were males—we think the increase was real and was accounted
for largely by an increase in male victims.

The data from the 1970s and the 1980s are from the same
populations and thus permit less problematic comparisons. Ta-

---

[++]We are grateful to Aaron Handler for providing us with these data. The
1960s homicide data in table 4.1 based on death certificates are from published
sources that do not include the sex of the victim and for which the original raw
data have not been found.

ble 4.4 shows a variable pattern of change in the age- and sex-specific average annual rates of homicide. For women the rates are essentially unchanged from one decade to the next. Among men there was a major decline in the 45–54 age group and smaller changes in other groups. The overall effect was a slight increase. The male-female ratio was about four to one in each of the two decades.

In table 4.5 we give the average annual age- and sex-specific rates of suicide for 1972–78 and 1985–88. In general there has been a slight and probably nonsignificant decline in rates at every age and for both sexes. No single age group accounts for most of the decline, unlike the case for cirrhosis.

We cannot explain these patterns of homicide and suicide. More particularly, we cannot explain them in terms of changes in patterns of alcohol abuse because of the serious deficiencies in the data. In addition, two others are noteworthy. First, all

Table 4.4 Average Annual Homicide Death Rates per 100,000, by Age and Sex, 1970s and 1980s

Age	Males		Females	
	1972–78	1985–88	1972–78	1985–88
<10	2.0–2.3	3.2–3.8	3.3–3.8	3.1–3.7
10–14	6.7–7.7	1.6–1.9	1.2–1.4	0
15–24	43–49	48–57	6–7	6–7
25–34	51–58	70–83	15–17	12–14
35–44	48–55	36–43	17–19	13–15
45–54	53–61	23–27	16–18	14–17
55–64	19–22	30–35	4–5	6–7
>65	33–38	28–33	5–6	6–7

the homicide information pertains to the victim, not the perpetrator. Second, none of the data of which we are aware (except our own early study of police files) assesses the association between homicide and suicide—whether causal or otherwise—on the one hand, and the presence of alcohol in the situation, on the other. It is dangerous and potentially misleading to assume that which has not been demonstrated.

ECOLOGICAL CORRELATIONS

One can, of course, attempt to show a relation between these various events and alcohol use at the ecological level by seeing whether these events differ from each other and from alcohol-related conditions in their distribution across the reservation. In

Table 4.5 Average Annual Suicide Rates per 100,000, by Age and Sex, 1970s and 1980s

Age	Males		Females	
	1972–78	1985–88	1972–78	1985–88
10–14		3.4–3.8		1.5–1.8
15–24	44–50	33–39	10–12	6–7
25–34	82–94	73–86	10–12	6–7
35–44	48–55	40–47	6–7	5–6
45–54	39–45	35–41	0	0
55–64	19–22	18–21	0	0
>65	23–29	11–13	5–6	0

previous studies we have compared the observed distribution of cirrhosis, suicide, and homicide across the reservation with the expected distribution as predicted by the distribution of the population. As already noted, we have found that cirrhosis was more common in border areas. The same was true in the 1980s, whether one considers cirrhosis alone or all alcohol-related deaths from disease (cirrhosis, alcoholic psychosis, alcohol-dependence syndrome, and chronic alcoholic liver disease). Criminal homicide in the 1950s and 1960s was not distributed in the same fashion, nor were all homicides in the 1970s and 1980s, though there was a nonsignificant tendency for homicides to be overrepresented in border areas (Kunitz 1983, 107). It was not possible to do the same analysis with the suicide data from the 1950s and early 1960s (Levy 1965, 313), although the impression was that there was no major difference in the distribution by type of reservation community. There was, however, a significant difference between the observed and the expected distribution of suicides in the 1970s (Kunitz 1983, 110); more suicides than expected occurred in the area near Gallup, New Mexico. Many more than expected, however, also occurred in the Chinle Service Unit, the Indian Health Service catchment area that includes Pinon—the isolated community from which most suicides were reported in the 1950s and early 1960s. By the 1980s the difference between service units was no longer significant.

Another way to analyze the data is to correlate the rates of death due to each of these causes. These data are shown in table 4.6. Cirrhosis and homicide deaths were significantly correlated, as were suicide and motor vehicle accident deaths. Motor vehicle accident and suicide rates were uncorrelated with cirrhosis and homicide rates.

That the ecological correlations are not all significant and that homicide rates increased, suicide rates remained virtually constant, and cirrhosis and motor vehicle accident rates declined (see table 4.1) suggest that they do not move together and are not caused by the same conditions. But the absence of both concomitant temporal variation and consistent ecological relations does not demonstrate that there are not important causal associations at the level of the individual between alcohol use, on the one hand, and homicide and suicide, on the other. It does suggest, however, that far more needs to be known at the individual level in order to better disentangle whatever relations do exist. For the present we suggest that alcohol abuse is more important as a cause of alcoholic cirrhosis than it is of motor vehicle accidents and probably more important as a cause of motor vehicle accidents than of suicide and homicide. If that is so, then the decline in both cirrhosis and motor vehicle accidents

Table 4.6   Average Annual Rates of Death from Various Causes in Navajo Reservation Service Unit Populations, Late 1980s

Service Unit	Estimated Population[a]	Cirrhosis (1985–88)[b]	Homicide (1985–87)[c]	Suicide (1985–87)[d]	Motor Vehicle Accidents (1985–88)[e]
Chinle	24,052	6.2	9.7	16.6	73.8
Crownpoint	13,256	16.9	17.6	15.1	84.8
Fort Defiance	24,199	13.4	26.2	5.5	78.5
Gallup	25,424	17.7	28.8	17.0	120.0
Kayenta	14,090	1.2	9.5	16.6	80.0
Shiprock	37,368	8.0	24.1	11.6	86.3
Tuba City	20,425	13.4	13.1	18.0	100.3
Winslow	12,397	12.0	18.8	5.4	66.5

[a] NAIHS 1990. Population estimates are based on census projections and are therefore likely to be low.
[b] NAIHS, unpublished data
[c] NAIHS 1990
[d] NAIHS 1990
[e] NAIHS, unpublished data

may well represent a profound positive change toward a more moderate form of alcohol consumption.

CHANGING PATTERNS OF ALCOHOL USE

In our first study, as noted, we reported the drinking status of people in three groups: the adult members of an extended kin group in a rural area, called the Plateau group; a random sample of adults living in the reservation administrative and wage-labor center of Tuba City, Arizona, called the South Tuba sample; and all the Navajo long-term (more than ten years) residents of the bordertown of Flagstaff, Arizona. These data are given in table 4.7.

It was striking that the prevalence of drinking was lower among Navajos than it was in nationwide samples of the U.S. population, largely owing to the number of people who had given up drinking. In each group significantly more men than women drank; there were significant differences between men across groups; but there were no significant differences between women across groups. A higher proportion of women in the Flagstaff and South Tuba groups were lifelong abstainers than was the case in the Plateau group, but a higher proportion of women was currently drinking in Flagstaff than in the other two groups.

These groups were not weighted random samples of the Navajo population, so they cannot be combined to give estimates of the overall prevalence of drinking among Navajos in the mid-1960s. They are nonetheless useful for comparative purposes. In 1984 May and Matthew Smith (1988) surveyed the patient population of the Indian Health Service clinic in Winslow, Arizona, a bordertown about 60 miles east of Flagstaff, serving a large rural population adjacent to the area where our field work had been carried out eighteen years earlier. They argued that

using a clinic population did not introduce significant bias into
their study since every measure they had, including previous
studies, suggested that clinic populations were indistinguishable
from the larger service unit population. Their prevalence data
are contained in table 4.7 along with the data from our original
survey. The proportion of Navajos served by the clinic in Winslow who were not drinking in 1984 (48 percent) was slightly
higher than the estimated proportion of abstainers in the state
of Arizona in 1986–88 (about 40 percent) (Williams et al. 1991,
36). Most remarkable is the apparent increase in drinking
among women from the mid-1960s to the mid-1980s. This is
consistent with the increased prevalence of fetal alcohol syn
drome and effect in the Navajo population during this period
(May et al. 1983).

Table 4.7 Prevalence of Alcohol Use in Samples of Navajo Men and
Women, 1960s and 1980s

Drinking Status	Plateau (1966)[a]	South Tuba (1966)[a]	Flagstaff (1967)[a]	Winslow (1984)[b]
	Women			
Lifelong abstainer	9 (37.5%)	9 (64.3%)	20 (66.7%)	
Stopped drinking	14 (58.3%)	4 (28.6%)	3 (10.0%)	
Total not drinking	23 (95.8%)	13 (92.9%)	23 (76.7%)	54 (60%)
Currently drinking	1 (4.2%)	1 (7.1%)	7 (23.3%)	36 (40%)
Total	24	14	30	90
	Men			
Lifelong abstainer	1 (5%)	0	2 (11.1%)	
Stopped drinking	12 (60%)	6 (31.6%)	7 (38.9%)	
Total not drinking	13 (65%)	6 (31.6%)	9 (50%)	30 (36%)
Currently drinking	7 (35%)	13 (68.4%)	9 (50%)	54 (64%)
Total	20	19	18	84

[a] Levy and Kunitz 1974, 136
[b] May and Smith 1988

CONCLUSION

In a series of papers, Martin Topper (1985; Topper and Curtis 1987) argued that as the Navajo population grew and diversified, so did drinking styles proliferate. He identified at least five types (including the female pattern) that are regarded as traditionally Navajo, several of which overlap with styles we described in our first study. The first type is the "house party," which occurred at home in the evening and involved the sharing of alcoholic beverages by all adults present. The second type involved drinking by groups of older men, usually when traditional ceremonies were taking place but at a place somewhat removed from the ceremony itself. The third type was similar to the second but involved younger men. The fourth type was alcoholic drinking, which for men usually meant isolated drinking. "The reason that his drinking was so heavily stigmatized was that it took the individual away from the economic tasks that he or she was obligated to perform and it did not involve any sharing of 'drinks' among kinsmen." Fifth, "The traditional female alcoholic was a person who drank in the company of men when they drank in groups in the desert or who hung around the bootlegger's house or in the trading post and traded sexual favors for liquor" (1985, 232–35).

Besides these older forms of drinking, new forms have grown up. "Drinking no longer occurs more or less exclusively among kinsmen or affines. The drinking cohort often forms more or less spontaneously at various events and places." That Navajos do not drink with relatives and affines is disruptive, Topper argued, because the socialization function of the drinking group vanishes and because many Navajos are suspicious of nonrelatives: "Strangers of any culture have not been easily accepted." This difficulty with strangers has been made worse by the boarding school experience, he wrote, and by wage labor, both of which are alienating and fail to meet deeply felt emotional needs.

The net impact of acculturation appears to be that only the escape or narcotizing function of alcohol remains for many young Navajos who drink in non-traditional environments. Given the fact that these people are an ever-increasing segment of the Navajo population, a major trend toward a new and dangerous form of drinking is under way. Those who drink for escape in non-traditional environments find themselves using a disinhibiting, depressant drug among strangers about whom they feel ambivalent. Furthermore, they drink in environments in which traditional Navajo rules for social control of drinking do not apply, and for which there has not been the development of non-traditional social controls. Finally, they frequently bring with them considerable anger and frustration concerning their economic and perhaps social condition. Given these factors, the increasingly high rate of alcohol-related morbidity and mortality among young Navajos is explainable. Many of these young people are neither culturally nor emotionally prepared either to tolerate the stresses of non-traditional drinking environments or to experience the emotional release or satisfaction that such drinking provides for people of other cultures. Clearly, then, these newer forms of drinking are not as therapeutic as the more traditional ones. (1985, 238–39)

It is important to distinguish between the causes and the effects of alcohol use. We have argued that the traditional patterns of alcohol use were not usually pathological in their causes, though they were often pathological in their consequences. The new form of "acculturated" drinking that Topper identifies is clearly pathological in its causes and consequences. Topper believes that the style of acculturated drinking is becoming increasingly common and accounts for the increase in alcohol-related morbidity and mortality. But alcohol-related mortality seems to have decreased from the 1970s to the 1980s, suggesting a more complicated process at work.

It is possible that the decline in mortality reflects the evolution of a more moderate and controlled style of drinking among people who drink for nonpathological reasons and that the pathological drinking Topper describes has either emerged over the past generation or two or has been newly revealed by the larger changes in drinking styles that seem to have occurred. The possible heterogeneity of drinking patterns among Navajos is important for reasons having to do with both prevention and treatment. The follow-up study of mortality reported in the next chapter speaks to this issue in more detail.

5

Survival Patterns of the Original Study Groups

Our field research began in the mid-1960s with people who were at least twenty-one years old, that is, the youngest members of our study population were in the highest risk age groups in the very period when the rates of death were increasing most dramatically. Our data therefore address the experience of cohorts whose youngest members were born no later than the early 1940s. As we have suggested, the cohort born between 1941 and 1953 seems to have had much lower death rates from alcoholic cirrhosis in the 35–44 age group (that is, in 1985–88) than those born earlier. This cohort is younger than all but our very youngest respondents, who were born no later than 1944. Most were born in the 1930s and earlier and thus are in the high mortality cohort. We emphasize this because our data speak to the experience of an older generation. In the absence of comparable recent surveys of the population, it is not clear that the survival patterns of younger cohorts will be the same as those we report for our original study group.

SAMPLES

The Plateau group: all adult members ($N = 46$) of a traditional stock-raising extended-kin group in an area called the Kaibito

Plateau. As recently as the 1960s there was no accurate count of the population from which a true random sample could be drawn. We elected instead to study a kin group that had been one of the largest and wealthiest in the area before stock reduction in the 1930s and among whose members were two ceremonialists. Although not representative of the general population of the area, the kin group was traditional in that none of its members was Christian or belonged to the Native American (peyote) Church, and only the youngest males were engaged in part-time wage work.

The South Tuba sample: a random sample of households, including forty adults, drawn from a census of the Navajo wagework settlement adjacent to the government agency town of Tuba City on the western end of the Navajo reservation. The census had been made by the Department of Environmental Health of the Public Health Service Indian Hospital in Tuba City in preparation for putting in a water system.

The Hospital group: thirty-five people (30 men, 5 women) who were referred or self-referred to the PHS Indian Hospital in Tuba City to be started on Antabuse to control their excessive alcohol consumption. These individuals constituted the entire population under treatment at the time. As the program had just been inaugurated, there was no roster of past patients from which a random sample could be drawn. It is possible that because these were the first patients admitted to the program and were voluntary, they differed from those who came after them, particularly if those who entered later were forced into treatment by the courts. It is likely that the major difference is between self-referred and court-referred rather than between early and late entry into treatment. We claim only that our respondents are representative of voluntary patients.

We also studied forty-eight Navajos who had lived for at least ten years in the off-reservation bordertown of Flagstaff, Arizona. This was the entire population of Navajo long-term residents of the town.

Only the first three study groups were included in the follow-up, primarily because tracking off-reservation residents would have been far more difficult. Reservation society is kin-based, and it was relatively easy to locate family members who knew the whereabouts of our original respondents. This was not true of off-reservation residents. Moreover, because the off-reservation sample was similar to working class Anglo-Americans in patterns of alcohol use, we felt that a follow-up study would not provide enough new information to warrant the effort required to collect it.

The three groups whose members were living on the reservation in 1966 were followed by having a local person who knew the community well search for them through family members and friends. Some had moved to other parts of the reservation or to bordertowns. The most difficult people to locate were men who had married into the area at the time of our first study, subsequently divorced, and moved away, leaving behind no kin of their own. Even in these cases, former wives and in-laws were able to give their general whereabouts.

Death certificates were requested from the state of Arizona for all people known to have died and for those whose status was unknown. Hospital records for people known to have died were also reviewed, though in a few cases they could not be obtained. Next of kin of all the people who had died were interviewed about the causes and circumstances of death. We are satisfied that we identified all the people in our sample who had died since 1966, though two remain about whom the relation of death to alcohol consumption is unknown.

There were 121 individuals in the three groups in 1966, including eight who had died within a few years before the study. In the original study, proxy interviews were done with their next of kin. These individuals are not included in the present study. Moreover, upon reviewing our original data we discovered that we had included the Hopi husband of a Navajo woman in the South Tuba sample. He has been dropped from the present analysis. Thus the size of the study population is 112.

Methods of Analysis

The survival histories of the 112 individuals in this study are analyzed by considering the number of years that each person has lived since the 1966 interview. For the 32 persons who have died, we have complete life histories; for the other 80 persons, the life histories stopped in 1990, when the present study terminated. In other words, the analysis took into account that those 80 people lived all the years up to 1990, but it made no assumption about when after 1990 any such person would die. Both the complete and the truncated life histories are analyzed by Cox's proportional hazard model, using the BMDP Program 2L, and taking into account the crucial variable of age, as well as other variables with likely effects on mortality, such as sex, drinking status, and sample group. Cox's model assumes that for any one level of a factor X, the survival function can be expressed by means of a baseline, or average, survival function and a conversion coefficient that converts the baseline to the survival function at that level of the factor X. The analyses produce estimates of survival curves—that is, plots of the function:

$$S(t) = \Pr \{\text{Length of survival in the study} \geq t\},$$

which is simply the proportion surviving t years after the initial interview in 1966. To study how this survival function depends on other factors, one may proceed in one of two ways.

The stratification approach is to fit separate survival functions to each level or category of the factor. Thus, one may fit a function for male survival, another for female survival, and a different function for each age group. The effect of the factors is then seen by comparing the survival functions fitted in the different strata, which are defined by the various levels of the factors. This would be a fine method, but it requires multiple stratifications, and the number of cases in each stratum rapidly becomes too small to allow for a trustworthy estimation, especially if cross-classifications by several factors are made.

The modeling approach to analysis incorporates data on factor levels by building them into the survival function, using Cox's model. If the model fits the data, the effect of factor X is estimated simply by a single conversion coefficient, whereas in the first approach to analysis the factor effect requires the estimation of an entire survival curve for each level of the factor.

With limited amounts of data, the Cox approach is clearly attractive. Its disadvantage is that it may be misleading if the model is inappropriate, which may happen if the configurations of the survival curves at different factor levels differ substantially. In such a case, the Cox model would obscure the differences because it assumes a simple relation between the curves.

We therefore use the Cox model cautiously and check its justification wherever possible. When the survival curves at different levels of a factor appear to have different patterns, we introduce that factor as a stratification rather than as a variable in the Cox model. Thus we find that age and sex can be used well in the Cox model, and we therefore include both as covariates in all analyses. Other factors, however, are not found to affect survival as suggested by the Cox model and are therefore used only to stratify the analyses. This is done with such factors as drinking status, sample, and type of family unit.

The analysis by sex, age, and drinking status is thus a mixture of stratification (of drinking status) and of estimating conversion factors by the Cox model (for age and sex). In other words, separate survival curves are estimated for abstainers, for former drinkers, and for drinkers, and the model is then used to estimate conversion factors for sex and age. For example, to obtain the survival curve for sixty-year-old female abstainers, we use the curve for abstainers and convert it exponentially by a factor for females (which increases survival) and a factor for age sixty (which reduces survival). For abstainers of other ages and for males, the conversion factors are different, but the same abstainers' survival curve is used as a baseline.

The analysis is mostly descriptive and exploratory rather than inferential and confirmatory. This is partly because the data are scanty and unlikely to yield definitive generalizations and partly because tests of significance are not readily available for some inferences on survival analyses, such as comparisons of the survival curves of different strata.

The results of the various analyses are presented graphically in the form of survival curves. Use of the Cox model means that we need to plot only one baseline curve for each stratum and list the conversion factors to adjust that baseline to different age and sex levels. The model has the different curves essentially "parallel," differing only in their individual conversion factors. We therefore see no point in plotting a lot of these very similarly shaped curves and limit our presentation to curves for men and women aged fifty. In view of our use of the Cox model, the shape of these curves is estimated from all the data, not merely from the data for fifty-year-olds.

RESULTS

Salient Results from the Baseline Study

The community samples were chosen to represent the range of socioeconomic and cultural variations on the reservation. It is thus not surprising that the Plateau group was less well educated than the South Tuba group, more likely to live in extended than neolocal family units, and more involved in livestock raising than in wage labor. On all these measures, the Hospital group was intermediate between the two community groups. With respect to age of the 112 respondents, among men the Plateau group averaged 44, South Tuba 37, and the Hospital group 33. Among women the Plateau group averaged 37.5, South Tuba 41, and the Hospital group 36.6.

Concerning the use of alcohol by respondents in the two community groups, at the time of our original study we found that more men than women had histories of consuming alcohol, and more were using alcohol at the time of the study. Almost no men were lifelong abstainers. Many women were. On the other hand, a high proportion of men in each group had become abstainers, often after years of heavy drinking and experiencing symptoms that would indicate excessive alcohol use. On a measure of intensity of drinking behavior (the Preoccupation with Alcohol scale), it was found that the Plateau and Hospital groups described far more extreme forms of alcohol use than the South Tuba (or Flagstaff) groups and that men and women differed only in the Plateau group.

Self-reports and life histories from our oldest informants were consistent with ethnographic reports going back into the late nineteenth century. These indicated that group drinking among young men at ceremonies was common, and those who did not wish to drink were forcibly encouraged to participate. In addition, however, since in the early years of the reservation alcohol was expensive and hard to get, it thus became a high-prestige consumption item.

It seemed to us that heavy drinking was the result of adherence to traditional values having to do with individual power, group solidarity, and the ability to purchase highly valued goods; that it was characteristic of young men; and that it tended to diminish markedly as they reached their late thirties and forties. Indeed, an eighteen-month follow-up using police records of the Hospital group and the two reservation community groups showed that the former had a significant decline in arrests, even though virtually none of them had taken Antabuse since discharge from the hospital (Kunitz and Levy 1974, 171).

That men seemed able to reduce their alcohol consumption as they entered early middle age was, we thought, the result of family pressure, witnessing the ravages of alcohol abuse (particularly violent deaths) among peers, and the assumption of new responsibilities as they entered a new phase of their lives. Until this occurred, however, alcohol use caused serious health and family problems, particularly since use had increased significantly when roads were improved and motor vehicles became more common. Drinking among women, however, seemed to be a very different phenomenon. As already noted, a much higher proportion of women than men were abstainers, but those who did use alcohol included many who led tumultuous lives and were widely regarded as deviant in the community.

Follow-up Results

In table 5.1 we give the distribution of deaths among men and women in each of the three groups. There are no significant differences between men and women overall or between men and between women in each of the three groups.

On the other hand, cause of death does differ significantly between groups, as table 5.2 indicates. More people in the Hospital group died of alcohol-related problems than did people in the other two groups. Age clearly confounds the analysis, however, since the Plateau men are so much older than the

Table 5.1   Deaths, by Sex and Sample Group

Men	Vital Status	
Group	Dead	Alive
Plateau	6	11
South Tuba	7	13
Hospital	9	21
Total	22	45

Women	Vital Status	
Group	Dead	Alive
Plateau	4	19
South Tuba	4	13
Hospital	2	3
Total	10	35

others. For that reason the following survival analyses control for age.

Figures 5.1 and 5.2 are survival curves for men and women at age fifty, which include age and sex as covariates in the Cox model and the sample group as the stratum. The striking feature of each figure is the more rapid drop in the proportion surviving among the Antabuse group than among the other two groups.

In the second analysis we substituted drinking status in 1966 for sample group. Figures 5.3 and 5.4 indicate that the results are essentially similar. Drinkers have lower rates of survival than others, although by the end of the follow-up period there was an unsurprising tendency for the curves to converge as survival among abstainers declines.

Finally, we combined sample groups and drinking status into the following categories: lifelong abstainers; those who had stopped drinking by 1966; drinkers in the Antabuse group; and other drinkers. Figures 5.5 and 5.6 show the models for men and women at age fifty. The patterns are essentially the same as reported above, but we now see that the Hospital group had slightly lower survival rates than the other drinkers.

We have noted previously that tests of significance are not available for comparisons of different strata's survival curves. Nonetheless, there are several important features of the curves shown. Note that the survival curves of the abstainers and

Table 5.2 Alcohol-related Deaths in Three Study Groups

| | Alcohol-related Deaths | |
Group	Definite and Probable	Not Alcohol-related
Plateau	1	8
South Tuba	5	6
Hospital	9	1

Chi-square = 11.03; df = 2; $p < 0.01$
Two unknowns (1 Hospital, 1 Plateau) omitted.

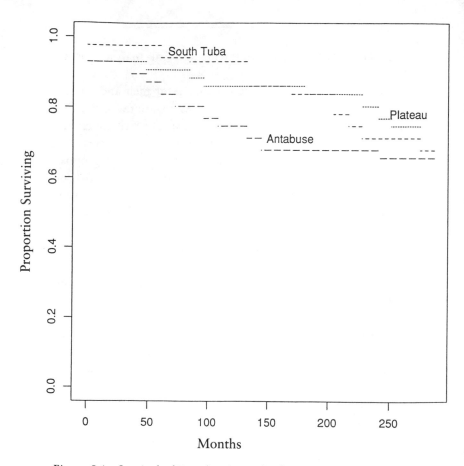

Figure 5.1   Survival of Females, Age Fifty, by Sample

former drinkers are invariably higher than the curves for the drinkers, indicating that a higher proportion of the first two groups survive than of the third group at each year of follow-up. These differences between the curves are most obvious in the first ten to twelve years, after which there is a distinct tendency for them to converge. In other words, by the end of the twenty-five-year period, the difference in the proportion

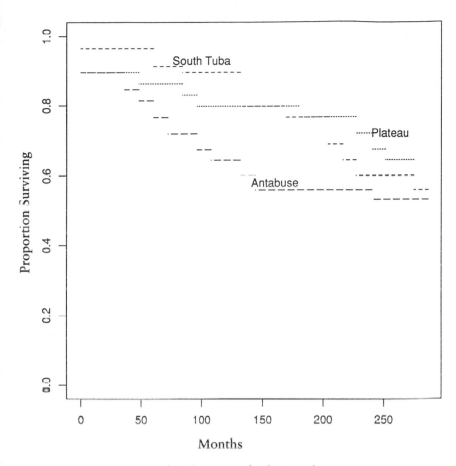

Figure 5.2   Survival of Males, Age Fifty, by Sample

surviving between nondrinkers and drinkers is considerably less than it was ten years after the initial interview.

If we consider mortality versus survival during the first twelve years of the study (up to and including 1977), we note in table 5.4 that the proportion surviving is highest among abstainers (100 percent), lowest among drinkers (81 percent), and intermediate among former drinkers (88 percent).

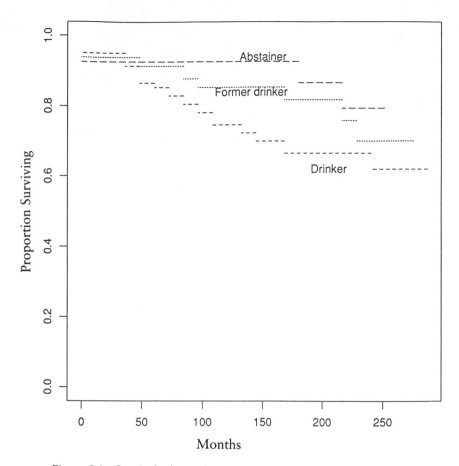

Figure 5.3 Survival of Females, Age Fifty, by Alcohol Use

This comparison is confounded with sex differences, but as table 5.4 indicates, a similar pattern is observed among both males and females. It is remarkable that this mortality pattern, which had been expected, is found for each sex. This in itself is highly unlikely to have occurred by chance. The numbers are rather small for formal significance testing, but the abstainer-versus-drinker comparison is significant at the 2 percent level

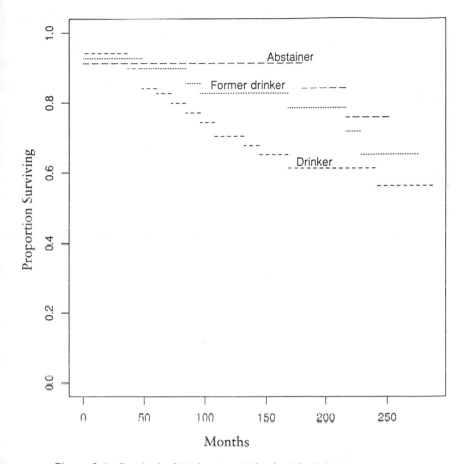

Figure 5.4 Survival of Males, Age Fifty, by Alcohol Use

for women (for men, with a single abstainer, such a test could not be carried out). If abstainers and former drinkers are pooled and the trend is tested within each sex, the result is significant at the 4 percent level, mostly because of the data for women—those for men are more equivocal.

Turning now to consideration of mortality within each of our sample groups, we note that the only significant differences we

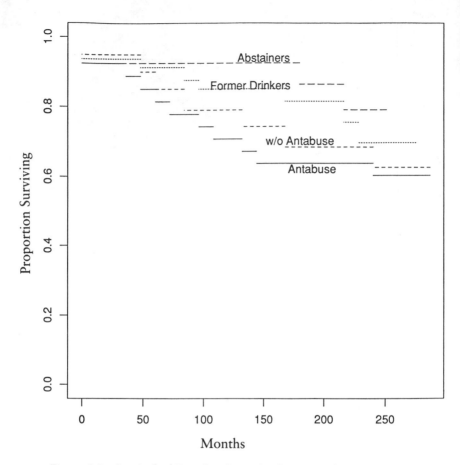

Figure 5.5 Survival of Females, Age Fifty, by Use and Sample

can detect between the Hospital men who died and those who are still alive are that the survivors were substantially older at the time of the first interview in 1966 and lived in larger households or camps. Those who have survived were on average 35 years old at that time (median 34), whereas those who died were on average 28.1 years old (median 29) (p <0.02 by Mann-Whitney U-test).* The men who survived lived in camps with a

*In a logistic regression with age, Preoccupation Score, and years of education

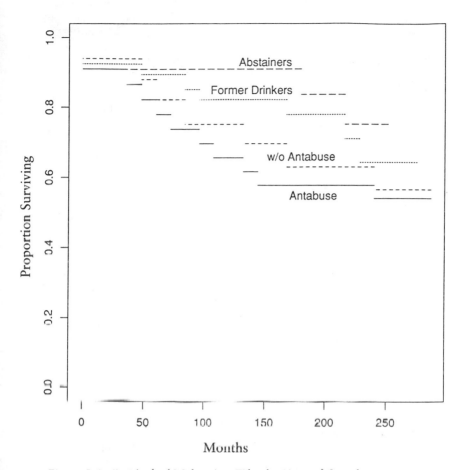

Figure 5.6 Survival of Males, Age Fifty, by Use and Sample

median number of eight people, whereas those who died lived in camps of median size of six ($p < 0.05$ by Mann-Whitney U-test). There were no differences in family organization, place of residence (South Tuba or elsewhere), the frequency of drinking, liver function studies, the experience of hallucinations after drinking, or any other reported sequelae of alcohol use.

as the independent variables and vital status at follow-up as the dependent variable, only age was significantly associated with an increased risk of death.

Table 5.3   Mortality 1966–77, by Sample Group and Sex

Men	Vital Status as of 1977	
Group	Dead	Alive
Plateau	14	3
South Tuba	18	2
Hospital	25	5

Chi-square not significant

Women	Vital Status	
Group	Dead	Alive
Plateau	21	2
.South Tuba	17	0
Hospital	3	2

Chi-square = 7.635; df = 2; p <0.05

Table 5.4   Mortality 1966–77, by Drinking Status (1966) and Sex

Men	Vital Status	
Drinking status	Dead	Alive
Lifelong abstainer	0	1
Former drinker	2	15
Current drinker	8	38

Women	Vital Status	
Drinking Status	Dead	Alive
Lifelong abstainer	0	18
Former drinker	2	16
Current drinker	2	5

Nor was there any difference between those who died and those who survived in the average age at which drinking began (19 for survivors, 17 for those who died), the average age at first arrest (23.7 for survivors, 23.2 for those who died—excluding five unknowns among the survivors), the decade of life in which alcohol became a problem, the average number of arrests in the five years before the interview, and the average Preoccupation with Alcohol score.

That average age distinguished those who later died from those who survived is congruent with the results of the first study. There we argued that if they survived their twenties and thirties, Navajo men tended to reduce or cease drinking sometime in their late thirties or forties and that enrolling in the Antabuse program provided a focus for that. Clearly, it was not the aversive conditioning of Antabuse that had the effect, for virtually none of these men had taken the medication long enough for that to have occurred. The results reported immediately above support that inference and suggest that the younger men who enrolled in the program were less motivated to cease drinking. These results are also similar to Ferguson's (1968, 1970), which showed that Navajo men whose drinking abated after Antabuse treatment were older than those who showed little or no change.

There were, of course, young men who did not die in the follow-up period. We wished to discover whether there was anything that distinguished them from those who died prematurely, and we therefore did a nested case-control study in which we matched these groups by age. There were nine in each group. Of those who died, eight died from alcohol-related causes. The ninth, who suffered from a painful, life-threatening chronic disease, had reduced (but not discontinued) his alcohol consumption and become addicted to an analgesic, with which he committed suicide.

There were few differences between the two groups. The median age at first arrest was 21 among those who died and 26 among those who survived ($p < 0.05$ by Mann-Whitney U-test). There was a tendency ($p > 0.05 < 0.1$) for those who died to have had more arrests between 1961 and 1966 than those who survived (median numbers, eight and four). The men who died had all attended school; five of the controls had not ($p = 0.05$ by Fisher's Exact Test). The median number of people in the camp tended to be greater for those who survived than for those who died (nine versus six; $p > 0.05 < 0.1$ by Mann-Whitney U-test).

On the other hand, there was no difference in the age at which drinking had begun; in the reported sequelae of alcohol use; in place of residence (South Tuba versus other more rural areas); in the quantity and frequency of alcohol use; in reported troubles due to drinking; or in arrests for assaults.

The arrest data are hard to interpret. They may be a reflection of more flamboyant early drinking among those who died than among those who survived, or they may be a reflection of the place of residence. If those who died lived in relatively heavily policed communities, where bootlegged liquor is also more accessible, premature death and early arrests may be the result of the place of residence. Such a result would be compatible with our early findings that alcoholic cirrhosis occurred at higher rates in communities near bordertowns, where alcohol is more readily available. We do not find such a difference in place of residence, however, although our numbers are obviously too small to detect all but the strongest effects. It is thus possible that there really was an important difference in drinking behavior between the two groups that is related to their survival patterns.

To explore this possibility further, we have considered the life histories of these men in more detail. Because our previous study of elderly Navajos (Kunitz and Levy 1991) suggested that there was a relation between depression and alcohol use, we looked particularly for evidence of depression in our interview material and in the medical records. Our previous work suggested that many men were unwilling to discuss the symptoms of depression even as their affect suggested that indeed they were depressed. Moreover, histories from informants about someone who has died are likely to be biased according to how people seek to explain to themselves and others the reason for a premature death. Depression is likely to be one of the reasons invoked. Both sources of bias would tend to inflate the difference between those who died and those who survived.

There is indeed a tendency for those who report deaths to describe the deceased as having been depressed—more than those still alive would be so described. Seven of the nine men who died were reported by informants, in the hospital record, or both as having suffered from depression. The drinking of the other two was attributed to the loss of a loved one. In one case, a man and his wife had both drunk to excess and then stopped after counseling and threats from social workers that their children would be taken from them. They had not drunk for several years before the wife died. Within six months the widower began drinking and continued until he died. He had had multiple episodes of alcoholic gastritis, which made serious respiratory problems worse. In the other case a man was said to have begun drinking after the death of his mother and continued for several years until he was killed in a motor vehicle accident. Both he and the driver were drunk. We have not counted these two men as depressed, although there is reason to believe that their drinking did originate at least in part in depression. Three of the nine controls likewise reported depression. The difference is not significant (by Fisher's Exact Test).

In addition to histories of depression, we felt that the context in which drinking was learned might explain the differences between those who died and the controls who survived. Our data are not adequate to allow us to do more than suggest that there is tenuous evidence that those who died began their drinking off the reservation (five of nine), whereas none, or at most two, of the nine survivors may have begun off the reservation.[†]

[†]If the two people who may have begun off-reservation in fact did, the

Small numbers and inadequate data preclude our pursuing this issue further here. In chapter 7 we describe in more detail the context in which several of the deceased men began to drink.

There is, then, suggestive evidence that the men in the Hospital group who died differed in their family backgrounds and drinking behavior—and perhaps in their reasons for drinking— from their age-matched controls who have survived. Those who died were more likely than the controls to have attended school, to have lived in a relatively small family group, and to have been arrested young and frequently. The differences in depression are not as compelling, partly because the numbers we have to work with are small, partly because the potential biases we have already mentioned may have led to an exaggeration of the presence of depression among those who have died.

Turning to the people in the community samples, recall that the proportion of drinkers surviving was essentially the same as observed among the Hospital sample (for both men and women). Six people in these two groups (three men and three women) died of alcohol-related conditions (one in the Plateau group, five in the South Tuba group). Among the alcohol-related deaths in the Hospital group were eight men and one woman.‡ The difference is not quite statistically significant (by Fisher's Exact Test) but suggests that women with alcohol problems

difference between the survivors and the deceased is not significant by Fisher's Exact Test. If none began drinking off-reservation, the difference is significant at the 5 percent level.

‡Of the nine men in the Hospital sample who died, one committed suicide with pain medication. Though he continued to drink excessively, alcohol was not involved in his death. He is described in more detail in a following section. Two women in the Hospital sample died, one from alcoholic cirrhosis, the other from carbon monoxide poisoning. It is not clear from the available records whether the latter was drunk or whether the death was a suicide. We have not considered it alcohol-related in the absence of evidence that it was. We coded as unknown the relation of her death to alcohol. She was a woman who had been diagnosed as both schizophrenic and epileptic. Alcohol abuse was not the worst of her problems.

serious enough to result in death may have been less likely to have had contact with the treatment system than men with equally serious problems.

When we compare the four women who died of alcohol-related problems with the eleven men who died of similar problems, we note that all four women were said to have been seriously depressed well before they died, whereas six of the eleven men were said to have been depressed. The difference is not significant (by Fisher's Exact Test), but these results too lend very weak support to the notion that drinking among women is different from drinking among men. This is a topic to which we shall return in the next chapter, when we discuss the life histories of people in our sample.

Finally, we return to an issue raised in our discussion of the changing rates of mortality due to a variety of conditions often considered to be alcohol-related. The two that are especially problematic are suicide and homicide. Although much of the drinking behavior of those who died was sufficiently self-destructive to raise the question of suicidal intent, we refer here only to those cases that were not caused by the physical complications of excessive alcohol consumption. By this criterion, two men, both in the Hospital group, committed suicide, and one woman in the Plateau group was the victim of a homicide.[5] We tell their stories briefly to illustrate the range of difficulty encountered in attempting to infer a causal relation between alcohol use, on the one hand, and suicide or homicide, on the other.

The homicide victim was a member of the Plateau sample and

---

[5]One woman who died of carbon monoxide poisoning (described in the preceding footnote) has been omitted because, though she had a history of depression and schizophrenia as well as alcohol abuse, there was no evidence that her death had not been accidental. Another woman, whose remains had been found four years after she disappeared, has not been considered a homicide victim since the forensic anthropologist who examined them could find no evidence of foul play.

twenty-two years old when we first interviewed her in 1966. At that time she was separated from her first husband and living with her parents. She said that when she was seventeen she had tried wine once with some older members of her family. It had tasted awful, and she had not had any since.

Shortly after we interviewed her, she began living with a man by whom she had four children. It was not clear to her sisters whether the couple had ever legally married. She and her husband both worked for the Bureau of Indian Affairs and lived in the community where she had always lived. Her sisters differed somewhat in their accounts of when she began drinking but seem to agree that it was several years before her death in 1981. One of the sisters reported that her sister told her that she began drinking because she could not persuade her husband to stop, but her drinking had been only occasional until a year or two before her death. Her young daughter had died in 1978, and her drinking seemed to become more severe after that. Whether it was unhappiness about her daughter's death, with her job, or both, her sisters could not say. Her sisters differed on the extent of her drinking, one saying that she drank several bottles of beer only on paydays, the other saying that she drank whiskey more than once a week.

On the day of her death, the woman and her husband and another couple had gone to a nearby bordertown to drink. On the way home they got into an argument, and she and the other woman got out and started walking. After a few miles, she sat down by the side of the road while her companion went into the bushes to relieve herself. While the companion was away, a car came by, and when the companion went back to the road she found her friend lying down, having been struck by the passing vehicle. She had a bottle of whiskey beside her. Shortly after, the two men came along, put the injured woman in the car, and set off for the hospital. They ran out of gas, however, and did not arrive until many hours later, by which time she had died.

The family clearly suspected that the husband had been the driver who had run down his wife as she sat by the side of the road. The woman who had been with the victim had not seen the accident. The husband was never charged and died some years later of alcohol-related problems of an unspecified nature. We have considered this woman to be a homicide victim, but the evidence is in fact ambiguous. If it was her husband who was driving the vehicle that struck her, and if he had been drinking, would those be sufficient grounds for saying that alcohol caused her death?

An equally ambiguous example is provided by the next case: a man who was thirty-one when we first interviewed him as part of the Hospital sample. At that time he had been drinking heavily for about ten years and reported a variety of family problems as a result, but he had continued to work steadily for the same employer.

About two years after our interview, he left the Tuba City area with his family to work for his employer off the reservation. They moved back to the eastern part of the reservation in the early 1970s, where he continued to work for the same company. He had continued drinking all through this period. Both informants (his wife and a cousin's wife who was also a close friend) agreed that frequently (more than once a week) he drank a great deal of any alcoholic beverage that came to hand. His drinking had increased in the early 1970s after he learned that he had diabetes. According to his cousin's wife, he was very depressed about his health, and she thought that contributed to his increased alcohol consumption.

In the autumn of 1977 several couples had gone out hunting in the mountains in eastern Arizona. All the men but he were out of the camp hunting. He had remained behind drinking. Suddenly he grabbed a gun, ran away from the camp, and shot himself in the head. His cousin's wife said she thought he drank because he was depressed and that the day he killed himself he had been drinking to give himself the courage to commit suicide.

His wife said he did not tell her much of what he was thinking, and she was unaware that he was depressed. Although she also thought that a passing deerhunter might have shot him when he left the camp, she had a copy of the death certificate, which stated that the death was a suicide, and did not disagree with (or accept) the diagnosis when asked.

Clearly, in this case alcohol was present in the situation, but it is not clear that the suicide would not have occurred without it. Both informants agreed that the man's health had deteriorated in the last years of his life, perhaps as a result of untreated diabetes, perhaps as a result of excessive alcohol consumption. One informant insisted that the man had become increasingly depressed as a result and was using alcohol to treat his depression, and finally, to give himself courage to commit suicide.

The second suicide was committed by a man who was twenty-nine years old when we first interviewed him as part of the Hospital sample. He had a painful, life-threatening chronic disease, which required many hospitalizations. His excessive use of alcohol was making his chronic disease condition worse, so the physician caring for him suggested that he be treated with Antabuse. He agreed, and indeed the medical record subsequently showed fewer visits in which alcohol abuse was mentioned as a cause for the visit. Nonetheless, according to both a brother and a sister, he continued to drink heavily and frequently. When we reinterviewed him in 1967, he denied drinking but was obviously drunk.

Because of the painful nature of his chronic disease, he was placed on pain medication, to which he became habituated. He also seems to have become habituated to the hospital, for he insisted on hanging around there and would often be found sleeping in the waiting rooms or halls when there was no medical reason for his being there. He became increasingly depressed in the few years after we first interviewed him and in 1969 attempted suicide with an overdose of pain medication.

A short time later he was admitted to the hospital for treatment of complications of his chronic disease. Aware of his previous suicide attempt, the staff attempted to keep all medications out of his reach. Nonetheless, he managed to get hold of an analgesic and took a second overdose. He died of asphyxiation due to aspiration, despite attempts at resuscitation. It is clear that alcohol was not involved in the immediate situation and cannot be implicated as a cause. Like the first suicide we described, however, alcohol seems to have been used to treat (unsuccessfully) an underlying depression, which in turn was the result of deteriorating health.

These examples require that we ask what we mean when we say that alcohol abuse causes a variety of untoward events. In the case of alcoholic cirrhosis, alcohol is obviously both a necessary and a sufficient cause. Without it, alcoholic cirrhosis cannot develop, and if enough of it is consumed in the right way, it is highly likely that cirrhosis will result. The same thing cannot be said of the association of alcohol use with motor vehicle accidents. The absence of alcohol does not ensure that an accident will not occur, and its presence does not ensure that an accident will occur, depending upon the amount consumed. The association is even more tenuous when homicide and suicide are considered. As the preceding examples suggest, even when alcohol is present in a situation, it is not clear that the situation would not have occurred without it or that its presence would make suicide or homicide probable. It is every bit as likely that such situations happen to people who drink and that the reasons they drink may be the same ones that put them at increased risk of being involved in a homicide or suicide.

So far we have discussed only alcohol-related deaths, but people in our study died of other conditions as well: non-alcohol-related accidents, heart disease, and cancer being most prominent among them. The people who died of these other causes were, with two exceptions, in the Plateau and South Tuba groups. The average ages at time of first interview and at death were significantly greater in these two groups than in the Hospital group (see table 5.5). The members of the Hospital group who died were significantly younger than those who survived, and the members of the other two study groups who died were significantly older than those who survived. The net result is that when we consider those who survived, the members of the three groups are indistinguishable in terms of age. The mean and median ages at first interview were respectively 35–36 and 33 in each. Twenty-five years later the survivors are on average in their late fifties.

At present, the survivors are indistinguishable in several other important respects as well. We consider several measures here: physical functioning, symptom scores of depression, the quantity and frequency of alcohol use, and the kind of beverage consumed.

The scales of physical function are taken from the Sickness Impact Profile (sip), which was developed in Anglo-American populations, but which we have used successfully in our study of elderly Navajos (Kunitz and Levy 1991). This scale does not

Table 5.5 Age at Time of First Interview and at Death in Three Study Groups

Study Group	Age at Interview		Age at Death	
	Mean	Median	Mean	Median
Plateau				
Deceased	50.6	48.5	62.3	55.0
Survivors	36.9	33.0	—	—
South Tuba				
Deceased	48.5	48.0	63.1	62.0
Survivors	35.1	33.0	—	—
Hospital				
Deceased	29.2	28.0	38.5	34.0
Survivors	35.4	33.5	—	—

allow one to diagnose any particular disease entity. It is, rather, a way of assessing the ability to carry out normal activities of daily living (dressing, toileting, walking, and so on). The higher the score, the greater the level of disability.

The measure of depression is derived from the Center for Epidemiological Studies on Depression (CES-D). It is a scale of symptoms commonly associated with depression. A high score is not equivalent to a clinical diagnosis of severe depression but is rather a measure of the severity of symptoms, which may be more or less transient and situational. We have also used this scale in our study of the elderly (Kunitz and Levy 1991, chapter 4). It allows for estimates of one-month and one-year prevalence rates.

The Quantity-Frequency measure of alcohol use requires knowing the beverage(s) an individual consumes (in order to know their alcohol content), the amount he or she consumes, and the frequency of consumption. In general, beer, wine, and liquor are the three beverage categories. Since fortified wine is the drink of choice for many people, we have added that category as well.

First, pooling data from all the survivors, there are significant rank-order correlations between most of these various scales. The SIP scales are correlated ($p < 0.001$); the two depression scales (one month and one year) are correlated ($p < 0.001$); the Body Care SIP scale is correlated with both depression scales for one month ($p < 0.005$) and one year ($p < 0.001$); age is correlated with both SIP scales ($p < 0.02$ for body care; $p < 0.001$ for movement) but not with the depression scales.

Second, there is no significant difference (by the Kruskal-Wallis Analysis of Variance) in scores of the survivors on the two scales from the Sickness Impact Profile, either between study groups or between men and women. Nor is there a difference in the depression scale scores.

Third, there are no significant differences in the proportion of people in each group who were currently consuming alcohol at the time of follow-up (see table 5.6). Nor were there differences in what they drank, the quantity, the frequency with which they drank it, or the proportions who considered themselves, or were considered by the interviewers, to have problems with alcohol.

Moreover, when we look back to the first interviews and ask whether there were at that time differences between surviving members of each group, the differences are not impressive. For example, Preoccupation scores of survivors (distinguishing between women and men) did not differ between groups, nor did the proportion of men who had been arrested at least once in 1961–66, nor the number of arrests for those who had been arrested. The three surviving women in the Hospital group had all been arrested at least once in those years, but 14 of the 19 women in the Plateau group (73 percent) and 9 of the 13 women in the South Tuba group (69 percent) had not been. There was no significant difference in the number of arrests of those few who had been arrested (by Kruskal-Wallis Analysis of Variance).

These results suggest, first that as a result of selective mortality the three groups began to look more and more alike and second, that there existed a segment of the young male population that was at especially high risk of death from alcohol-related conditions. It is their attrition from the population that accounts for the increasing homogeneity of those who survived. This is a potentially important observation, for if there is a segment of

Table 5.6 Drinking Status of Survivors in Three Study Groups, 1990

Drinking Status	Plateau	South Tuba	Hospital
Currently drinking	2	8	6
Currently not drinking	28	17	18
Totals	30	25	24

the population that is at especially high risk of alcohol-related death, then efforts to identify them and prevent their self-destructive drinking would be valuable.

Finally, by the time our follow-up study was under way, in 1990, the American Psychiatric Association had formalized the diagnosis of psychoactive substance dependence in its manual of mental disorders, known as DSM-III-R (American Psychiatric Association 1987). Using those criteria, we reviewed our original interviews and medical and police records to determine whether it was possible to make a retrospective diagnosis. The criteria and the information we used to apply them to our respondents appear in appendix A. All but one member of the Hospital sample met the criteria of alcohol dependence. The one exception was a woman who had been admitted to the program with her husband, a long-time government employee who was threatened with loss of his job if he did not seek treatment for his heavy drinking. Because the diagnosis was all but universal in this group, it was not predictive of mortality in the follow-up period.

We also applied the same criteria to all nineteen people in the other two groups who were known to have been consuming alcohol at the time of interview in 1966. For three of them the records were not adequate to make a retrospective diagnosis. Of the sixteen for whom data were sufficient, eleven were diagnosed as alcohol-dependent and five were not. Four of the eleven diagnosed as alcohol-dependent died in the follow-up period, all of alcohol-related causes. Three of the five nondependent drinkers died, none of alcohol-related causes. The difference in cause of death is statistically significant ($p < 0.05$ by Fisher's Exact Test).

When the differences between men and women are considered, we note the following: Of five women in the Hospital sample, four were diagnosed retrospectively as alcohol-dependent. One woman in the South Tuba sample was also diagnosed as alcohol-dependent. Of these five alcohol-dependent women, three died of alcohol-related causes in the follow-up period, and one had become an abstainer by 1990. Of forty men who were retrospectively diagnosed as alcohol-dependent (all three study groups combined) in 1966, thirteen had died by 1990, nineteen were abstainers, four were still drinking but were not alcohol-dependent, and four were still alcohol-dependent. The survival of alcohol-dependent men was greater than for women with the same diagnosis, but with so few women the difference is not statistically significant.

Small numbers require caution in interpreting data, but our results do suggest several points. First, in the nonclinical population, the diagnosis of alcohol dependence was predictive of death from alcohol-related causes—though it was of no value in the clinical population. This is not particularly surprising and indicates simply that people with a diagnosis of alcohol dependence are at higher risk of dying of alcohol-related conditions than people without such a diagnosis, but that within the alcohol-dependent population more refined criteria are necessary to predict outcome.

Second, alcohol-dependent women seem to have a greater risk of dying of alcohol-related causes than men with the same diagnosis. This accords with observations we made in the original study, where we showed that women were much less likely to drink than men, but that when they did drink, they were much more likely to encounter severe problems. Third, there is evidence that some men, once diagnosed as alcohol-dependent, can subsequently drink in a nondependent fashion. We consider these issues in more detail in the next chapter.

6

Navajo Drinking Careers

In this chapter we turn our attention to the characteristics of problem drinking regardless of whether the individual died before the restudy in 1990. Instead of using alcohol-related mortality, we initially take drinking status (currently drinking or abstaining), either at the time of restudy or at the time of death, as an indicator of persisting drinking problems. In the same way that an alcohol-related death was not always a sure sign of problem drinking—one could be killed by a drunken driver without being drunk, for example—so it is possible to have continued to drink for many years in moderation. But because the alcoholic is said to be unable to stop drinking, those in our study who continued to drink over a period of twenty-five years would certainly include all he alcoholics.

In 1966, we were impressed by the fact that the men in the more traditional Plateau group appeared to drink as heavily as those in the South Tuba and Hospital groups. Moreover, the Plateau men, along with those in treatment, scored more in the "alcoholic" range on the Preoccupation with Alcohol scales than did the men in South Tuba or Flagstaff. Of the four measures, the Preoccupation scale was considered the most effective in identifying alcoholics in the general population. In our study, however, these questions identified the self-referred problem

99

drinkers as alcoholics and incipient alcoholics but failed to distinguish between them and a group of men in the community samples who were not regarded as alcoholic. It seemed remarkable to us that many of the men who would be labeled alcoholic by this index were able to give up drinking entirely at some point in their lives.

At that time, the Plateau group included more men who had stopped drinking than did the South Tuba and Flagstaff groups. On the reservation, one drank either rather heavily or not at all. In Flagstaff and the nation generally the largest proportion of people fell in the light-to-moderate drinking range. We were left with the conviction that the instruments used to identify alcoholics and incipient alcoholics in the general population could not be used with the same confidence in Indian populations.

We have seen that, controlling for age, the only factors that seem to discriminate between those who died from alcohol-related causes and those who did not were: age at time of first arrest, number of arrests between 1961 and 1966, and average household size. Those who died were also more likely to have attended school and to have begun drinking off the reservation. There was only one male lifelong abstainer. The rest of the men in the three groups drank for varying periods, and for most, their drinking was considered normal. In our earlier work we argued that Navajos learned how to drink from contact with Anglo-Americans in the nineteenth century and that this style of heavy binge drinking has persisted among the Indians, while most Anglos changed their drinking habits during the years of Prohibition. Navajo men drank together with kin or with friends. The amounts consumed were considerable, but the crucial factor in the Navajo view was that the drinking was social. In the Navajo context, this was as acceptable as Anglo-Americans having a few drinks before dinner or wine with a meal. Every man in the study started drinking in this manner regardless of how old he was when he started. Just as Anglo-Americans ask how one can tell which social drinkers will ultimately become alcoholics, so Navajos are concerned about what distinguishes a "normal" Navajo drinker from one who continues to drink until it has destroyed his life.

In chapter 4 we described several Navajo styles of drinking: (1) the house party, which included family members both male and female, (2) drinking by groups of older men, (3) drinking by groups of younger men, (4) drinking in isolation, which was considered deviant, and (5) deviant drinking by women who drank in the company of drinking men. In this chapter we classify drinkers as either social or solitary at the time of the first study. The solitary label was applied to people who combined solitary and social drinking as well as to those who only drank alone. We obtained no accounts from men that told of starting to drink in order to drown their sorrows. The vast majority of men began their drinking at home on the reservation with friends or with family members. Some men drank first while in the armed forces or while away from the reservation as laborers, but here too the reasons given were ones of sociability. In the service an Indian could drink with Anglos, and drinking served to strengthen a sense of belonging. One younger man who began drinking while in the navy mentioned that drinking gave him the feeling that he was freed from family restraints and a sense of being in charge of his own life. We suspect that solitary drinking develops after a period of social drinking and that it signals, as the Navajos believe, a more serious drinking problem.

Our solitary drinking label also included a few individuals who drank much like the casual or light Anglo drinker. In 1966, we found that many of the men in the Flagstaff group would drink a beer or two while at home in the evening watching television. There was also one highly educated woman who might have a cocktail before dinner, alone or with friends. There were so few drinkers of this light type that we felt they would not appreciably weaken any correlations between drinking status and style and could in any event be readily identified.

Women who drank with men and traded their favors for

alcohol presented a somewhat different problem. They would be labeled social rather than solitary drinkers but would nevertheless be considered deviant by other Navajos. In the event, there were so few women who continued to drink for any length of time, and in fact so few women who ever drank that statistical analyses were of little value. For this reason, as well as because women generally seemed to have different drinking careers, we discuss them separately from the men.

Although there is a feeling among some individuals that women ought not to drink, it is still considered normal for a woman to drink at home with her family or, in recent years, when away from home with her husband. All but three of the women in the study began drinking in this manner. Some had their first drinks at home because their parents drank and they were curious. Many of these young women did not like the taste of alcohol and never repeated the experience. We have classed these women as lifelong abstainers. Others continued to drink after marriage if their husbands were also drinkers. A number of women who had not been drinkers before marriage started to keep company with their husbands, who were drinkers.

First, we examine factors that might predict problem drinking. We hypothesize that drinking style is the major predictor of whether a person stops or continues drinking. Subsequently, we look for factors that might predict the style of drinking itself and, finally, at case histories to see whether there are typical reasons for the development of problem drinking.

Because the Plateau group differs greatly from the other groups on so many variables, any significant differences between those who stopped and those who continued to drink may well be accounted for by the nature of the sample group itself. In all the analyses, therefore, the influence of residence on the outcome is assessed. The difference between the education levels of drinkers and abstainers, for example, might be a result of the fact that the people in the Plateau group are generally less schooled than those in South Tuba and most of the Hospital group, who also come from South Tuba. If the effect of residence were not taken into account, one might conclude that the stresses of acculturation led to the greater prevalence of drinking problems in South Tuba. If, on the other hand, residence is an important variable, one must look for characteristics of the area—such as the availability of alcohol and the emigration of younger, more educated individuals from the rural areas—as having an important influence on outcome.

THE MEN
Drinking Status

Eighty-seven percent of the Plateau men had stopped drinking at the time of restudy or at the time of death, compared to 53 percent of the South Tuba group, 33 percent of the Hospital group from South Tuba, and 75 percent of the men in the Hospital group who lived in rural areas. These differences in recovery rates are considerable and indicate that, whether in treatment or not, those living in traditional, rural areas have better recovery rates than those in the wage-work communities. More detailed analysis by logistic regression of drinking status as the dependent variable and group and drinking style, age, and level of education as the independent variables shows that only drinking style has a significant influence; social drinkers have better recovery rates.*

When drinking style is the dependent variable, however, sample, level of education, and camp size all had significant effects.†
Men in the Plateau group, as compared with the other study groups, were most likely to drink socially, to have less education,

---

*The partial logistic regression coefficients of these factors have the following p values: sample = .57; style = <.01; age = .57; level of education = .13.

†The partial logistic regression coefficients of these factors have the following p values: sample = .05; level of education = .03; camp size = .02.

to have lived in larger camps in 1966, and to have stopped drinking (table 6.1). There was no difference, however, between the two styles with respect to the age at which drinking started, as we found in our examination of those who had died of alcohol-related causes. Nor did drinkers differ in respect of their scores on the Preoccupation with Alcohol and Definition of Alcohol scales or the number of withdrawal symptoms they experienced.

Because the symptoms of withdrawal are most often considered prime indicators of physical dependency on alcohol, it is important that there were no significant differences between social and solitary drinkers or between abstainers and drinkers in 1990 for any of the symptoms reported in 1966. Ninety percent of solitary drinkers and 76 percent of social drinkers had experienced one or more withdrawal symptoms. Most of the reported experiences were of the minor phase; that is, they occurred from six to eight hours after the last drink and rarely lasted as long as forty-eight hours. This type of episode may

Table 6.1   Men's Drinking Style

	Drinking Style	
Sample	Social	Solitary
Plateau	14	2
South Tuba	8	11
Hospital-Tuba	7	7
Hospital-other	6	6
Drinking status		
Abstains	28	10
Drinks	7	16
Education		
No	14	3
Yes	20	23
Mean camp size	9.6	7.7

include tremors, hallucinations, convulsions, and minimal disorientation. The major phase occurs between thirty-six and forty-eight hours of cessation of drinking and includes, in addition to tremulousness and hallucinations, delirium tremens, psychomotor activity, autonomic activity with much sweating, and profound disorientation.

Although there is a tendency for those who still drink and for solitary drinkers to experience delirium tremens more often than social drinkers and people who have become abstainers, the differences are not statistically significant. Six percent of social drinkers experienced delirium tremens compared to 21 percent of solitary drinkers. With considerably larger samples, it is likely that the expected differences would be found. The importance of these findings, however, is not that steady problem drinkers may be more prone to the major withdrawal symptoms but that symptoms of withdrawal cannot be used for prognostic purposes.

In our earlier study we noted that a high proportion of Navajos who reported tremulousness also experienced hallucinations of some sort (Levy and Kunitz 1974, 157). In other studies, 25–30 percent of alcoholics who reported tremulousness also reported hallucinations, either auditory or visual. Of the 42 men who reported tremulousness, 10 reported only auditory hallucinations and 18 reported visual hallucinations either with or without auditory hallucinations. This high proportion (67 percent) is due primarily to the settings in which Navajos drink, settings that differ greatly from those of non-Indian drinkers.

Withdrawal symptoms are less frequent and less severe among alcoholics who can control the tapering-off process. Those who cannot stop their drinking gradually but who pass out, get sick, or suddenly run out of liquor suffer a far higher incidence of withdrawal symptoms. The major precipitating factor is the suddenness of the withdrawal (Wolfe and Victor 1970). The onset of alcohol withdrawal states has been noted within two weeks of the start of a drinking bout among British seamen, beginning when they return to their ship and are without a continuing source of supply (Marjot 1970). The crucial element appears to be the sudden cessation of drinking.

The reservation style of drinking among the Navajo fosters sudden withdrawal. After ingesting large amounts of alcohol at one time, people often pass out or find their supply exhausted. Especially on the reservation there may be no readily available supplies to help them taper off. In bordertowns Navajos are arrested or wake up with no money after drinking. In contrast, the middle-class non-Indian drinker often has a liquor cabinet at home and can take the hair of the dog in the morning to stave off tremulousness. Even on skid row, an alcoholic can get a drink because the bars typically open early in these locales. Thus, by the time the non-Indian drinker develops symptoms of withdrawal, it is clear that he or she has long tolerated high alcohol levels in the blood and can do without alcohol for only very short periods. It seems that some of the most characteristic signs of addictive drinking are themselves influenced by the social environment and cannot be taken as true gauges of what Anglo-Americans think of as alcoholism.

Depression

We have seen that the men who died from alcohol-related causes tended to have suffered more from depression than the controls matched for age, although the difference was not significant. There were ten questions in the interview schedule dealing with depression (appendix B). For each affirmative answer a score of 1 was given if the symptom persisted for two or more weeks even though, as was most often the case, there were symptom-free periods of from one to five days. The maximum possible score was 10. Although the questionnaire was based on the Diagnostic Interview Schedule for Depression (DIS-D) developed by the National Institute of Mental Health (Robins, Helzer, Croughan, Williams, and Spitzer 1981; Robins, Helzer,

Croughan, and Ratcliff 1981), we did not attempt to diagnose clinical depression according to the *Diagnostic and Statistical Manual for Psychiatric Disorders* (DSM-III). Instead, we followed the practice of most epidemiological studies of depression, which use symptom-scale scores to identify depression. The majority of these studies consider a score of about one-third the maximum possible—in our case a score of 4 or above—as the cut-off point indicating the probable existence of clinical depression (Ensel 1982; Zung 1965). This method was used to ascertain the prevalence of depression at one month and one year before the interview. To assess the lifetime history of depression we also used material from the medical charts. A symptom-scale score cannot distinguish between transient episodes of bereavement, major depressions, or dysthymic disorders. Nor is it clear that the way we measured the lifetime history of depression would yield the same results if diagnoses were made according to DSM-III criteria.

More solitary than social drinkers had experienced episodes of depression, although the difference was statistically significant only for a lifetime history (table 6.2). Depression in association with suicide or a suicide attempt was also found more often among solitary (seven) than social (one) drinkers. There was no

Table 6.2 Men's Drinking Style and Depression

	Lifetime History of Depression				
	No		Yes		
Drinking style	Observed	Expected	Observed	Expected	Total
Social	29	(24.1)	6	(10.9)	35
Solitary	13	(17.9)	13	(8.1)	26
	42		19		61

Chi-square = 7.51; df = 1; p = <.01

association between depression and drinking status, however. The two men who committed suicide were both in the Hospital group, and both were drinking at the time of their deaths. Of the six men who attempted suicide, only one had stopped drinking before making the suicide attempt. The episode was precipitated by his wife's leaving him. Although he had been abstinent for many years, his life continued to be troubled by personal and family problems. In all, six of the eight men who attempted or successfully committed suicide were from South Tuba.

Whether drinking causes depression or is itself caused by depression remains moot. In several cases a drinker's depression was precipitated by the loss of a loved one, but because we have no knowledge of the respondents' early years we cannot know whether a depressed personality led to drinking and thence to a more acute episode of depression when faced with a stressful event. There were also several cases in which the depression seemed to be caused by the drinking itself as well as by the deleterious effects it was having on the respondent's life.

Self-perceived Problems with Alcohol

The majority of men—74 percent of the social drinkers and 77 percent of the solitary drinkers—regardless of drinking style, reported that drinking had been a problem for them at some time in their lives. On the other hand, alcohol was still a problem significantly more often for solitary than for social drinkers, which is consistent with the finding that more social drinkers were abstainers by 1990 (table 6.3). All but one of the solitary drinkers who claimed that alcohol use had never been a problem were clearly denying the true state of affairs in the interview and sometimes to themselves as well. The one South Tuba man for whom drinking was never a problem reported drinking fairly heavily in his twenties, but once steadily employed, drank very lightly. Of the remaining five, only two were abstainers, and all had trouble with their families, frequent arrests for alcohol, and all had withdrawal symptoms.

The Diagnosis of Alcohol Dependence

We retrospectively diagnosed all those who were drinking in 1966 by the criteria for alcohol dependence developed by the American Psychiatric Association. As we saw in chapter 5, people so diagnosed were at a higher risk of dying from alcohol-related conditions than people without such a diagnosis. Within the alcohol-dependent population, however, more refined criteria were necessary in order to predict outcome.

We wondered whether prediction would be improved if style of drinking was used in conjunction with the diagnosis. In table 6.4 we show the status in 1990 of all men studied, including those diagnosed as alcohol-dependent in 1966. Social drinkers were far less likely to die from alcohol-related causes, and all those still drinking in 1990 were drinking in a controlled manner. The difference in outcomes was statistically significant, although many solitary drinkers were also abstaining in 1990.

The two social drinkers who had died of alcohol-related causes were only twenty-two and twenty-three years old in 1966, and although they had not yet begun to drink alone, were already heavy drinkers. Thus, even style in conjunction with a diagnosis of alcohol dependence may not work as well for the very young as it does for those over twenty-five. The solitary drinker whose death was not due to alcohol was still drinking

Table 6.3   Men's Drinking Style and Problems with Alcohol

| | Drinking Still a Problem | | | | |
| | Yes | | No | | |
Drinking style	Observed	Expected	Observed	Expected	Total
Social	2	(7.35)	24	(18.65)	26
Solitary	11	(5.65)	9	(14.35)	20
	13		33		46

Chi-square corrected for continuity = 12.48; df = 1; p = .001

when he committed suicide and thus his death may be thought of as alcohol-related. The high proportion (42 percent) of solitary alcohol-dependent men who were abstainers in 1990 is still impressive and suggests that even with this more accurate method of predicting outcome the careers of alcoholic drinkers are not foreordained. Only one of these men was in the Hospital group from South Tuba. Four were in the Hospital group from other areas, and three were in the South Tuba group. It is also important that, despite the notion that the alcohol-dependent cannot control their drinking, four of the social drinkers were able to drink in a controlled fashion by 1990.

Reasons for Abstaining

Men gave various reasons for stopping their drinking. There was little difference between styles of drinking, but there were significant differences between the study groups (table 6.5). Men from the Plateau gave up drinking primarily for religious reasons, while those in the South Tuba and Hospital groups did so mainly for reasons of health. Five of the six Plateau men who gave up drinking for religious reasons listed the Native American Church. Only one attributed his stopping to an established Prot-

Table 6.4 Men's Drinking Style and Status in 1990

	Drinking Style				
	Social		Solitary		
Status	Observed	Expected	Observed	Expected	Total
Died of alcohol-related causes	2	(3.66)	6	(4.34)	8
Alcohol-dependent	0	(1.83)	4	(2.17)	4
Died of other causes	0	(0.46)	1	(0.54)	1
Controlled drinking	4	(1.83)	0	(2.17)	4
Abstinent	10	(8.23)	8	(9.77)	18
	16		19		35

Chi-square = 11.05; df = 4; p = <.03

estant church. The Other category included family and job responsibilities and finding that drinking had become unrewarding
or less pleasurable. The difference remains significant even when
only the social drinkers in the Plateau and South Tuba groups
are compared.

The reasons that were given for stopping drinking varied. The
Native American Church was given as a reason to stop problem
drinking as well as all drinking (table 6.6). Treatment programs
helped many to stop problem drinking but not to stop drinking
entirely. Nevertheless, men often stopped all drinking for reasons of health but never gave health as a reason to stop problem

Table 6.5 Men's Reasons for Stopping All Drinking

	Reasons						
	Religion		Health		Other		
Sample	Observed	Expected	Observed	Expected	Observed	Expected	Total
Plateau	6	(2.15)	1	(6.82)	7	(5.03)	14
South Tuba	0	(1.69)	9	(5.36)	2	(3.95)	11
Hospital	0	(2.15)	9	(6.82)	5	(5.03)	14
Total	6		19		14		39

Chi-square = 20.59; df = 4 p = <.001

Social Drinkers in Plateau and South Tuba Samples

	Reasons						
	Religion		Health		Other		
Sample	Observed	Expected	Observed	Expected	Observed	Expected	Total
Plateau	5	(3.25)	1	(3.9)	7	(5.85)	13
South Tuba	0	(1.75)	5	(2.1)	2	(3.15)	7
Total	5		6		9		20

Chi-square = 9.499; df = 2; p = <.01

drinking. Just deciding on one's own was cited as a reason to stop problem drinking but not all drinking.

The decade of the 1960s saw many Plateau families join the Native American Church (the peyote religion), and several men felt that the church helped them achieve abstinence. That "Indian" religion (traditional ceremonies and the NAC) is found more often in the Plateau group while Christianity prevails in South Tuba is to be expected (table 6.7). Why the Native American Church is mentioned more than the others as helping men to attain abstinence is less obvious because the Christian churches also preach against alcohol use.

The ethical code of the peyote religion—known as the "Peyote Road"—has four main parts: brotherly love, care of family, self-reliance, and avoidance of alcohol (Slotkin 1956, 71). Although much of the peyote experience is individually oriented—"the user is prompted to ask of everything, 'what does this mean for me?'" (Aberle 1966, 6)—the ethical principles as well as the experience foster the creation of community feeling. Many pey-

Table 6.6 Men's Reasons to Stop Drinking

	To Stop Problem Drinking		To Stop All Drinking	
	1st	2d	1st	2d
Native American Church	7	2	5	4
Established Protestant	1	0	1	1
Treatment program	13	1	0	0
Health	0	0	19	0
Family support	5	7	0	0
Responsibilities	0	0	6	2
Found unrewarding	0	0	2	2
Own Decision	7	5	0	0
Other	1	0	6	2
	34	15	45	11

otists claim that they can read one another's mind during the ceremony. This feeling of intimacy with fellow members, moreover, lasts for a considerable time after the meeting.

That Christianity does not serve a function similar to that performed by the Indian religions may be explained by the fact that Christian congregations did not, until recently, create a feeling of community among their members. In 1966, most Christian ministers on the Navajo reservation were non-Indians. The only ordained Navajo in Tuba City was the Baptist minister, who was not from the local community but commuted from Flagstaff. By 1990, however, the situation had changed considerably as evangelical Protestant sects had ordained many Navajos. Established Protestant churches lost more than half their members in all groups by 1990. Among men, the evangelical churches lost members in all groups except the Hospital, Other.

Table 6.7 Religious Affiliation, 1966 and 1990 (as percentages)

| | Men | | | | | |
| | 1966 | | | 1990 | | |
Sample	Navajo*	Christian	None	Navajo	Christian	None
Plateau (17)	76.5	23.5	0.0	82.3	17.7	0.0
South Tuba (19)	27.8	66.7	5.5	36.8	42.1	21.0
Hospital Tuba (17)	29.4	58.8	11.8	81.2	18.8	0.0
Hospital Other (12)	33.3	58.3	8.4	30.0	70.0	0.0
	Women					
	1966			1990		
Sample	Navajo*	Christian	None	Navajo	Christian	None
Plateau (23)	78.2	21.7	0	69.6	26.1	4.3
South Tuba (16)	6.2	81.2	12.5	56.2	37.5	6.2
Hospital (4)	25.0	50.0	25.0	100.0	0	0

*"Navajo" includes traditional and Native American Church

As men aged, they tended to return to the traditional Navajo religion. Membership in the Native American Church also grew, although usually in combination with traditionalism.

Traditional Navajo healing ceremonies are performed for the benefit of the individual patient. A diagnostician divines the cause of the disease and suggests the appropriate ceremonial cure. The ceremony is performed by a "singer," who is contracted by the family for this one performance. The "doctor-patient" relationship is relatively impersonal and short-lived. Introspection and ethical principles, moreover, play little role in ceremonial life. Unlike the Native American Church, the traditional Navajo religion has not adopted a uniform position vis-à-vis alcohol use and abuse.

According to Topper (1985, 231), Navajos have always viewed drinking as being undesirable although less so than mental illness or witchcraft. On the one hand, drinking facilitated conviviality at social gatherings. Several Plateau men mentioned that when they drank with other males, alcohol promoted a feeling of solidarity, and this gave them a sense of power and fearlessness. On the other hand, intoxication involved the loss of one's faculties and led to wild and reckless behavior. Terms used to describe such behavior use the thematic prefix *tsi'*— literally, to walk aimlessly in every direction. *Tsi'naagha,* for example, connotes both drunkenness and going to sexual extremes (Young and Morgan 1980, 734). Chaotic and purposeless behavior is characteristic of Coyote, the trickster figure of Navajo myth, so that excessive drinking may also be considered a Coyote-caused disease. How many Navajo drinkers actually regard their drinking as a disease is another matter.

Ceremonial Treatments for Alcohol Abuse

We have seen that treatment programs have helped a number of men to stop problem drinking and that participation in the Native American Church helped others to stop drinking entirely. To determine whether those who felt a church helped them to achieve abstinence also made use of Navajo ceremonial treatments, the number of Navajo ceremonies (sings), minor rituals, and peyote meetings performed for the respondent in the five years before the interview in 1990 and the reason for each type of treatment were tabulated.

Given the number of men in the Plateau group who claimed that the Native American Church was the major reason for them to stop drinking, it came as a surprise that no one in any of the samples had a peyote meeting performed specifically for either alcohol or mental problems. Sings and minor rituals, on the other hand, were used by 15 percent (10) of all men with drinking histories to treat alcohol or mental problems. (As alcohol is thought to affect the mind, we felt that mental problems were virtually synonymous with alcohol.)

That individuals did not have peyote ceremonies performed specifically for their problems with alcohol should not be taken to mean that participation does not have beneficial effects. We have mentioned that peyote meetings heighten a sense of communion with others who do not drink and help the drinker to create a new social environment. Men who had peyote ceremonies performed for them, regardless of the reason, were more likely to be abstainers in 1990 than those who did not (table 6.8). Whether, however, this may be attributed to the effectiveness of peyote meetings is moot. A significantly high proportion of church members were in the Plateau group, and, as we have seen, most Plateau men drank socially, and recovery rates were highest in this group.

Men who had sings or minor rituals performed for them but had not had peyote meetings were no more likely to be abstainers in 1990 than those who had sought no treatment. Ten men had sings or rituals specifically for alcohol or mental problems, and their recovery rates were no different than those who had not sought such treatment. They were interesting in another respect, however: six were in the South Tuba group, and five were Christians who had left their churches by 1990. It is possible that they found Christianity wanting and sought other means to combat their drinking problems.

We have seen that only drinking style predicted whether men were still drinking or abstinent in 1990, and that place of residence, level of education, and camp size were all associated with drinking style. Men in the Plateau group were most likely to drink socially, to have less education, to have lived in larger camps in 1966, to have stopped drinking by 1990, and to give religion as a reason for stopping, than were the men in the other groups.

But style of drinking in and of itself is not a protection against sustained problem drinking. Two social drinkers died from al-

Table 6.8 Men's Ceremonial Treatments (number of men)

| | Peyote Ceremony | | | | |
| | Yes | | No | | |
Sample	Observed	Expected	Observed	Expected	Total
Plateau	7	(3.86)	10	(13.14)	17
South Tuba	1	(4.32)	18	(14.68)	19
Hospital	7	(6.82)	23	(23.18)	30
	15		51		66

Chi-square = 6.6; df = 2; p = .04

| | Peyote Ceremony | | | | |
| Drinking status, 1990 | Yes | | No | | |
	Observed	Expected	Observed	Expected	Total
Drinks	2	(6)	24	(20)	26
Abstains	13	(9)	26	(30)	39
	15		50		65

Chi-square corrected for continuity = 4.42; df = 2; p = .03

cohol-related causes; both were from South Tuba, and one was in the Hospital group. Of the social drinkers who were still drinking in 1990, only one was in the Plateau group, and he was drinking lightly. In the 1960s, he had spent much of his time as a laborer off the reservation and tended to drink more heavily when away from home. Three other social drinkers were still drinking in 1990; all were in the Hospital group, and two were from South Tuba. All three were drinking in a controlled manner by 1990. In addition, there was one social drinker from the Plateau group who had experienced delirium tremens. He had been a very heavy drinker until he married, at which time he tapered off and drank only occasionally. He quit drinking entirely ten years before the reinterview. There were two Plateau men who were classed as solitary drinkers. Both were able to stop drinking completely despite having been heavy drinkers and in many respects resembled what we would call alcoholics in the general population.

When we recall that only drinking style predicted drinking status by 1990, but that sample, level of education, and camp size all had significant effects on drinking style, we find that the as-yet-unresolved question is whether problem drinking is primarily a result of the type of community in which one lives or of drinking in a socially approved style. Before addressing this issue, let us look at the women's drinking patterns to see how they parallel or diverge from those of the men.

THE WOMEN

Of the forty-five women in the study, seven Plateau and five South Tuba women were lifelong abstainers. Of those with drinking histories, only one Plateau and six South Tuba women were drinking at the time of restudy or at the time of death. Both style of drinking and years of education have significant effects on drinking status; that is, women social drinkers were more likely to be abstainers in 1990, but, unlike the men, those who still drank were less educated than the abstainers.[‡] There were, however, too few women for a logistic regression analysis to reveal significant results on the joint effects of residence, drinking style, age, and level of education.

When the women's drinking histories and behavior are compared to those of the men, they appear to be similar in most respects despite the fact that the differences between the female social and solitary drinkers are rarely significant (table 6.9). Solitary women drinkers, however, tended to have fewer years of education than the social drinkers although about the same proportion had no education at all. Whether these nonsignificant differences would be found among larger samples is moot. Solitary women drinkers, however, had significantly more arrests, liquor violations, and assaults than did the social drinkers.

Table 6.9 Drinking Styles of Men and Women

| | Drinking Style | | | |
| | Men | | Women | |
Mean averages	Social	Solitary	Social	Solitary
Age in 1966	39.7	33.0*	41.2	36.0
Yrs, Education	4.7	6.7*	4.2	2.0
Age started	19.2	18.2	20.9	26.6
Number in camp	9.6	7.7	10.7	7.4
Preoccupation scale, 1966	5.9	6.3	5.2	7.4
Number arrests	7.1	9.8	0.8	12.3**
Number liquor violations	1.5	1.8	0.1	1.1**
Number assaults	0.1	0.5	0.0	0.3**
Age, 1st arrest	27.2	24.4	39.0	30.2

* $p = \leq .04$ by the Mann-Whitney U-test.
** $p = \leq .001$ by the Mann-Whitney U-test.

[‡]The partial logistic regression coefficients of these factors have the following p values: style = .04; years education = .03.

Solitary drinkers experienced auditory and visual hallucinations after drinking significantly more often than social drinkers. This is markedly different from the men, who showed no differences with regard to the sequelae of drinking (table 6.10).

Proportionately more women than men had experienced depression at either one month or one year before the interview. The one-year prevalence was 12 percent for men and 24 percent for women, a ratio of two to one, which is also found in the general population. The ratio, however, is almost equal for lifetime history of depression—30 percent of men, 38 percent of women. In large part this is due to the greater number of men in the Hospital group. When the Plateau and South Tuba groups are considered separately, only 14 percent of the men and 32 percent of the women had any history of depression. We have already seen that alcohol abuse contributes significantly to the level of depression among men. That a similar correlation is not found among women is due primarily to the fact that so few women were solitary drinkers.

Unlike the men, most of whom reported that drinking had

Table 6.10 Women's Drinking Style and Withdrawal
            Symptoms

	Style	
Auditory Hallucinations	Social	Solitary
Yes	3	4
No	14	1

Chi-square corrected for continuity = 4.35; df = 1; p = <.04

Visual Hallucinations		
Yes	0	2
No	17	3

Fisher's Exact Test p = .04

been a problem at some time in their lives regardless of their drinking style, solitary women drinkers were far more likely than social drinkers to report that drinking had been a problem (table 6.11). There was no significant difference between types of drinkers reporting that drinking was still a problem in 1990. Again this is most likely because so few women were solitary drinkers; 67 percent of solitary drinkers said alcohol was still a problem compared to only 22 percent of the social drinkers.

Five women were retrospectively diagnosed as alcohol-dependent. None of these was a social drinker. Three died of alcohol-related causes, and two were abstinent by 1990. Four were in the Hospital group, and one was in the South Tuba group.

For men, residence was highly correlated with reasons to stop drinking. The same was not the case among women drinkers because of their small number. The overall pattern was similar, however; only women who were social drinkers gave religion as a reason to stop all drinking, and none was from the Hospital group.

As with the men, peyote meetings were held mostly for Plateau women. Although women who had peyote ceremonies were more likely to be abstainers, the difference did not reach a level of significance. Nor were recovery rates different for women who had sings. When all ceremonies for alcohol and mental problems were combined, women who had no ceremonial treatments for those reasons were more likely to be abstainers than

Table 6.11 Women's Drinking Style and
Problems with Alcohol

	Drinking Ever a Problem	
Drinking Style	Yes	No
Social	9	17
Solitary	6	0

Fisher's Exact Test p = <.01

the women who had had ceremonies. Again, however, the difference was not statistically significant. Male social drinkers
were as likely as solitary drinkers to believe they had a problem
with alcohol. Women social drinkers, on the other hand, were
less likely to have had problems with their drinking and, in
consequence, would be less likely to have had ceremonies performed.

Navajo men start drinking because it is expected of them, and
considerable social pressure is brought to bear on those who do
not participate willingly in group drinking bouts. Referring to
the period between 1871 and 1878, a Navajo telling his life
history recounted how "friends would come around with whis
key and would try to make me drink. They would try to pour
it down my throat but I would let it run out on the ground"
(Dyk 1947, 19). Peer pressure was a problem for many of the
men in this study, who complained that even when they were
trying to stop drinking, their "buddies" would come to their
homes and pressure them into drinking. One of the younger
men in the Hospital group from Tuba City was persuaded to
go with his friends to an off-reservation bar. He intended not
to drink as he was on Antabuse but thought he could enjoy the
company of his friends without imbibing. In the event, he was
taunted and teased until at last he took a drink. He suffered the
inevitable consequences.

Most of the women also started their drinking in a socially
approved manner—that is, at home with their families. This
pattern was found significantly more often among the Plateau
women than among the others (table 6.12). The majority of
South Tuba women began drinking after marriage in order, as
several said, "to keep my husband company." Drinking in public, even with one's husband, is a relatively recent pattern, and
although not wholeheartedly approved, it has come to be recognized as common and not necessarily deviant. Some of the
women from South Tuba came from drinking families. Some
who had not, raised children who became drinkers.

Although fewer women than men had drinking histories, approximately the same proportion of women were able to stop drinking over time. Both women and men tended to drink more heavily after divorce or the death of a spouse or a child. Several women said they drank to assuage loneliness. Although it is clear that some men and women who became heavy drinkers had personality problems, it is not possible to identify preexisting psychological factors as the primary reason to start drinking. Severe personal problems, however, were the reason for starting to drink for three of the women in the Hospital group, all of whom were solitary drinkers. No similar cases could be identified among the men.

One woman was an adopted orphan who while still a child helped to raise the children of her adoptive family. By all accounts she was a kind and caring person during her youth. At age 12 she was given in marriage to a man thirty years her senior. It was a violent marriage; her husband drank and beat her often. She started drinking at age twenty-three. Later, after separating from her first husband, she married a nondrinker who was a member of the Native American Church, and for three or four years she remained abstinent. Finally, however, she became exasperated because her husband rejected her children and refused to help with their upbringing. When she realized

Table 6.12 Women's Reasons to Start Drinking

	Reason					
	Family		Husband		Problems	
Sample	Observed	Expected	Observed	Expected	Observed	Expected	Total
Plateau	13	(7.5)	3	(7.0)	0	(1.5)	16
South Tuba	2	(5.16)	9	(4.81)	0	(1.03)	11
Hospital	0	(2.34)	2	(2.19)	3	(0.47)	5
Total	15		14		3		32

Chi-square = 30.45; df = 4; p = .0001

the situation would never change, she began drinking again, and the second marriage broke up. Her periods of drinking were separated by several weeks of sobriety so that she was able to hold jobs as a dishwasher. Finally, however, her children were taken from her. She had severe bouts of depression, attempted suicide once, and developed delirium tremens. She never stopped drinking and died from alcoholic cirrhosis at age forty-two. All nine of her children are doing well, and although two had some problems with alcohol, they appear to have handled them.

The second woman told us she started drinking heavily at age twenty-nine to drown her loneliness and to forget her worries. This coincided with her return from a tuberculosis sanatorium to find that her relatives had taken her valuables from the trading post where she had left them in pawn for safekeeping. She felt alienated from her family, which was never supportive. Her husband also drank heavily, and after his death she entered the Antabuse treatment program in Tuba City. She married a second time, but this husband, also a drinker and wife beater, died as well. She gave birth to fourteen children and had a history of abandoning her infants. By all accounts she was never a sympathetic person. We feel the underlying cause of her drinking was her psychiatric condition; she was given the diagnosis of psychotic schizophrenia in 1970, when she was thirty-seven years of age. She was able gradually to attain abstinence by the time she was fifty-one, but she has always resisted psychotherapy and has suffered severe bouts of depression in recent years.

The third woman, also from South Tuba City, had suffered from grand mal epilepsy since she was a child but was not brought to medical attention until she was twenty-one years old, just five years before she was admitted to the Antabuse program.[5] By age seventeen, she had a lengthy police record. At eighteen she was apprehended while having intercourse with an

---

[5]The case history of this woman has been described in detail elsewhere (Levy, Neutra, and Parker 1987, 140–42).

older, married brother who had a long history of drinking. The succeeding years were marked by a series of arrests for drunken and disorderly conduct with many references to promiscuity. In 1963, at age twenty-five, she left the reservation to live with an Anglo in a bordertown. She maintained that she was happy for the first time in her life. Nevertheless, the couple drank heavily and were soon separated. Over the three years they were together, she took her antiepileptic medication erratically and suffered frequent seizures, especially when in jail. After the separation, she returned to Tuba City and entered the Antabuse treatment program but did not take the medication regularly and continued to drink.

According to her medical chart she was immature, impulsive, and given to temper tantrums. There was a long history of depression and suicidal ideation as well as one suicide attempt. In addition to her heavy drinking, she was a chain smoker, a habit not often found among the Navajo. At some point she contracted tuberculosis. She had also experienced all the withdrawal symptoms, including delirium tremens. Her chart notes that during the time she lived with her common-law husband she managed to drink somewhat less and to suffer fewer seizures. She never stopped drinking, however. She returned to the bordertown where she had worked as a domestic and was found dead from carbon monoxide poisoning in 1969 at age thirty. The death was listed as accidental, and alcohol was not mentioned, although she may have been drunk. It is also possible that she committed suicide.

This unfortunate woman's story is important for two reasons: the negative beliefs that Navajos have concerning seizures and the background of her family, which together go a long way toward explaining her alcoholism. The symptoms of the grand mal epileptic seizure are believed by traditional Navajos to be the consequences of sibling incest. Sexual intercourse, whether with a true sibling or a member of one's clan, is strictly forbidden and its "punishment" in the form of seizures is perhaps the most dreaded of afflictions (Levy, Neutra, and Parker 1987). An epileptic child, of course, will not be suspected of incest. Instead, its parents will be suspected, either of incest or of an especially malevolent act of witchcraft. The child and its family are stigmatized. In the case under discussion the incest was a self-fulfilling prophecy as it took place after the onset of seizures. The epileptic female loses all social status, and, unable to attract a marriage partner, becomes vulnerable to rape by others as well as to incest.

Not all female epileptics become alcoholics, however. Much depends on the social standing of the family. High-status, wealthy families have traditionally been able to shield an epileptic from the community, provide healing ceremonies, and most often direct the blame onto witches, whom they believe are trying to destroy the family out of envy. In this case the family was, if not poverty stricken, certainly poor. The father always claimed he was too poor to pay for the ceremonial treatments his daughter needed, although poverty does not explain why she was brought to medical attention only after she was an adult.

The community believed, of course, that she was '*iich'ah*, the disorder caused by incest, but not because of the incestuous act for which she and her brother had been arrested. Instead, it was said to have been caused by her father, who had transgressed a tabu before her birth. We were never able to learn exactly what the father had done, although it appears to have been serious because he was forced to leave his home community the year his daughter's seizures began. There was reason for the family to guard its reputation closely: it was one of a group of related families with a tradition of marrying back into a father's clan, also a proscribed form of marriage. In addition, theirs was the only kin group in the area with a *nádleeh,* a berdache. The family was not well off despite the fact that the father's father and two brothers were ceremonialists.

Here we have an example of how a deviant and poor family

may be driven from the home community and forced to migrate to a wage-work settlement. In this instance, the father and all his offspring took to drink, and at least one of the sons married into another family of heavy drinkers. Again, the question arises, to what extent does the nature of the community account for the extent and type of drinking found among its members?

Before turning our attention to this problem, it is important to remember that although we have been treating Navajo drinkers as a special population, in many ways they are much like drinkers in the general population. Those who appeared to be alcoholic in our samples were often able to moderate their drinking drastically, or even to achieve abstinence without specific treatment for alcoholism. Similar observations have been made by others. Vaillant (1983, 144–45, 160), for example, has shown that alcoholism is not always a progressive disease that must end in either abstinence or death. Others have shown that large proportions of heavy drinkers are able to continue drinking at various levels without experiencing further problems (Helzer, Robins, and Taylor 1985). Spontaneous remission is also common: "In the largest study yet mounted of nontreatment populations, the so-called Epidemiologic Catchment Area (ECA) study, fully 84 per cent of those who met DSM-III lifetime criteria and had reported especially heavy consumption at some time (7 or more drinks daily for two or more weeks) reported no periods of such drinking during the past year. Rates of remission (defined as the proportion of lifetime that [a person] had no alcohol problems in the past year) were found to be high, ranging from 45 to 55 per cent across the different sites of the study and averaging 51 percent for the study overall" (IOM 1990, 34).

Female alcoholics also constitute a heterogeneous group, and many of the differences found between male and female Navajo drinkers are also found in the general population. Women drinkers are more likely than men to suffer depression and to have serious liver disease, a spouse with an alcohol problem, a history of sexual abuse, and a pattern of drinking in response to major life crises (Beckman and Amaro 1986; Braiker 1984).

Given these similarities, one must ask to what extent Navajo drinking is different from that found in the general population. Is it, as we have suggested (Levy and Kunitz 1974), more a matter of style than substance, a style that involves public intoxication and group bingeing that deviate considerably from urban Anglo drinking?

Community Influences

Indian or even Navajo drinking patterns are often described as typical of the entire group. That is, it is generally believed that all Indians drink more than non-Indians and that Navajos typically indulge in binge drinking. In our earlier study we labeled the style of drinking we found among Plateau men traditional Navajo drinking, implying that this style described the vast majority of Navajo male drinkers before their contact with wage work and Anglo-Americans. Yet, the Plateau group is not typical of all pastoral areas of the reservation, so that one must question whether the style we characterized as normative can be used as a marker of nonalcoholic drinking. This is especially important when we recall that the six men in the Hospital group who came from rural pastoral areas drank socially and yet had significant problems with alcohol.

The Plateau group constituted a single large kin group from the area known as the Kaibito Plateau, the best grazing land on the western half of the reservation. The kin group was led by the second wealthiest stock owner in the area before the stock-reduction program of the 1930s. Differences in wealth are not a new phenomenon. The Navajos' subsistence economy underwent several shifts during their history in the Southwest, but by 1850 more than half their subsistence was obtained from stock raising, and differences in wealth had become marked (Aberle 1966, 25). Pastoralism continued to be the major source of subsistence during the reservation period until the stock-reduction programs. Differences in wealth persisted during the entire period. In 1915, a survey of the Southern Navajo Reservation reported that 24 percent of families owned no sheep at all, and

42 percent had fewer than a hundred (Navajo Year Book 1958, 375). Aberle (1973, 187) has reviewed the data for family composition and concluded that approximately 53 percent of all family units were independent nuclear families immediately before stock reduction.

Eric Henderson (1985) has reconstructed the history of the Kaibito Plateau. It was settled by two groups of Navajos immediately after their release from Fort Sumner and the establishment of the original reservation in 1868. From that time until 1930 the population grew, augmented by immigration from what is now the eastern part of the reservation. Use of the range intensified, and the northern reaches of the plateau were a favorite winter pasture of the wealthy descendants of the original settlers. Differences in livestock holdings increased throughout the period. By 1930, families with larger flocks tended to travel greater distances between winter and summer locations, while families with smaller flocks had more restricted seasonal movements. The cooperating kin groups of the wealthy were larger than those of poorer stock owners. Most of the poorer families, perhaps as many as half of all camps, cooperated little with kinsmen who were not resident in the camp.

The elite was composed of families descended from leaders of the Fort Sumner period; most of those of lower status were more recent immigrants; those in the middle were from the poorer Fort Sumner families as well as immigrant families. By the late 1930s, the wealthiest owners, some 7 percent of all owners, held over a third of all livestock in the district; the wealthiest 25 percent owned over two-thirds, and the poorest 50 percent owned only 15 percent. It was during these pre-stock-reduction years that most adults in the kin group learned to drink.

Only the wealthy could afford liquor at that time; it was therefore a luxury item that represented wealth and social standing. The leader of the kin group would send a young relative to trade young steers for whiskey in southern Utah. A gallon of whiskey was traded for a steer. One middle-aged informant told us that the head of the kin group would dole out drinks to the younger men in a tin cup after the whiskey run had been made, and in the evening the leader and his family would drink together in private. As a young man he dreamed of one day being able to afford whiskey and to drink in this manner.

Because whiskey was not only costly but difficult to obtain, few could drink to insobriety except on rare occasions. And because drinking took place within the family and always involved sharing with relatives, drinking behavior was defined and controlled by traditional Navajo values. Cooperation in all family activities and responsibility toward kin were instilled early. The individual strove for material wealth that was shared with relatives. Hospitality, generosity, and care for relatives who were less well off were highly valued.

The economic changes that came about after stock reduction in the 1930s were accompanied by a gradual shift to a cash economy and to road improvements, which made alcohol increasingly available. Over the years, we can trace the changes in drinking behavior brought about by these developments. After livestock reduction there were no longer any wealthy families, only the poor and the very poor. There was no longer any reason for wealthy families to undertake long seasonal moves. Seasonal shifts in residence had been one of the prime means by which families kept in contact over long distances. Families that summered together and cooperated in farming no longer had any economic reason to move to winter pastures, where they would cooperate with a different configuration of kin. With smaller flocks there was less need for manual labor. Sheep shearing and lambing operations were no longer occasions that required the cooperation of more than a few families. The nature of relations between the wealthy and those of lesser means was altered; there were no longer wealthy owners to whom the poor could turn for herding and construction work. The wealthy had lost not only their ability to sell their surplus in the market, they had no surplus to redistribute locally out of generosity or in sponsoring ceremonials.

Young men, even those from poor families, were increasingly able to pay for fortified wine, which, following World War II, began to take the place of the more prestigious but still expensive whiskey. Groups of young men could now drink together because those with some wage income could share with their friends. Sharing with friends beyond the kin group began to be more common. It was the young wage earner who could afford a pick-up truck and who could drive to an off-reservation bar to obtain wine. And it was his age mates who could reciprocate.

Despite the steady erosion of the kin group, the tradition of responsibility to kin was one that the adults in this study have retained and passed on to many who were in their teens and twenties in the 1960s. We note the man who had been a heavy drinker but who tapered off and than stopped after marriage and the assumption of family duties. We note also the man who stopped drinking when, after his brother died in an accident, he assumed responsibility for his widowed sister-in-law and her children. There was also the young man who returned to the reservation to work when his father died, to take care of his aging mother. Although he did not abstain entirely, he never drank at home and was careful not to squander his pay on drink.

After stock reduction, the families that made up the kin group remained near their farms in the southern portion of the district. Even what winter graze they still needed was eventually denied them as the population grew and more district grazing lines were drawn. Increasingly, grazing land was in short supply even for the small flocks that some of these families were still able to maintain. The kin group no longer cooperated with the leader's sisters. Herds, in fact, had become so small that there was no longer a compelling need for several camps to cooperate regularly.

By 1960, when we first became acquainted with them, the

extended families, or camps, that made up the kin group had already drifted apart. Nevertheless, four camps constituted a core of regularly interacting families, and four other camps cooperated with this core on a less regular basis. Together the eight camps included twenty-one households with a total population of 105, of which 64 were minor children. The eight camps owned a total of 1,890 sheep.** This averaged 18 head per capita, well below the amount necessary to support a family. Social Security and Aid to Families with Dependent Children were major sources of income. None of the young men had steady wage work although several worked for a few months each year away from the reservation. The average annual per capita income from all sources was about $360.

There were few economic activities that demanded the cooperation of all or most of the camps. Shearing was most often done within a single camp or by two cooperating camps. Similarly, there was no need to pool the flocks of several camps during the lambing season. Gelding horses was the only ranching activity we were able to document that involved men from all the camps. There were still seasonal moves to winter pasture, but these involved single households leaving the camps to take the flocks a few miles to the north. Transportation was a major problem, however. Only one man owned a truck, and this was used extensively by the four core camps for hauling wood and water and for trips to town, trading post, and hospital. The other four camps relied on help from neighbors and from children who lived off the reservation but who came home weekends to help out. Most of the camps worked small dry farms that did not require assistance from outside the extended family. The original fields of the senior man (the oldest in the kin group), however, were more extensive and better watered. During planting, five families from four camps stayed by the fields until the

---

**This includes cattle, each equivalent to four sheep, but does not include horses which were not sold or consumed.

job was done. A similar pattern was followed during the harvest, which was shared by all the camps that had contributed labor.

Most of the curing ceremonies involved only a single camp, or one camp with the assistance of individuals from another. Because there were three ceremonialists in the kin group, many of the sings were "in house" affairs with only a few relatives coming to attend rather than to help out. The only ceremonies that called for hosting large numbers of guests were three Enemy Way sings given by three camps in the early years of the decade. Each of these events involved six of the eight camps as well as clan relatives of the patient. Between 1956 and 1960, eighty ceremonies were performed for adults of the eight camps. For the years 1965–69, the total number of ceremonies remained the same but sixty-two (77 percent) were peyote meetings. For all but two of the adults this did not represent a religious conversion so much as a shift to a cheaper and shorter (one-night) healing ceremony that required little cooperation from kinfolk (Levy and Kunitz 1974, 129).

By the early 1970s, the kin group had shrunk to eleven households grouped into six camps. The decrease in the number of households was due as much to the emigration of young couples as to death. Among the forty-seven adults aged twenty-one and older in 1967, there were only six who had steady wage work and seven who combined seasonal wage work with stock raising (Levy and Kunitz 1974, 115). Twenty-nine (57 percent) thought of themselves as full-time stock raisers. Only five (10 percent) were retired or unemployed receiving social welfare or Social Security. By 1973, the number of retired and unemployed had risen to 33 percent, and although the proportion of adults with wage work had not changed, as many women as men had steady employment. Most striking was the growth in the number of women heads of household—from one in 1960 to four in 1973. The young adults who remained at home were most often divorced mothers with their dependent children. Of the six camps, only one had households headed by active males with wage work. This was also the largest camp, containing three house-holds. Three camps comprised two households each; three of these households were headed by unemployed women, and three by unemployed men (one of whom had an employed single daughter). The two single-household camps were headed, re-spectively, by a widow and by a retired stock raiser who now lived alone with his wife.

The number of sheep per capita had not declined appreciably (from eighteen to sixteen) over the years. Nor did the economic profile of the six camps differ radically from that of the sur-rounding area. The average annual per capita income for the group from all sources in 1973 was $749, only $100 less than it had been in 1960, although purchasing power had declined appreciably owing to inflation. The proportions of the total derived from wage work (40 percent) and unearned income (50 percent) was the inverse of the community average (Callaway, Levy, and Henderson 1976, 67). Wealth differences among the camps had become marked, however. One camp derived 76 percent of its total income from all sources from wage work and had a per capita income of $1,098. In sharp contrast, the camp of a widow and her divorced daughter relied primarily on unearned income and had a per capita income of $491. It is abundantly clear that Social Security and welfare had become the major means of support of several families.

Even in this formerly wealthy set of related families the dis-integration of the kin group was well advanced by the early 1980s. In 1985, there were ten households grouped into seven camps, only two of which contained more than one household. Five households were headed by men, three of whom were over sixty-five years of age. Three of the five households headed by women were led by widows who were still active, two of whom had divorced daughters and minor children living with them. Four of the camps were totally dependent on welfare and Social Security.

Routine cooperation with relatives in other camps is a thing of the past. Anglo-style family reunions celebrating an older person's birthday and Thanksgiving dinners are the only occasions attended by relatives from other camps. These expressions of sentiment, however, are not satisfactory substitutes for the sense of kin solidarity that once provided support and security. Social support provided by kinfolk was predicated on the possession of sizable stock holdings before stock reduction. Camp size was only one measure of this support; the other was regular cooperation between a number of related camps.

The stock-reduction programs destroyed the pastoral economy without providing an alternate means of making a living. It was not until the 1960s that most children in an age cohort were receiving an education to prepare them for wage work. But wage-work opportunities existed almost exclusively in off-reservation towns or agency towns on the reservation. In consequence, the better-educated, newly formed families most often had to leave their homes to make a living. Today intercamp cooperation is virtually nonexistent, and multihousehold camps are all too frequently composed of families headed by the unemployed and underemployed. The subsistence economy is still, fifty years after stock reduction, as much dependent on unearned as on earned income.

The drinking patterns displayed by the men and women of the Plateau group developed during the nineteenth century and were characteristic of the wealthy. Poor families may have aspired to drink in the same manner but were unable to do so until paved roads, cash income, and inexpensive wine were widely available after 1960. Every household in the Plateau group today owns its own pick-up truck regardless of the source or amount of family income. One or two of the women were able to obtain alcohol and to drink heavily after the loss of a spouse, despite the fact that they were entirely dependent on welfare income.

Whether the traditional restraints placed upon drinking in the past can survive in the years to come is doubtful. Alcohol is no longer expensive or difficult to obtain. Cooperative kin-based subsistence activities no longer exist, making it doubtful that traditional values and attitudes can long survive. With jobs scarce in the rural areas, the better educated and more skilled are increasingly forced to seek employment in the growing wage-work settlements, if not away from the reservation entirely. Despite the economic and social erosion we have observed over the past thirty years, we have been impressed by the successful adaptations made by a number of the younger members of the kin group, who were either children or teenagers when we first knew them in the 1960s.

Henderson (1985) compared the adaptations made by families of differing status after stock reduction in the 1930s and concluded that members of formerly wealthy families have been more likely to achieve educational and occupational success in the wage economy than have members of poorer families. He could find no economic reasons for this but noted that the wealthier stock owners saw the benefits of education in a changing world very early. Conversely, poorer families saw education as an intrusion and did everything they could to keep their children from being sent away to school. By the 1960s, a higher proportion of descendants of the wealthy had left the reservation than of descendants of poorer families.

Younger members of the kin group continue this trend in the 1980s. The older children of one couple have remained in the home area, but their younger siblings, with more education, have completed college. Two brothers work for the Navajo Tribe and have relocated to the tribal headquarters in Window Rock. A sister has married an Anglo and relocated to a large urban area, where she works for a community college. A cousin, after completing college, married an Indian from an eastern tribe who is a professor at a leading university. Those who have left the reservation appear to be doing well and raising families of their own.

We do not know enough about the children of South Tuba

families who have left the reservation to be able to say whether Henderson's observations continue to be true even for those poorer families living in communities that provide easy access to public schools and more interaction with non-Indians. It is possible to say, however, that the disintegration of the social fabric and the economic decline of the rural pastoralists has not resulted in anomie, a sense of despair, or any noticeable stress from the conflicting demands of two culturally different worlds. We were startled, for example, when a child one of us had known as a two-year-old from the traditional family of a ceremonialist in the kin group suddenly appeared in one of his university classes some twenty years later as a young adult and an "A" student.

South Tuba City

South Tuba City has come to be more representative of the environments in which increasing numbers of young Navajos learn about drinking. Growing up in a wage-work community like South Tuba is qualitatively different from growing up in the pastoral hinterlands of the reservation and may represent the future of Navajo drinking more accurately than any rural area of the western part of the reservation.

Tuba City, first settled by Mormons, became the site of the Western Navajo Agency after the area was incorporated into the Navajo reservation by Executive Order in 1900. From the start it was a source of wage work for both Navajos and Hopis. The Navajo settlement became known as South Tuba to distinguish it from the government "compound" just to the north, which contained the boarding school, offices, and housing for non-Indian employees, with a trading post separating the two areas.

By the 1960s, when we originally conducted our research, we wrote: "In the case of Tuba City, it is not clear that a real community exists in the sense that we think of it in Anglo-American towns of comparable size. The town now contains between 800 and 1000 people. About half of them are Anglos who are employed by various federal agencies. Even though some of these people have lived in the area for more than 20 years, the majority are transients. In general, the Anglos make up several subcommunities depending on the agency that employs them, either the Public Health Service, the Bureau of Indian Affairs, or the Arizona Public School System. The entire Anglo population has little to do with the Indian population, which lives in an area called South Tuba" (Levy and Kunitz 1974, 42–43).

The population of South Tuba has always been heterogeneous. The earliest settlers were from the eastern reservation who came specifically for federal employment as range riders and police. Over time, families from almost every part of the western reservation came for jobs, both temporary and permanent. Although some families were related to each other and some maintained ties with relatives in the hinterland, the trend was toward the proliferation of independent nuclear families. Not only wage work but the zoning of South Tuba into individual lots and the completion of a federally financed low-cost housing project has increased the trend toward the development of nuclear families.

Wage labor has not been the only attraction of Tuba City, however. The availability of state and tribal welfare services and the presence of a hospital have drawn many families to the area who rely on welfare checks and medical care. Finally, towns like Tuba City are, like off-reservation towns, places where "problem" families no longer tolerated in the home communities must find ways to survive. In all our research, with Hopis as well as Navajos, we have observed that more traditional communities tend to eject deviant families, who must migrate to more acculturated areas. Among the Hopis we have had occasion to observe that the higher prevalence of suicide, homicide, and alcoholic cirrhosis in transitional villages and off-reservation towns has often been taken as evidence of the stressful nature of the acculturation process, when in reality, such deviance is generated in all types of communities (Levy, Kunitz, and Henderson 1987). For some, transitional communities like South Tuba serve the same function as the skid rows of America's cities.

It is not surprising that we found more heavy drinking in South Tuba and more men from South Tuba in the Hospital group. The elements that foster drinking and problem drinking in Tuba City are: (1) easier access to sources of alcohol, (2) greater availability of cash, (3) the absence of functioning kin groups and the responsibilities and values they foster, (4) the density of the settlement, which makes it impossible for the drinker to avoid the pressure to drink from his drinking buddies, (5) the growing prevalence of the empty-nest phenomenon among women in nuclear families whose children have grown and left home, and (6) the absence of a sense of community, making it difficult to foster new attitudes and cooperative activities.

In stark contrast to the Plateau, South Tuba was home to several families in which almost all the adults drank heavily, and three of these families were virtually destroyed by alcohol abuse. One was the family, mentioned earlier, that had been forced out of the home community. The source of the others' problems was not discovered. Nor are we able to guess just how prevalent or how recent this phenomenon is. But because such families may tell us much about the genesis of destructive drinking patterns and because they tax the resources of health providers and social welfare agencies, they deserve more attention than they have received. It is to a description of one such family that we turn in the next chapter.

7

A Family History
of Alcohol Use

TRACY ANDREWS

Several South Tuba men were from families
known in the community for their drinking. Three brothers from
one of these families died of alcohol-related causes during the
course of the study, and although we did not interview all of
them, all had sought treatment at one time or another. Other
members of the family continued to experience problems, including possible fetal physiological damage to a few members
of the youngest generation. On the other hand, a sister was a
lifelong abstainer and often assumed responsibility for the children and grandchildren of family members mired in alcohol
abuse. Even the lives of nondrinkers have been affected by the
family legacy of alcohol abuse that many say began with the
father before alcohol was widely used or available on the reservation. In general, family members were very much concerned
about the high toll alcohol abuse had taken on them and their
relatives. They asked repeatedly whether we could explain why
so many of them had become problem drinkers, and sometimes
they offered theories of their own.

There was no ready answer to these questions. The "found-
ing" couple were not problem drinkers, and the family did not
appear to have any outstanding psychological problems. It was
not one of the many poor families that had come to Tuba City
in search of wage work. Nor was it one of the deviant families

that sought refuge in Tuba City after having been driven from the home community. The answer, if there is one, must be sought in the changing social contexts of drinking experienced by later generations. In addition to the information obtained from interviews with respondents and their medical charts, fifteen relatives were asked to recall their earliest awareness of and experiences with alcohol, their parents' attitudes, and the part alcohol played in their childhood.

THE FIRST GENERATION

The history of alcohol use in this family begins with the man we shall call Medicine, who was born in the early 1890s and died in the mid-1970s at age eighty-two. The son of poor parents from the eastern part of the reservation who came to the area early in the century, he married an older woman from a well-to-do family living near Tuba City. His in-laws owned irrigated fields and grazed their livestock to the west. If not wealthy, Medicine was certainly not poor. His father was a ceremonialist, and Medicine learned a minor ceremony from him. Around 1918, at twenty-six, he married his wife's ten-year-old daughter by an earlier marriage, and it was this wife who bore his children.*

Medicine's Wife, as we shall refer to her, does not recall being aware of alcohol or seeing anyone drink, let alone her husband, until about ten years after their marriage. Medicine seldom drank at home and rarely came home drunk. He told her about alcohol and occasionally suggested she try it, but she never took alcohol from him. The first time she can remember tasting alcohol was in the late 1930s, when their oldest child, Julia, was a teenager. Julia stole a little of Medicine's home-brew to see how it tasted, and Medicine's Wife also tried some but thought

*This was a common form of marriage among the Navajo.

it was horrible. She never wanted any again until she was much older and was feeling distressed by her husband's death and her children's many problems.

Julia's recollections about her father's early drinking behavior agree with those of her mother, although Julia told of one occasion when her mother unknowingly accepted alcohol from Medicine. Medicine's Wife was in labor with one of her sons and was having a difficult time during the home birth. Medicine helped her drink some home-brew from a buckskin bag, saying that this "medicine" would help her labor. This was around 1932, when Julia was about ten years old and thought that the home-brew was, in fact, medicine.[†]

During the early years of their marriage, Medicine's main occupation was that of ceremonialist, or singer, although the family also had about 150 sheep and 15 acres of farmland. The minor ceremonies he conducted lasted no more than three nights, and Medicine said drinking home-brew helped him to stay up all night. He could not have maintained his reputation as a respected healer, however, if drinking had diminished his ability to perform ceremonies.

Medicine never told his Wife about when he first started drinking, and she had only occasional contact with his parents so was unaware of their attitudes toward or involvement with alcohol. Julia, however, lived much of her early life with Medicine's parents because they were elderly and needed her to assist with their personal care and to tend their livestock. Julia does not think they drank, because they never spoke to her about alcohol, and she never saw it around during the time she lived with them.

During these early years, Medicine's Wife never saw him buy

[†]"Home-brew" known as *tol'pai* was brewed from maize and was supposed to have been quite intoxicating. It was out of favor in the eastern portion of the reservation by 1910, although its use in the west, as late as 1954, has been reported by Adams (1963, 217).

alcohol. He would take pack mules or burros to an off-reservation town where he purchased bootleg whiskey from an Anglo who had his own still.‡ Medicine brought the whiskey home in barrels, which he hid underground. Julia also remembers once coming upon her father and his friends unexpectedly when she was herding sheep at a distance from anyone's camp. She heard them talking and laughing from behind a hill. She thought they were cooking coffee in a huge pot and did not recognize the smell or the equipment they were using until much later, when she was told how home-brew was made.

Eventually, Medicine's Wife realized that he was selling and trading the home-brew and bootlegged liquor. He would bring home coffee, flour, fresh meat, and cash. Medicine never sold the liquor from their home, so his Wife was unsure how long he was a bootlegger.

In the early 1950s, Medicine obtained a job with a government agency, and the family moved from their grazing area and farmland to live in Tuba City. Not only did they want their children to be closer to schools, but one of their sons had health problems that required easy access to the hospital. With a steady income there was no further need for Medicine to bootleg, and any illegal activity would have jeopardized his job. Commercially produced alcohol was also more available on the reservation at this time, and it was always possible to find someone who had liquor for sale in Tuba City. Drinking was increasingly common at social gatherings, fairs, and traditional Navajo ceremonies. Although residence in town offered Medicine's children many opportunities, it also exposed them to widespread excessive and public drinking behavior.

Medicine's Wife and their children all agreed that, as they

---

‡National prohibition lasted from 1918 until 1933 which accounts for the illegal stills. Even after prohibition was repealed, the possession and sale of alcohol on the Navajo reservation was illegal, and remains so by choice of the Tribal government.

grew up, he rarely drank around their home. His Wife can remember only one time when Medicine offered alcohol to their children, and on this occasion only a few of their sons were present. Medicine's Wife had prepared dinner, and Medicine was obviously feeling tipsy when he came home. He set a bottle of alcohol on the table and said that everyone should try some, that it was good to have with food and after finishing a meal. Medicine's Wife did not drink any of the liquor, although her sons did. This was the only occasion when she remembers seeing Medicine drink with his children, and by this time (the early 1960s) he was nearly seventy and in declining health.

In fact, the family rarely saw Medicine actually consuming alcohol until he was older and the youngest children were in their early teens. At that point he began to spend long periods at home since he needed more bed rest. One of them remembers seeing him drink at home on occasion, but never to excess. As his eyesight deteriorated, he stopped drinking because being tipsy would have made it more difficult for him to get around. As far as his Wife knows, Anglo doctors never told him that drinking alcohol was hurting his health.

In her youth, Medicine's Wife said that "there was no place for alcohol in my life." She was the oldest child, so she was responsible for caring for her family's livestock. She does not remember people drinking when she was young, and as far as she knows her parents did not drink. They never spoke to her about alcohol, mainly, she thought, because it was not available. With all of her children to take care of and the whole family to look after, she did not have time for alcohol during her youth or middle age.

Medicine's Wife was sixty-seven when her husband died; by that time most of her children had persistent or periodic drinking problems. She thinks she began to drink alcohol because of "loneliness in my mind and body." But she could not get very involved with alcohol because her oldest daughter was adamantly opposed to drinking and repeatedly told her mother to stay away from liquor. She was eighty-three when interviewed and had continued to drink occasionally "to get out of my moods." There was always someone who would drive by and give her a cup or two of wine. But her eyesight began to fail and she did not want to hurt herself, so she rarely drinks anymore.

Medicine's Wife said that during her lifetime there had been a real change in the way people, especially women, use alcohol. Women were drinking more and in public, which she considered improper. When she was younger, women conducted themselves "like men" when they drank. They went somewhere private, away from family and social gatherings. After the family moved to Tuba City, she began to see women drinking in public for the first time. The inappropriateness of drinking in public was repeatedly mentioned in discussions about changing patterns of alcohol use in the community.

A glimpse of Medicine's drinking behavior was provided by Julia. In the mid-1930s, when Julia was a young teenager, she remembers her father visiting once with another man, who arrived on horseback with a wooden barrel tied to the side of a donkey. When she went into the hogan, her grandmother said, "Your father brought some more whiskey." This was the only time her grandmother spoke to Julia about liquor, and nothing was said about what it was or about drinking. Her father went into a separate hogan to drink with the other men. Julia recalls that "they conducted themselves well," and the family could sleep even though the men were drinking nearby.

What, then, was the legacy of alcohol use passed on to Medicine's children? Medicine was a well-known, respected, and active ceremonialist whose Wife first became aware of his drinking around 1928, when he was about thirty-five. He described drinking as improving his stamina during the rigors of conducting ceremonies, and on one occasion he referred to alcohol as a medicine. He was characterized as most often drinking appropriately—that is, away from the family with other men. Only once did he encourage his sons to drink, and only as an accompaniment to a meal, as a social activity. He was rarely, if ever, drunk around his children. Medicine bootlegged alcohol, exchanging it directly for food and eventually receiving cash, at least part of which he gave to his Wife and children, but he quit selling alcohol after taking on a full-time government job.

The picture that emerges agrees with statements made by Anglos who had lived for many years in and around Tuba City. One maintained that she had not seen any drunken Navajos until around 1917 and, even then, it was so uncommon that she had to be told what was wrong with the man. A trader who had grown up on the western end of the reservation said that drinking became more common in the 1930s, during the Depression, when cash had become more available (Levy and Kunitz 1974, 66).

Medicine's belief that drink enhanced rather than diminished his ability to conduct ceremonials was also held by many others. A ceremonialist once told us that he could pray and perform his chants more effectively when he had something to drink. And an informant related how a ceremonialist once asked him to drink at a healing ceremony so that he could "devote" his songs. In this context, the references appear to be, even if vaguely, to a facilitation of supernatural power (Levy and Kunitz 1974, 74–75). Opinion varied greatly, however. One participant in the original study was an active and respected medicine man throughout his life, rarely taking even seasonal wage work to supplement his patients' payments. He died at age seventy-nine, about five years before our follow-up study. Several family members described him as a lifelong and adamant abstainer. This singer felt that traditional Navajo religion did not allow healers to drink and that a practitioner who would do so was neither a serious professional nor dedicated to his healing profession.

There is no evidence that Medicine provided a role model for the excessive drinking of his children, although it is clear that the oldest of them were aware of his drinking and bootlegging by the time they were in their teens. Medicine's Wife was uncomfortable with the public drinking that had become increasingly common but had no sense that consuming alcohol might be injurious to health. She said that when their children began to drink excessively, Medicine would preach to them about not using alcohol, but they did not listen.

Medicine and his Wife could not have anticipated the emerging challenges to the norms governing alcohol consumption that had largely conditioned their own behavior. Medicine's drinking never impeded his ability to support his family. In the rapidly changing economic environment, it was a sign of success for the household head to have cash with which to buy goods at the trading post.

THE SECOND GENERATION

Medicine and his Wife had twelve children, ten of whom lived to adulthood. All but one of these children experienced serious drinking problems at some time in their lives, and the deaths of five were alcohol-related. Although the siblings included in the Hospital and Tuba City samples were males, three of Medicine's daughters were also problem drinkers.

The Daughters

Medicine's oldest child, Julia, was born in the early 1920s. Because she lived with her grandparents, she never went to school. Today she rarely speaks English, although she understood many questions during interviews. Her younger siblings respected and even feared her because she forcibly expressed her strong disapproval of their drinking.

Julia married when she was in her late teens, around 1940, and it was her husband who first discussed alcohol with her. He described it as being a man's drink: "Women especially should never drink when they are bearing children." Her husband drank occasionally, even to drunkenness, but mainly when he

was working away from the reservation. She described him as
having a more respectful attitude toward liquor than people
have today. He never explained why women should not drink,
but she held him in high regard and took his words seriously.
With one notable exception, Julia never drank more than an
experimental sip or taste of alcohol. Following a disagreement
with her husband, Julia bought some wine and went to a friend's
home, where they got drunk. After this she never wanted to
drink again.

Julia and her husband lived for several years in a small bordertown, where they worked at entry-level jobs created by the
defense industry during World War II. After the war and the
death of her husband, she returned to Tuba City, where for the
first time she saw Navajos drinking in public. She says she was
able to remain abstinent because she believed her husband when
he told her that alcohol was not meant for women and because
she was made strong by her father's and grandfather's prayers.
Her respect for these three men and the teachings of the Native
American Church gave her "the strength to stay away from
alcohol."

At the time Julia first became involved with the NAC, the use
of peyote was illegal. Before 1967, when its use in religious
ceremonies was decriminalized on the Navajo reservation, she
and other NAC members were occasionally jailed for their use
and possession of peyote. Julia first attended a peyote meeting
because of some serious health problems. She was told by a
physician that she needed surgery. A friend who was a peyote
leader, or road chief, arranged for her to have a ceremony before
the surgery. When she returned to the hospital several days later,
she was told there was no longer any sign of the problem, and
the operation was canceled. After learning that she had taken
peyote, the doctor warned her against using it because he believed it could harm her. Julia said she did not know what to
think about the doctor's advice, nor was she sure that the NAC
ceremony had caused the problem to disappear. But the cere-

mony did make her feel better, and she has continued her NAC participation ever since.

Through her involvement with the NAC, Julia's life has improved, she says, "both in material goods and within myself." Her traditional Navajo prayers and the white and yellow corn pollen associated with them have relieved the stress in her life; she knows NAC supplies further support. Her current husband used to drink, but he believes that joining the NAC helped him to stop. Although Julia has never attended a church where they "preach from a bible," on the basis of others' descriptions she thinks it is similar to the NAC: "You have to believe in it, and pray a lot for a better way and for others."

When asked whether she knew anyone who took peyote just to feel high, Julia replied that the effects of alcohol are in no way similar to the religious experience of a peyote meeting. She noted, however, that individuals are different, and those who abuse alcohol might also abuse peyote. Julia never tried to convert any of her siblings to the peyote religion, which was not introduced to their community until after several of them had died. All three of her sisters were drinkers. Alice and Belle were already dead at the time of the follow-up; only Cora was interviewed.

Although Julia was just four years older than Alice, their childhood and early adolescence were markedly different. Alice lived with her parents and siblings throughout her childhood and attended the Tuba City boarding school for a few years. She met her husband while attending this school and moved to his family's home community some forty miles away.

Alice began to drink only after she married. Her father-in-law used to make home-brew and was known for his drinking. Although she lived much of the time with her in-laws, Alice also had a hogan at her parents' camp, where she stayed occasionally when she had a job in Tuba City. Before she remarried and established a separate camp of her own, Julia also stayed at her parents' camp when she returned from working off the reservation. It was at this time (about 1951) that she first knew of

Alice's drinking. There were occasions when Alice drank openly at their parents' camp. She was in her midtwenties and pregnant with her fourth child at that time.

Julia does not know for how long or how frequently her sister had been drinking, but she repeatedly told her that women should not drink, especially when pregnant. Despite these admonitions, Alice continued to drink during this and her final pregnancy a year later, often driving away in her pick-up truck when inebriated. After Alice's youngest children were born, Julia cared for them. Then, as Julia remembers it, her sister drove off one day in 1954 and never came back. She died in an automobile accident at twenty-eight, and Julia continued to care for several of her children.

Belle was more than twenty years younger than Julia, and the family had moved to Tuba City by the time she reached high school age. She was among the first of Medicine's children to attend the public high school but left home before graduating to work as a seasonal farm laborer. Julia does not think Belle started drinking while still in school, although she was involved with a man who drank and abused her, and both were drinking when they returned to the reservation.

Belle continued to drink even after her second marriage. She was alone when she died in her sleep, and although Julia does not think she had been drinking, the family never inquired about the cause of death.

Cora was almost sixty in 1990 and through an interpreter described her long and continuing struggle with alcohol abuse. She knew that her father drank occasionally but rarely saw him drinking while she was growing up. She never knew her mother to drink until after her father and several of her brothers had died. Because it was such an infrequent occurrence, she does not remember thinking much about her parents' drinking as a child. During her high school years, she was sent to an off-reservation boarding school but did not begin drinking until she had returned to the reservation.

Cora remembers stealing some of her father's pint bottles of wine in her midtwenties while he was away conducting sings. She and her girlfriends had observed how alcohol caused other people in town to act, and they were curious about how it would make them feel. Her parents, however, were very upset when they found out about her drinking, so she would sneak drinks only when they were away. She never drank with her parents, but she occasionally drank with one of her brothers.

Cora said she did not drink during the year she worked in a large city, and although her first husband drank, initially she did not join him. She would, however, drink with her girlfriends but could give no reason for doing so. After her first child was born, she stopped drinking for a while but gradually started again with her husband. Her drinking became more frequent and excessive. The tribal social service department threatened to take her children away if she did not stop drinking, and she was urged to enter the Antabuse program at the hospital. She refused to do so because a nephew had cautioned her against it, telling her that Antabuse was too potent and could harm her. Rose never participated in traditional Navajo ceremonies or NAC to attain abstinence, but she did go to an alcohol-recovery program off the reservation.

Cora believes the treatment program was helpful: she was released into the care of her sister Julia and regained custody of several of her children. Julia also raised one of Cora's children. With her family back together, Cora and her husband went to southern Arizona for the onion harvest. There her husband became involved with another woman, so, with money from Julia, Cora and the children returned to the reservation. She did not start drinking again immediately, but after several relatives died, she began to drink because, "It made me feel better and helped ease my mind."

There are times when Cora believes she could stop drinking completely but feels pressured to drink by neighbors, who are always dropping by to offer alcohol. She usually stays at her parents' camp in a section of Tuba City where liquor is easy to obtain and where people looking for alcohol tend to congregate.

But when she leaves that area of town to stay with Julia, a few miles away, or with the daughter raised by Julia, she is able to stop because neither of them drinks. She has found that "alcohol doesn't really taste good unless I have something bothering me—when I have something on my mind or my knees are really hurting." No one ever told her that alcohol would make her feel better, she just found this out from her own experience. She tries to quit, but when she feels overpowered by loneliness or physical pain, she finds herself opening her door to drinkers again.

The Sons

Medicine's daughters' problem drinking began under the influence of their husbands. For the sons, on the other hand, pressure to drink came from their peers. Medicine's oldest son, Frank, was in his late sixties in 1990 and had recently returned to the camp where his mother lived with her current husband. His first marriage was to a woman who lived over one hundred miles from Tuba City. She did not drink, and he began using alcohol only upon returning home after some fifteen years of marriage. After his second wife's death, which his family thought was related to his alcohol abuse, Frank began to sell liquor and to drink more himself. Currently, he does not often stay at his mother's camp during the day, but even when he is there he prefers to be left alone and keeps to himself.

Ray was born in 1935 and died in 1986 at age fifty-one from pneumonia and alcoholic cirrhosis. He was the oldest of the three brothers who participated in the original study. He began drinking when he was fourteen, before the family moved to Tuba City, but Julia claims he was not allowed to drink at home while a teenager. Medicine was strict with his older children, and if he saw his sons drinking would "whip" them. His daughters, on the other hand, were lectured. Julia contends that her brothers did not feel that Medicine was mean and stayed with him, caring for him as he got older.

Julia believes that her brothers did not drink much when they were in their teens and that it was not until they left the reservation in their late teens and early twenties for boarding school, job training, or seasonal farm labor and were exposed to different styles of drinking, that alcohol became a problem in their lives.

Ray attended boarding school off the reservation for four years and first married in his late teens, soon after the family had moved to Tuba City. Ray was in his twenties when he met his second wife, who said that his drinking was "not a problem" in those years. She remembers him drinking about once a week or every two weeks and noted that sometimes he would be abstinent for months at a time. Ray was employed full time as a maintenance man during the early years of their marriage, and the family was financially stable. Several of their children, however, died in infancy or early childhood. Ray, who had been drinking heavily, was responsible for the death of one child in an accident.

Ray's drinking increased during his second marriage. His wife said that he drank regularly at home as well as with his friends and that he became increasingly short-tempered and angry. She noted that she did not drink when they first met and married, but after she turned twenty he wanted her to drink with him and became angry if she refused. She also recalled that several years after they were married Ray began bootlegging. He had his own vehicle, so once in a while he would obtain alcohol off the reservation and then sell it from the trunk of his car in Tuba City.

By his late twenties, he already had a history of heavy drinking associated with episodes of vomiting blood. Alcoholic cirrhosis was diagnosed when he was thirty-one. He had many arrests for drunk and disorderly conduct, driving while intoxicated, and transporting and selling liquor on the reservation. His second marriage gradually disintegrated, and he lost his steady job.

During the late 1960s and early 1970s, Ray began to haul hay from out of state for resale on the reservation. He increasingly added to his income by bootlegging, reportedly at the encouragement of his third wife. At first he bootlegged only at the beginning of the month, when many people received their assistance or Social Security checks. Bootlegging, however, was lucrative in comparison to the locally available wage jobs and soon became his major source of income.

Ray and his third wife established their own home and were considered comparatively well off. They lived near his parents in a part of town that had become known as a place to obtain alcohol. One of Ray's children recalled that her father and stepmother took trips to off-reservation towns where they would purchase liquor for resale on the reservation and enjoy drinking with friends. Ray would leave instructions with his older children about how to conduct transactions with customers who came by their house and the appropriate amount of liquor to dispense with each sale.

Ray periodically took Antabuse when he wanted to stop drinking but remained abstinent only for several months at a time. His third marriage was turbulent. His siblings and children from his other marriages tended to blame his continued abuse of alcohol on his wife's infidelities, her willingness to join him in drinking, and her desire for a high standard of living. During this troubled marriage, several of Ray's younger siblings and numerous friends died. He sporadically worked at local, part time jobs. He hurt his back on one job about five years before his death. Although he did not drink while working during the day, his back was very painful at night and was one reason for his drinking.

Ray's pattern of bingeing to the point of unconsciousness, however, was well established before his injury. During the last six years of his life, he increasingly experienced problems with gastrointestinal bleeding after drinking. He was also diagnosed as diabetic and often did not take his insulin when drinking. In the final months before his death, he was living alone, although one of his daughters checked on him regularly. He became very jaundiced and weak and finally required assistance for all daily functions. At age fifty-one, Ray died in the local hospital; pneumonia complicated by hepatorenal syndrome and end-stage alcoholic liver disease were listed as the immediate causes.

Lester, born in the early 1940s, began drinking at about age ten and drank heavily from the time he was eighteen until he first took Antabuse, at twenty-three. While still in his teens he married the daughter of a local medicine man. Although he did not tell his wife much about his early life, he did say that his father was very strict, which, he felt, was for his own good. She said Lester never spoke in anger about his father. While they were married, Lester would sometimes come home from his parents' camp and say that they had been drinking, but he never voiced an opinion about it. She believes that while Lester was growing up, his father did not drink much and that his mother did not drink at all until after Medicine died.

Lester's wife was an abstainer. She knew he drank when they married, but she felt his alcohol use was not a problem at that time. When he left the reservation for a year of job training, however, he began to drink heavily. He returned to the reservation after trouble with the police. A few years later, he enrolled in the Tuba City Antabuse program because he felt drinking was hurting him and his family. Although he was not totally abstinent over the following six years, he appears to have experienced few if any major problems associated with his drinking. He joined the Protestant church his wife attended and was considered a good worker at the several temporary jobs he held.

Lester never drank at home, although he would return inebriated after drinking with his friends. He was not abusive toward his wife or their children, but after many short periods of abstinence and relapses, she finally told him he could not live with them until he stopped drinking completely. He entered the Antabuse program for a second time and worked for a while as a counselor at the local alcohol recovery center. Although he felt it was fairly easy to maintain periodic sobriety, he also spoke with physicians and family members about his great distress over his marital problems and the violent deaths of several close friends. Lester was particularly depressed after the deaths of his sister Belle and brother Herbert and began to binge with increasing frequency. He was generally in good health, although his drinking eventually resulted in alcoholic liver disease. During the six months before his death, he had a number of unexplained seizures despite having severely curtailed his drinking.

A few weeks before his death, Lester expressed a desire for a reconciliation because, he said, the only thing that mattered was being with his family. He had a job and had been abstinent for several months. He proposed to continue living with his parents while remaining abstinent to prove he was serious about reuniting the family. He apparently died in his sleep of cardiopulmonary arrest due to choking. Although alcohol was not listed as a direct cause, alcoholic cirrhosis had been diagnosed just five months before he died at age thirty-five.

Herbert, the youngest of the brothers in the study, died before his older brothers, at age thirty-one. He was one year younger than Lester, and their drinking histories were similar in many ways. He was described as an attractive and genial person who drank abusively at times but who had periods of abstinence lasting several months and, once, over a year. Julia believes that Herbert first learned about drinking by observing Cora drinking at home while he was growing up.

Herbert married his first wife when they were both about twenty years old, at which time he did not have a drinking problem. Shortly after their marriage, they moved to a farm in Phoenix, where they worked as field hands. There was a bar just down the road from where they lived, and Herbert began to go there frequently. Julia does not know why he began drinking more often, but he eventually lost his job because of it. Within two years Herbert had developed a pattern of heavy binge drinking that continued after they returned to the reservation.

His wife's family were devout Christians. Through church counseling and attendance they kept their marriage together for a while longer, and Herbert was abstinent for several months at a time. His wife said he did not drink at home but would go off somewhere with his friends. After about five years they separated permanently, although he continued to visit their children. Subsequently, he had a number of failed relationships and intense grief reactions to the deaths of several of his siblings and close friends within only a few years. The duration and frequency of his binge drinking increased, and medical records indicate that he also suffered bouts of depression, expressed suicidal ideation, and made several suicide attempts.

Herbert admired his older brothers and looked to them for advice and support. They often rebuffed him, however, and Herbert was stung by their rejection. He was on Antabuse several times and once expressed interest in going to an alcohol treatment center. He died in his sleep at his second wife's rural camp, where he had been herding sheep for several months, having curtailed his drinking considerably.

As an adolescent, Herbert had been hospitalized with acute rheumatic fever. Although the immediate cause of his death was unclear, a rheumatic heart condition, congestive heart failure, and chronic alcohol abuse were listed in the medical records.

Jackie was Medicine's youngest living child in 1990 and was the first in the family to graduate from high school. He spoke thoughtfully and at times intensely about his and his family's history of alcohol abuse, expressing sadness and regret as well as hope for the future. Although Herbert and Lester were only about five years older than Jackie, Ray was nearly fifteen years and Julia more than twenty-five years his senior. Jackie's childhood was quite different from that of his older siblings in some important ways. Medicine was in his midfifties when Jackie was born, and within ten years his health had begun to decline: He spent more time at home and for the first time in his life began to drink regularly in front of his children. Jackie thought that his father drank because he got tired, and after he finished a ceremony, "drinking helped him rest up. Like anyone else, when he was working hard he needed to relax afterwards."

Jackie remembers that his father sometimes yelled at his older brothers and sisters and was "kind of mean to them when they misbehaved." But he was always kind to Jackie and never yelled at him. As Medicine's health declined and he was drinking more at home, several of Jackie's older siblings were drinking heavily. As they moved in and out of troubled relationships, or when they came to town for temporary work, Jackie's siblings often stayed at Medicine's camp. At this time Jackie was in his mid-teens, and as a high school sophomore, he began to think about experimenting with alcohol.

He emphasized that no one in his family forced him to drink. Jackie's initial experience with peer pressure kept him away from alcohol. He was very involved in sports during high school and was told that if he was caught drinking he would be kicked off the team. He needed a place where he could study, so he decided to live with a friend who also was involved in sports and who did not drink. Jackie was afraid that if he stayed with his parents and his brothers he would "take up the bottle—who would tell me to stop?"

He knew he did not want to go through the same problems with alcohol that had plagued his brothers' lives. After graduating from high school, he attended two years of vocational training off the reservation. Occasionally he would drink two cans of beer after work or school with the other people in the program. At the time, he worked during the day and went to school at night. When he was employed as an ironworker off the reservation, he would normally work for a few days and then have several days off. During his free time he would drink with friends but never on the job or the night before, because he considered it much too dangerous. After a job was over he would drink, either alone or with friends. He did not think about it much; the alcohol was readily available, and on the weekends a group of friends would go camping. How much they drank depended on how much money they had.

Jackie was drinking rarely when he returned to Tuba City in the early 1970s. The friend he had lived with during high school had become a member of the Native American Church, and with this friend's encouragement, he also joined. Soon afterward, he married a woman who did not drink. He stopped drinking completely for several years, attributing his abstinence to his use of peyote.

Jackie worked for a while as a laborer but lost his job. With his children in school, his wife working, and nothing to do, he and his wife began to argue about his unemployment. Eventually his wife "took the house and the children" and obtained a divorce. According to a member of the family, Jackie lost his job in part because he was drinking again, and Jackie himself said his drinking was a factor leading to the divorce. In any case, he said he started to drink more often because he was lonely. After the divorce he felt he did not have anything to work for, stopped going to NAC meetings, and "went on my own."

Unlike his brothers, Jackie never became a bootlegger, because he feared arrest and believes he might have drank even more if alcohol had been around all the time. Nevertheless, he has been drinking fairly steadily since the divorce, and although he knows alcohol is bad for his health, he says it improves his mood.

Recently, he has considered trying to stop drinking. He knows about the available treatment programs and that he could go to a rehabilitation center, but he wants to see whether he can quit on his own. He described how two of his brothers had gone to rehabilitation centers without becoming abstinent. He has heard about Antabuse and knows that one should not drink while taking it. He is afraid to take it, however, because his brothers told him that if he drank while on the medication it would kill him. Thus he has never thought seriously about going to a rehabilitation center himself except on those occasions when he "gets to really hurting from too much drinking." His final comment on the idea of seeking professional help was, "The pills took my brothers' lives."

Jackie believes that if he remarried he would be motivated to stop drinking. He wants to marry a woman from a different community and move to where her family lives. He feels he needs some help to stop drinking and that it would be too easy to start again were he to stay in Tuba City. So many of his friends in the area drink that it is hard to stay away from alcohol. He has worked at odd jobs for a couple of years and was in the process of applying for employment with the Navajo Tribe. On the day he was interviewed, he had been abstinent for a week, the longest he had refrained from drinking for a long time.

Medicine's youngest child, Nelson, married as a teenager and was described by the family as an occasional problem drinker and bootlegger. Nelson's death at thirty-five, however, was not due to alcohol.

THE THIRD GENERATION
Herbert's Children

Medicine's children have over sixty offspring of their own, ranging from very young to middle-aged. Although Herbert never drank in front of his children, he was sometimes drunk when he came home. His widow says the children continue to feel anger toward him and remember how he sometimes mistreated them. One son is drinking now, and when his mother, a lifelong abstainer, tries to persuade him to stop, he says, "Well, my dad drank," as if to offer both an excuse and an explanation.

Lester's Children

Lester's wife never drank. She always hoped that he would quit drinking and was always willing to allow him to return home if he would abstain. When sober, he was a good father, and his children loved him. Their oldest child, a son who is now in his late twenties, has severe drinking problems. He did very well through junior high school but dropped out of high school when he was fifteen, shortly before his father died. Lester's widow often talks with her son about quitting, and although he says he wants to stop, she does not think he is really trying. He will stop for several months but then gets involved with friends who drink or finds a new girlfriend and begins to drink again.

According to her mother, Lester's oldest daughter "partied" in high school but stayed home and "straightened out" after an alcohol-related accident. She was very close to her father and missed him terribly after he died; it is still hard for her to speak about him. Her mother talked to her a lot when she was drinking and told her that her father would not want her to have the same problems he had. The other children do not drink, perhaps because their mother talked with them about alcohol, constantly telling them that if they wanted to make a living, they had to stay away from alcohol, and that alcohol had killed their father.

Ray's Children

Gail, Ray's daughter by his first marriage, described her mother as an alcoholic; she died when Gail was about twelve years old. During her early childhood, Gail and her parents lived with Medicine and his wife in Tuba City. She does not remember seeing much drinking then, and her grandparents never spoke with her about alcohol. She believes they did not want her to know about it. In the traditional Navajo way, Gail said, the elderly did not talk with children about problems until they were older.

Gail remembers Ray as a "very authoritarian" father who whipped his children to make them behave. After their mother died, the court asked Gail and her younger brother to choose the person they wished to live with, and they decided to stay with their aunt Julia. In contrast to her grandparents' silence on the topic of alcohol, Julia lectured them regularly about staying away from alcohol and finishing high school. Gail graduated from high school and has held a local government job for many years. She drank once in her life and felt it relaxed her. Because of this positive experience, she sometimes considers drinking again but then thinks about all the problems it has caused her family.

Gail's brother never finished high school but sought work away from the reservation, where he started to drink. His drinking increased after his father died until at last his wife took their children and left. The threatened divorce made an impression on him: he joined the Native American Church and quit drinking completely. Although Gail talks with him and encourages him frequently, she fears his grasp on sobriety is tenuous.

For nearly ten years, Gail also raised her half brother, Dennis. He is one of Ray's youngest children and had experimented with alcohol by the age of seventeen. Dennis was very close to his father and was devastated by his death. In recent years, when visiting his mother (Ray's third wife) he has found her drunk, so he does not go to see her anymore. Nor is she allowed to visit him at Gail's home if she has been drinking. At first his grades at school were mainly C's and D's, but now he gets A's and B's and is on the honor roll. Gail said Dennis will not or cannot talk about his father without becoming distressed and sad.

At Julia's urging, several of Ray's younger children were taken from him and his third wife. Several of his daughters met their future husbands when they came to the house to purchase alcohol. Although two of these daughters do not drink, one bootlegs occasionally, and their husbands drink abusively. The other daughters have had severe drinking problems since adolescence. One of them, LaVerne, was about thirty when we interviewed her in 1990.

Ray and his second wife were divorced when LaVerne was five. She lived with her mother until age eleven but then returned to live with her father and his third wife. She does not think he was drinking heavily at the time: at least she did not see him drinking around the house. He was earning more from hauling hay than from bootlegging, and the family was fairly well off. Neither Ray nor her stepmother drank for two years after LaVerne came to live with them. Ray spent much of his spare time building their large new house.

After about two years, Ray and his wife began going to a nearby bordertown with increasing frequency, and he told the children that if someone came to the house wanting alcohol they should make the sale. As long as LaVerne remained with her father she was involved in the bootlegging. She never felt it was wrong, only that it was the way they made money, and none of her school friends ridiculed her because of it. To the contrary, she remembers being one of the few high school students whose parents gave them a car. When she left home at age eighteen, her father was drinking heavily and his marriage was deteriorating.

LaVerne drank first with some of her high school friends. She was curious about how alcohol would make her feel, and she remembers getting very sick from the wine she drank. Several of her friends drank regularly and knew where they could buy alcohol, but she never acquired any from her father, who was opposed to her drinking. She began to drink heavily during her senior year because she felt depressed and resentful. Her parents were gone much of the time and depended on her to care for the younger children and to do the housework. Moreover, Ray was very strict, and she was afraid of him because "he used a belt a lot when he whipped me and the other kids." She believes her father may have hated her. "I had to do chores to his idea of perfection and he was always cussing us out." She wanted to be living somewhere else.

As a teenager LaVerne tried to hide her drinking, but when her father found out he took her to her mother in Utah, where she lived for several months at a time during the next two years.

She never finished high school, and in her early twenties returned to Tuba City, where she married a man from another family of problem drinkers. Her husband was employed when they married but has not worked much since. There were times when they fought and occasionally lived apart. Although they are living together now, their children have been taken from them and sent to live with her mother, who also drinks occasionally.

LaVerne and her husband have both experienced delirium tremens, and recently she has been frightened by her husband's seizures during alcohol withdrawal. Several years ago she entered a treatment program off the reservation, where she received support from other women her own age. After about six months, she returned home, where she attended several Alcoholics Anonymous meetings. She thinks these were worthwhile but that too few were offered. She stopped attending the meetings and has been reluctant to return because the other attenders know she has resumed drinking. She noted with a sense of hope, however, that it had been three weeks since she last had taken a drink. Three years later, she was encountered in another residential treatment program.

THE FOURTH GENERATION

Despite the fact that one of Medicine's granddaughters received counseling to stop drinking during her pregnancy, she failed to do so. Until the early 1980s, little was known about the physiological damage that can occur to a fetus when a woman drinks alcohol during pregnancy. Over the past ten years, however, there has been growing awareness that a related series of physical, mental, and emotional abnormalities, found among children of women from all ethnic backgrounds who drank while pregnant, is associated with alcohol toxicity. Depending on the severity of the physiological impacts, the resulting conditions are termed *fetal alcohol effect* (FAE) or *fetal alcohol syndrome*

(FAS). One of Medicine's great-grandchildren has been diagnosed as "probably" suffering from FAS; it is suspected that another may also be affected. Although it is too late to repair the damage done these children, the fourth generation of the Medicine family may have available the best tools to fight alcohol abuse, to manage its consequences, and to lay the groundwork for preventing future family members from experiencing similar problems.

DISCUSSION

It is clear that the heterogeneous population of Tuba City, with access to sources of alcohol and the cash to purchase it, never became a community with shared attitudes toward drunkenness or with the authority to control it. To identify this social environment as the only cause of unrestrained drinking, however, would be a mistake. Families are the primary environments in which individuals are first socialized, and many Tuba City families are abstinent.

Only one of Medicine's children was drinking heavily before the family moved to Tuba City, and this began only after her marriage to a man who drank. Nevertheless, all the children except Julia, who was raised by her grandparents, became problem drinkers, and the Tuba City environment aggravated the problem. Even in this environment, the drinking behavior of the parents was important in influencing the later careers of the children. The children of the third generation were reared in homes where bootlegging and abusive drinking were the major focus of family life, and many had lost a parent through death or divorce. All their fathers came home drunk regularly, and some were physically abusive. Some of the mothers, however, did not drink, struggled to keep their children abstinent, and in many instances were successful.

As far as we have been able to determine, Medicine did not drink abusively or at home in front of his children. Nor, at this late date, can we identify any stresses within the family that might have predisposed the children to drink. That Medicine was one of the early bootleggers in the area, however, meant that all the children were exposed to alcohol use to some extent. In Tuba City, the family lived in a setting where the children were not only surrounded by drinking during their formative years, but also had no other established "culture" to define for them the limits of appropriate drinking. In contrast, among the Plateau drinkers, it was accepted that young men would drink, but also that they would become abstinent once they assumed the responsibility of raising a family.

Medicine's family history suggests that the move into an agency town, in a context free of the restraints of kinship obligations, led to the use of alcohol. It was a context, moreover, in which alcohol was readily available and selling it was one of the few ways to earn money in a labor-surplus economy. Furthermore, it was striking how little awareness there was among the people we interviewed of the untoward health effects of excessive alcohol use. This suggests yet another reason why heavy drinking increased so explosively in the second generation of the family. Not only were there few social restraints and many opportunities to drink, but the very real dangers of heavy drinking were largely unknown.

There is hope that alcohol treatment and prevention programs may help to develop new attitudes and values. The first alcohol treatment program in Tuba City was the Antabuse program run by the Indian Health Service Hospital in the 1960s. There was no outreach program, no counselors, and no means to follow patients after they left the program. Since that time, the Navajo Tribe has developed local treatment centers with counselors who attempt to follow their clients.

Initially, these programs focused on male drinkers and employed only male counselors. Fortunately, increased attention is now being paid to the problems of women, and the hospital has developed a fairly extensive program to educate and counsel women considered to be at risk of giving birth to children with fetal alcohol syndrome.

Navajo tribal alcohol programs are also aimed at incorporating the more successful features of the Alcoholics Anonymous philosophy, especially the recognition of a spiritual component. Experience has led most local recovery programs to refrain from pushing any particular denomination, but rather to ask the client which is most important for him or her before encouraging greater involvement.

Tribal programs also have begun to emphasize that alcohol abuse is a family problem, rather than simply an individual problem. Family participation is emphasized because recovery is threatened if the client returns to a home environment where others drink or where family members remain distressed by the client's past behavior. Local programs are creating ways to gain social support as well as laying the foundation for redefining norms and attitudes toward alcohol, and it is possible that the decline of alcohol-related deaths in the past decade is partly a result of these programs.

Finally, in light of the current interest in the extent to which alcoholism may be an inherited phenomenon (Cotton 1979; Devor and Cloninger 1989), we emphasize that because our research was not designed to examine this question, we cannot comment on it definitively. We do, however, point out that despite the fact that Medicine had access to alcohol, he never became an abusive drinker. Nor is there evidence that he or any of his sons had antisocial personalities, which recent research has identified as a marker of inherited alcoholism (Cadoret et al. 1985; Cloninger et al. 1978; Helzer and Pryzbeck 1988; Hesselbrock 1986). In fact, some recent twin studies have concluded that inherited alcoholism appears to affect only males and that women who become alcoholics do so because of factors in the social environment—that is, because male family members drink excessively (McGue, Pickens, and Sivkis 1992). In sum, we tend to the opinion that we are observing primarily environmental rather than genetic effects.

8

Navajo Mortality
in Its Regional Context

"Indians, Eskimos die in car wrecks at three times national rate, CDC says," announced a recent headline in the *Arizona (Tucson) Daily Star*. And the *Journal of the National Center for American Indian and Alaska Native Mental Health Research* tells us that in 1987 Indians and Alaska natives died from alcoholism at almost five times the national rate (May 1992, 16). Such statistics not only give cause for concern but also shape the way the problem of Indian drinking is perceived. Moreover, the way data on Indian drinking are presented reflects our assumptions about the nature of alcohol, our image of the American Indian and ourselves as a people, and our ideas about the nature of society. In our earlier study (Levy and Kunitz 1974, 1–2), we wrote: "It can be argued that in all periods of our history the Indian has been used as a screen on which white America has played its own dramatic presentation of America's changing image. This presentation is replete with doubts, internal contradictions, and no little sense of guilt." But whether this image and our concern are directly related to an objective assessment of Indians' use of alcohol or to more subtle involvements between whites and Indians has never been determined.

In chapter 4 we examined mortality rates from cirrhosis and a number of pathologies thought to be affected by alcohol abuse in the Navajo service area. We pointed out the difficulties of counting the Navajo population and reporting mortality statistics. The populations of most Indian tribes are so small that relatively infrequent occurrences like deaths from cirrhosis and suicide vary widely from year to year. The need to avoid bias caused by these fluctuations and to use population denominators sufficiently large to obtain statistically meaningful results leads most investigators to aggregate data at the global level (all Indians) or regional level (IHS service areas). In this chapter we present data on Navajo mortality from causes traditionally thought to be alcohol-related, using as comparison populations the non-Indians in the same region. By so doing, we hope to be more sensitive to cultural and environmental factors that are obscured by studies that compare all Indians or all Navajos to national averages.

Not only are there considerable differences in culture, environment, and interethnic relations among the many Indian groups, but non-Indians also exhibit considerable cultural variability. For example, Shore (1975) has shown that although the annual suicide rate in the Portland Indian Health Area from 1969 to 1971, was 28 per 100,000 population, somewhat higher than the national Indian rate of 23 and considerably higher than the 11.6 reported for the nation, the regional rate was considerably distorted because more than half of the suicides were committed by members of one tribe, the Shoshone-Bannock, which had a rate of 122. When the suicides from this one tribe were omitted, the area rate was reduced to 14, and one coastal tribe, with a rate of 8, was considerably below the national average. Similarly, we have shown elsewhere that homicide rates during the seven-year period 1883–89 ranged from a low of 1.9 for the Eastern Pueblo Agency and 5.9 for the Navajos to highs of 165 for the Western Apaches and 130 for the Nevada Paiute (Levy and Kunitz 1971).

Despite such evidence, however, the image of the drunken Indian has persisted since the earliest contacts between Europeans and Indians. Either "Indians cannot hold their liquor" because of some unspecified racial difference, or, in the more sympathetic eyes of social scientists, because of the social disintegration and consequent anomie they have suffered since their conquest by Europeans.

The considerable cultural, economic, and environmental differences that characterize the major geographic regions of the nation are less often considered. The earliest and arguably the most persistent regional division in the United States is that between North and South. Even such an authority as Thomas Jefferson "characterized Southerners as hotheaded, indolent, unstable, and unjust; Northerners as cool tempered, sober, persistent, and upright" (McWhiney 1988, xiii). In contrast to prevalent opinion, Grady McWhiney and Forrest McDonald have attributed these differences to: (1) the settlement, during the seventeenth and eighteenth centuries, of the American colonies south and west of Pennsylvania mainly by "immigrants from the 'Celtic fringe' of the British archipelago—the western and northern uplands of England, Wales, the Scottish Highlands and Borders, the Hebrides, and Ireland . . . the culture these people brought with them and to a large extent retained in the New World accounts in considerable measure for the differences between them and the Yankees of New England, most of whom originated in the lowland southeastern half of the island of Britain"; and (2) "the material culture underlying the traditional folkways, values, norms, and attitudes both in the upland areas prior to the eighteenth century and in the antebellum South was primarily related to herding, in contrast to the commercial mixed agriculture that was the norm both in southeastern Britain and in New England" (McDonald 1988, xxi).

The South has retained the image of an area more given to violence "so pervasive that it compels the attention of anyone interested in understanding [it]" (Hackney 1969). As McWhiney argues for a cultural explanation, so does Hackney, who demonstrates that even after place of residence, race, and economic factors are controlled, the regional difference remains. The role alcohol plays in inflating violent death rates remains arguable, but the ratio of homicides to suicides is far higher in the South than in the North, indicating a predilection for outwardly expressed aggression. As the association between alcohol and homicide is said to be greater than that between alcohol and suicide, alcohol may very well be a part of the total mix.

Regional differences in drinking styles were also marked during the antebellum years; southerners preferred whiskey while northerners preferred beer and hard cider (Lender and Martin 1987, 9). In 1789, a proposed levy on domestic distilled spirits was supported by most northern representatives but opposed by most southerners. "At the roll call, the measure was approved, with a unanimous New England casting half the ayes (17–0), the middle states splitting (13–8), and the South standing in opposition (5–13)" (Rorabaugh 1979, 53).

Heavy drinking was common among southerners: "It was expected that a man attending a southern barbecue would follow the 'barbecue law,' which required that everyone drink to intoxication. The only excuse for refusing a round was passing out. In Mississippi . . . drinking to excess had become so fashionable that 'a man of strict sobriety' was considered 'a cold blooded and uncongenial wretch.' To refuse to imbibe gave 'serious offense,' suggesting a lack of respect and friendship. It was sometimes dangerous. A gang of lusty Kentuckians angry with an abstinent comrade is reputed to have roasted him to death" (Rorabaugh 1979, 151).

In contrast, northern farm owners were noted for their sobriety, although there were many in the north who also drank (Rorabaugh 1979, 248). It was, perhaps, the style of drinking and the values attached to it and not the absolute quantities imbibed that made the regional differences so noticeable.

As the frontier moved westward, however, whiskey increasingly became the preferred drink (Lender and Martin 1987, 30–40). There were economic as well as cultural reasons for this shift in taste. Settlers crossing the Appalachians were cut off from the East and were forced to develop their own products and markets. The soils of the Ohio River valley were far more fertile than those of the East and produced bumper harvests of grain that were difficult to dispose of. "To market their surplus grain more profitably, western farmers turned to distilling," which reduced the bulk of the grain (Rorabaugh 1979, 78).

The rise of grain alcohol notwithstanding, northerners and southerners tended to retain their old ways when they moved westward. Ohio was called a Yankee state because of the New England institutions that prevailed in the northern three-quarters of its territory. "Copies of New England were as solidly entrenched in the upper Midwest as southern ways were along and below the Ohio River" (McWhiney 1988, 268–69).

As the frontier moved westward to the Plains and to the Rocky Mountains, whiskey became the means by which the fur companies kept the trappers and Indians working for them. A trapper could earn enough in a year or two to retire. By paying trappers in whiskey and inviting them to an annual "rendezvous," where the furs were collected and paid for, the companies were able to enhance their profits by distributing diluted spirits. After days of gambling, fighting, and drinking, the trappers had consumed their annual profits and were forced to trap for another year. "Whiskey that cost 25 cents a gallon in Missouri was hauled to the rendezvous, cut ten to one with water, and sold for $4 per 4-ounce glass, a price increase of more than 5,000 to one. Without liquor sales, the fur companies would have made no profits" (Rorabaugh 1979, 159). The drinking habits of later western ranchers, loggers, and miners were formed, in large part, by those that prevailed during the nineteenth century.

Today, not only the southern states but also those of the Rocky Mountain West have high rates of death from alcohol-related causes, a circumstance often attributed to our frontier heritage (table 8.1). In general, urban areas have lower mortality rates from these causes than rural areas, and regional differences are even greater in rural areas owing to the persistence of older cultural factors as well as several environmental variables. When rural areas of the northern and southern Mountain region are compared, the northern tier has considerably lower mortality rates than the southern (table 8.2). With the exception of suicide rates, which increased steadily from 1960 to the present, rates for all pathologies rose between 1960 and 1970 and declined after 1980. Nevada not only has the highest mortality rates from all causes but is difficult to class as a definitely southern Mountain state. Even when Nevada is omitted from the calculation, however, New Mexico and Arizona are still higher than the states to the north.

The rural areas of the Southwest are generally poor and at some distance from health and other services. That medical attention is less readily available suggests that accident victims are more likely to die than their counterparts in or near urban areas. The western states are so huge that rural residents must travel long distances for most purposes, thus exposing themselves to a greater risk of vehicular accidents. The correlation

Table 8.1 Average Age Adjusted Regional Mortality Rates from Alcohol Related Causes, All Ages, 1979, 1980, 1983–85

Regions	N	Mean	Low	High
Northern[a]	21	44.8	30.2	55.4
Southern[b]	16	57.9	48.5	67.7
Mountain	8	65.9	48.8	87.6
Pacific	5	54.26	37.8	64.1

Source: Fe Caces, Stinson, and Elliott 1991

Note. Selected alcohol-related causes coded as underlying or contributing—cirrhosis, alcohol dependence syndrome, motor vehicle accidents, suicide, and homicide

[a] Northern = New England, Middle Atlantic, East North Central, West North Central

[b] Southern = South Atlantic, East South Central, and West South Central

Table 8.2 Mountain States Rural Populations: Mortality Rates per 100,000 Population

	Cirrhosis			
	1959–61	1969–71	1979–81	1987–88
Northern[a]	9.0	14.5	23.2	11.6
Southern[b]	18.8	27.8	30.4	25.1
Nevada	22.4	39.9	57.2	43.8

	Motor Vehicle Accidents			
	1959–61	1969–71	1979–81	1987–88
Northern	53.1	70.0	66.4	44.1
Southern	77.9	86.7	86.7	72.5
Nevada	85.5	104.5	120.1	85.2

	Other Accidents			
	1959–61	1969–71	1979–81	1987–88
Northern	64.7	72.3	63.3	38.3
Southern	76.1	83.1	59.7	50.8
Nevada	79.1	139.8	74.2	53.8

	Homicide			
	1959–61	1969–71	1979–81	1987–88
Northern	4.7	5.4	9.0	6.1
Southern	9.8	12.7	21.0	18.0
Nevada	12.4	16.5	38.5	19.7

	Suicide			
	1959–61	1969–71	1979–81	1987–88
Northern	19.4	22.3	25.4	29.6
Southern	17.8	23.0	30.5	38.9
Nevada	33.6	43.9	79.9	84.8

Note. Population calculated from U.S. Census and Vital Statistics

[a] Colorado, Idaho, Montana, Utah, and Wyoming
[b] Arizona, New Mexico

between miles driven and accident fatalities is demonstrated in table 8.3. Deaths per 100 million vehicle miles are estimated annually from the amount of gasoline consumed nationally. Unfortunately, a better indicator of exposure to the possibility of accidents—deaths per person-miles driven—is not available.

In 1967 the southern and Mountain states had above-average accident deaths per 100,000 population and per 100 million miles driven but lower than average rates of death from cirrhosis. Northern states tend to have lower than average accident deaths but higher than average rates of death from cirrhosis. Either alcohol is of less importance in contributing to vehicular accidents or rural populations contribute a high proportion of

Table 8.3 Accident and Cirrhosis Mortality Rates, by Region

Area	All 1969[a]	Motor Vehicle Accidents [yrs] 1951–61[b]	Mileage 1967[c]	Cirrhosis 1969[a]
United States	57.6	21.2	5.5	14.8
North				
New England	46.3	13.0	4.1	17.6
Middle Atlantic	41.8	14.0	4.7	20.2
East North Central	54.2	20.2	5.2	14.0
West North Central	63.3	24.1	5.7	9.7
South				
South Atlantic	63.7	23.1	5.9	13.4
East South Central	71.4	25.8	7.4	7.7
West South Central	65.7	25.9	6.2	10.6
Mountain	75.9	32.4	6.0	13.6
Pacific	61.3	24.5	5.1	19.0

[a] U.S. Bureau of the Census (1973, 62–63)
[b] National Center for Health Statistics (1970)
[c] National Center for Health Statistics (1970). Deaths per 100 million vehicle miles estimated annually from the amount of gasoline consumed. Vehicular mileage can be taken as an indication of exposure to the possibility of accidents. A high-mileage death rate therefore indicates a high proportion of deaths per miles driven.

alcohol-related deaths. At the national level, cirrhosis mortality rates for the forty-nine continental states were positively correlated with homicide rates (p = <.01), weakly associated with suicide rates (p = 0.07), and unassociated with deaths from motor vehicle accidents (p = 0.9).*

That environmental variables are the major causes of motor vehicle accidents in the forty-eight contiguous states is further demonstrated by the fact that in the period 1979–81, mortality was highest in counties of low population density (r = −0.57; p = <.0001) and inversely related to per capita income (Baker, Whitfield, and O'Neill 1987). This suggests that using accident rates as a marker of alcohol abuse without isolating those accidents associated with alcohol is not warranted.

The proportion of traffic accident deaths in the United States that were alcohol-related rose from 37 percent in 1977 to 41 percent in 1988 (Zobeck et al. 1991). This increase reflects the fact that alcohol-related fatalities per 100,000 population decreased by only 2.48 percent, whereas the rate for all traffic fatalities decreased by 11.97 percent in the same period. The decrease in accident fatalities, then, is due more to improved driving behaviors (seat belts and the like) and safer cars than to significant changes in drinking behavior. And this is true despite the growing number of campaigns against drunken driving.

Because the majority of Navajos live in rural areas in a region of high death rates from cirrhosis, suicide, homicide, and accidents, all thought to be alcohol-related, we have compared the Navajos to their rural neighbors in the hope that more accurate inferences may be made about the level of alcohol involvement as well as other contributory factors. We chose to compare the rural populations in several counties in New Mexico and Arizona. County census data were used for the years 1960, 1970,

---

*Simple regression analyses using cirrhosis as the independent variable. The data were from Fe Cases, Stinson, and Elliott (1991)

1980; 1988 data was estimated from the 1990 census. Crude death rates were calculated from three-year averages of the number of deaths for 1959–61, 1969–71, 1979–81, and for the two years 1987 and 1988. In the published volumes of data, cause of death in these rural counties is not categorized by age and sex, so it is impossible to adjust for these characteristics. Deaths are reported by place of residence rather than where the event occurred. Counties were labeled Navajo or Anglo. Rates for the urban populations of each state were also calculated (U.S. Bureau of the Census, 1960–90; National Center of Health Statistics, 1959–88).

County Classifications

Rural Navajo: These are counties in which 75 percent or more of the rural population is Navajo—Apache County in Arizona and McKinley County in New Mexico. Virtually all the Zunis in McKinley County (about 8,000) are classed as urban, so the rural population is almost entirely Navajo. The figures do not include the agency towns of Crownpoint, Fort Defiance, and Window Rock after they reached populations of 2,500.

Rural Anglo: Counties in which 75 percent or more of the rural population is Anglo ("whites not of Hispanic descent") but which are *not* called urban—that is, Bernallillo (Albuquerque), Pima (Tucson), and Maricopa (Phoenix). Included are Cochise, Mohave, and Yavapai counties in all years in Arizona; in New Mexico in all years—Catron, Curry, Hidalgo, Lea, Luna, Roosevelt, and Sierra; from 1960 to 1980—DeBaca, Quay, and Union; and only in 1987 and 1988—Los Alamos. We have combined the rural Anglo counties in New Mexico and Arizona in our analyses.

Urban: The populations in all counties (regardless of race) living in places with populations of 2,500 or more.

POPULATION

Both states have grown rapidly since 1960. Arizona has more than doubled its population; New Mexico has increased by 65 percent. Population increases have often led to declines in rural populations in many counties as locations that once were rural grew and were classed as urban in later censuses (table 8.4).

Yet the rural populations of Apache and McKinley counties have continued to grow, despite the fact that several places once classed as rural are now considered urban. Apache County, for example, was 100 percent rural in 1960 but only 76 percent rural in 1980. The rural population was 75 percent Indian in 1960 and grew to 84 percent by 1980. Only 15 percent of the county's urban population was Indian, however. In contrast, only 52 percent of McKinley County was rural in 1960, but by 1980 it had grown to 58 percent. The proportion of the rural population that was Indian remained almost constant at 83 and 86 percent.

Apache and McKinley counties include some of the most densely settled areas of the Navajo reservation and are the closest to large off-reservation towns: Gallup, New Mexico, and Holbrook, Arizona, to the south, and Aztec and Farmington, New Mexico, to the north. Some of the larger Navajo agency towns are also in these counties: Fort Defiance–Window Rock, Chinle, and Crownpoint. In our analyses, we have combined these two counties since the differences between them for the most part are not significant.

Table 8.4 Rural Populations

	Navajo	Anglo
1960	49,973	95,128
1970	56,952	100,309
1980	72,440	137,234
1988	73,497	129,148

Major road building programs on the Navajo reservation, begun in the 1950s, have greatly increased access to off-reservation centers over the years. Many of the roads were so heavily traveled that they were dangerous regardless of weather conditions. It is only in recent years that the roads connecting Window Rock and Fort Defiance to Gallup have been widened and improved. These developments have implications for changing accident rates as well as for alcohol use. Despite the existence of tribal and federal centers, however, travel is still made largely on unpaved roads, and the area is sparsely settled.

Several caveats must be stated. First, as discussed in chapter 4, the U.S. Census undercounts the Navajos by as much as 15 percent. As a result, the Navajo mortality rates reported below are probably higher than they are in reality. Second, rural deaths are not reported by race. It is assumed that in counties with 75 percent or more of the rural population drawn from a single ethnic or racial group, the majority of deaths will be accounted for by the numerically dominant population. Finally, there are substantial age differences between the Navajo and Anglo counties. In general, Navajo populations are younger. In 1960, 56 percent of the rural Navajos were under twenty years of age. By 1980, this had declined to 49 percent. The rural Anglo populations of people under twenty years had declined even more: from 41 percent to 32 percent during the same period.

CIRRHOSIS

Urban mortality rates for cirrhosis in Arizona and New Mexico followed the general pattern of the region and the nation, rising from about 11 per 100,000 population in 1960 to 16.2 in 1970, then declining to about 9.5 in 1988. Age-adjusted rates for the nation, which are slightly lower than the crude rates, were 10.5 in 1960, 14.6 in 1970, 12.2 in 1980, and 9.2 in 1987.

In table 8.5 we have shown the average annual crude mortality rates for rural Navajos and Anglos along with relative risks and 95 percent confidence intervals. In 1959–61 the rates of the two races did not differ significantly. By 1969–71 there was a significant difference: rates were higher in the Anglo population. There is no question that age structure confounds the analysis. Assuming that no cirrhosis deaths occurred below the age of twenty and that half the Navajo population and a third of the Anglo population were below twenty, the rates no longer differ. What is important, however, is that the Navajo rates are not significantly higher than the rates for the neighboring Anglos.

The general pattern for Indian deaths from cirrhosis in Arizona is that they are highest among groups living closest to sources of supply. Although alcoholic beverages are prohibited on the reservation, deaths from cirrhosis continue to be higher in areas closest to bordertowns. Thus, as roads continue to improve it is conceivable that areawide rates may continue to rise in a manner similar to that of Apache County, where rates rose from 7.7 in 1960 to 19.5 in 1980. McKinley County, in contrast, already had a rate of 20.5 in 1960.

It is also possible that new drinking styles—solitary drinking and drinking with nonrelatives—have developed more rapidly among the eastern Navajos. In chapter 4 we saw that for the Navajo Area as a whole mortality rates increased in the 1970s

Table 8.5 Crude Average Annual Death Rates per 100,000 owing to Cirrhosis

	Rate			
Year	Anglos	Navajos	Relative Risk	95% Confidence Interval
1959–61	15.4	12.6	A:N = 1.22	0.71, 2.06
1969–71	27.9	15.8	A:N = 1.76	1.13, 2.69
1979–81	31.8	14.2	A:N = 2.24	1.52, 3.27
1987–88	35.2	22.4	A:N = 1.57	1.05, 2.32

A Anglo, N Navajo

but have declined since. We are at a loss to explain this discrepancy, except to note that the increased urbanization of Indian populations and milder drinking styles among Navajos living permanently in off-reservation towns may be having an effect as they are included in the IHS Navajo Area statistics.

Note that at present alcohol problems among the Navajos as measured by deaths from cirrhosis are certainly not greater than those of their non-Indian neighbors despite any opinion those neighbors might hold. Thus, the question of whether Navajo drinking is a response to the stresses of acculturation or a general adaptation to the non-Indian culture around them must be taken into account in future research.

ACCIDENTS

Motor Vehicle Accidents

Fatal traffic accidents are said to be high among Indians. In 1971, the age-adjusted mortality rate for all Indians was 96.5 per 100,000 population, more than three times the national average. In 1974, the crude mortality rate on the Navajo reservation was 91 per 100,000 (Katz and May 1979). Rates in the United States climbed from 21.3 in 1960 to 26.2 in 1970 but have declined since then to 20.4 in 1987 (U.S. Bureau of the Census 1973; World Almanac 1989). The decline, however, has been among those over 45. After age 55, age-specific rates have decreased by about 10. Between ages 15 and 34, the rates have increased.

The trend for the urban populations of Arizona and New Mexico parallels that for the nation: an increase from 28 in 1960 to 34 in 1970, decreasing to 19 in 1988. The rates for rural Anglos, although considerably higher than urban rates, also follow this trend, as do the rates for the Navajo Area as a whole (see table 4.1). The rate in the rural Navajo population, however, rose from 1960 to the late 1980s. We believe that the road-building programs, which paved the roads to the west and south of Apache.County, and the increased number of automobiles were the major contributors to this increase.

The question arises of whether high Navajo traffic fatalities in general as well as the rate increases may be accounted for by alcohol use, given that the cirrhosis rates in Apache and McKinley counties also rose during the 1980s. May (1992) has estimated that 65 percent of fatalities are alcohol-related but suggests that actual Indian involvement is higher and national involvement lower. In an earlier study of accidents on the Navajo reservation, Katz and May (1979, 52–55) reported that for the three-year period 1973–75, 41 percent of Navajo single-vehicle accident fatalities and 46 percent of multiple-vehicle accident fatalities involved alcohol, proportions that are not much different from those for the nation.

In the United States, the proportion of motor vehicle accidents in which alcohol was involved rose from 36.5 percent in 1977 to almost 43 percent in 1987 (Zobeck et al. 1991). In Arizona between 1979 and 1981, the proportion of rural traffic fatalities in which alcohol was involved was 33 percent in Apache County and 34 percent in the rural Anglo counties (Arizona Department of Transportation 1979–81). With motor vehicle–accident fatality rates of 140.4 and 72.6, respectively, in these counties, the

Table 8.6 Crude Average Annual Death Rates per 100,000 owing to Motor Vehicle Accidents

Year	Rate			
	Anglos	Navajos	Relative Risk	95% Confidence Interval
1959–61	78.1	76.7	N:A = 0.98	—
1969–71	92.0	131.1	N:A = 1.42	1.19, 1.69
1979–81	77.5	119.6	N:A = 1.54	1.3, 1.64
1987–88	87.1	129.9	N:A = 1.49	1.34, 1.64

N Navajo, A Anglo

fatality rates associated with alcohol were 46 and 24.7, respectively. Thus the Navajo rate is about twice the Anglo rate for alcohol-related deaths. In table 8.6 we give the average annual crude death rates from 1959–61 to 1987–88. The risk of death is significantly greater among Navajos than Anglos for all periods but the earliest. We have not attempted the same rough age adjustment here as we did with cirrhosis, since accident victims are found in all age groups (see chapter 4).

Rural accident fatality rates are higher than urban rates for several reasons, including greater distance from medical care, fewer medical facilities, greater distances traveled at a higher speed, and lower quality of rural roads. In Apache County 4.2 percent of all traffic accidents are fatal compared to only 1.9 percent in the three Anglo counties and less than 1 percent in the metropolitan counties of Pima and Maricopa (Arizona Department of Transportation 1979–81).† These differences are considerable, and although some bias may be introduced if rural, especially Navajo, nonfatal accidents are reported to authorities less frequently, it is reasonable to infer that those factors that make driving on rural roads more dangerous are even more in evidence on the Navajo reservation.

Although there were eight locations where physicians were available in Apache County in 1987, only two were on the reservation compared to six in the Anglo counties (Gordon 1987, tables 14, 39). In the same year, the Anglo counties had 98 physicians and 57 emergency medical technicians per 100,000 population certified to administer advanced cardiac life-support techniques, basic airway maintenance, and intravenous fluid therapy. These figures contrast with 51 physicians and 8 emergency medical technicians per 100,000 population in all of Apache County (de Gennaro 1990, 25). Considering

---

†In Navajo County, with Navajos accounting for more than 60 percent of the rural population, the proportion of all traffic accidents that are fatal is also high (3.6 percent).

also the rarity of telephones in the rural areas of the reservation, it is reasonable to infer that the high Navajo case fatality rate is largely a result of the relative lack of emergency medical care. Rural population density is essentially the same for Apache and the Anglo counties (3.5 and 3.2 persons per square mile, respectively) so that it is not easy to estimate whether Navajos are at greater risk for accidents because they travel greater distances. Calculating fatality rates by miles driven based on gasoline consumption is highly inaccurate when computed at the county level. We arrived at a fatality rate of 10.6 per 100 million vehicle miles for Apache County in 1980.[‡] Apache County is traversed from east to west by two of the most dangerous roads on the Navajo reservation—U.S. Route 160 and State Route 264—which in 1973 had fatality rates of 16.35 and 16.26 per 100 million miles driven, respectively (Katz and May 1975).

A study conducted on the western Navajo reservation in the early 1970s reported that many vehicles were driven between 30,000 and 50,000 miles a year and that an average of 25,000 would definitely be low (Callaway, Levy, and Henderson 1976). Moreover, the cost of transportation accounted for more than 40 percent of the incomes of the more rural families. Accidents are more likely for vehicles that are driven many miles and are poorly maintained owing to the poverty of their owners. Half of all noncommercial vehicles registered in Apache County in 1980 were half-ton pick-up trucks compared to 22 percent in the Anglo counties (Valley National Bank of Arizona 1984). Pick-ups are less safe in an accident than sedans because passengers in the open bed are unprotected and without seat belts. Fifty-three percent of the vehicles involved in fatal accidents on the Navajo reservation in the 1970s were pick-up trucks (Katz and May 1979). We suspect that rural Navajos drive more trucks and carry more passengers in them than rural Anglos do.

[‡]Fuel consumption for 1980 from Valley National Bank of Arizona 1984.

In addition, 33 percent of Navajo drivers involved in fatal single-vehicle accidents had invalid driver's licenses in the 1970s.

In sum, although Navajo fatality rates owing to drunken driving are higher than Anglo rates, most of the difference in motor vehicle accident rates are attributable to distance from medical facilities, distances driven, unsafe and poorly maintained vehicles, and unsafe drivers. If alcohol were the major factor, the proportion of fatalities involving alcohol would be higher than in the Anglo counties and would have risen as the Navajo motor vehicle fatality rates rose between 1960 and 1988.

Other Accidents

May (1992) estimates that, in contrast to motor vehicle accidents, only 25 percent of other types of accidents involve alcohol. Table 8.7 shows that after a peak in 1970 accident rates have decreased steadily in Arizona and New Mexico, although Navajo rates remain higher than those of the other groups. There are no data concerning the extent to which alcohol is involved in these fatalities.

Case fatality rates are higher in rural areas owing to the nature of the environment as well as to the difficulty of obtaining emergency medical care; farm accidents in particular make rural areas more prone to fatal accidents. Living conditions of rural Navajos are still more primitive than those of rural Anglos despite the measurable improvements made since 1960. Our

Table 8.7 Crude Average Annual Death Rates per 100,000 owing to Other Accidents

Year	Anglos	Navajos	Relative Risk	95% Confidence Interval
			Rate	
1959–61	80.9	103.0	N:A = 1.27	1.03, 1.55
1969–71	78.0	109.4	N:A = 1.4	1.15, 1.58
1979–81	60.0	77.7	N:A = 1.29	1.05, 1.56
1987–88	55.3	82.3	N:A = 1.48	1.23, 1.78

N Navajo, A Anglo

impression is that burns caused by unprotected fires in hogans have contributed significantly to high fatality rates, although they have been declining in recent years as housing conditions improve. It is also likely that deaths from accidental poisoning are higher among rural Navajos. It is remarkably difficult to keep poisonous substances out of reach of children in hogans without storage containers and medicine cabinets. Aspirin poisoning of children was a major concern of pediatricians in the Tuba City hospital during the years we worked there, and we doubt that the situation was different in other parts of the Navajo reservation.

Because "other" accident rates are falling among the Navajo, in contrast to cirrhosis and motor vehicle accident rates, we are inclined to attribute the high Navajo rates to environmental factors more than to alcohol.

HOMICIDE AND SUICIDE

National rates of suicide and homicide have been rising steadily since 1960; homicide from 4.7 to 9.0, suicide from 10.6 to 12.3. Table 8.8 shows that both rural Anglos and rural Navajos have followed this national pattern. Moreover, the crude rates do not

Table 8.8 Crude Average Annual Death Rates per 100,000 owing to Homicides

Year	Anglos	Navajos	Rate Relative Risk	95% Confidence Interval
1959–61	8.05	10.6	N:A = 1.32	0.7, 2.48
1969–71	11.6	14.0	N:A = 1.2	0.72, 2.02
1979–81	16.5	17.0	N:A = 1.03	0.9, 2.0
1987–88	15.9	14.9	A:N = 1.06	0.35, 1.76

N Navajo, A Anglo

differ significantly in any year. Since homicide victims are found in every age group, we have not attempted the age adjustment we used with cirrhosis, but because the vast majority of victims are aged over twenty, we think such an adjustment would increase the rate among Navajos more than it would among Anglos.

A similar picture of secular change is evident for suicides in each population, as table 8.9 indicates. The suicide rate among Anglos is significantly higher than among Navajos. Because suicide among Anglos occurs at substantially older ages than among Navajos, and because the rural Anglo population is so much older than the Navajo population, age adjustment would have the effect of reducing the differences between the races. In the case of both suicide and homicide, however, the available data suggest that Navajos do not differ substantially, if at all, from neighboring rural Anglos.

Discussion

We have compared rural Navajos from the eastern end of the reservation to rural Anglos. Apache and McKinley counties include those service units with the highest mortality rates from cirrhosis; therefore they are not representative of Navajos

Table 8.9 Crude Average Annual Death Rates per 100,000 owing to Suicide

	Rate			
Year	Anglos	Navajos	Relative Risk	95% Confidence Interval
1959–61	16.5	15.3	A:N = 1.07	0.65, 1.75
1969–71	32.5	23.4	A:N = 1.39	0.96, 2.0
1979–81	36.7	19.8	A:N = 1.85	1.56, 2.19
1987–88	54.5	29.9	A:N = 1.82	1.3, 2.55

N Navajo, A Anglo

generally. The Navajo counties have higher mortality rates due to accidents of all types and rates equal to those of the Anglos for cirrhosis, homicide, and suicide. We have argued that environmental conditions account for the higher accident rates better than alcohol abuse does, although, clearly, if Navajos were to become abstinent the rates would decline.

We have also questioned the extent to which alcohol has a causal effect on rates of homicide and suicide. That it sometimes does, as when an intoxicated man kills a friend over a trivial matter, is not in question. Most often, however, it is no more than a complicating factor. An earlier study found that before 1945, when the proportion of suicides associated with alcohol was low (8 percent), murder before suicide occurred in 37.7 percent of all cases. After 1945, however, the proportion of suicides associated with alcohol rose to 47.2 percent, whereas murder before suicide declined to 7 percent without an increase in the overall rate of suicide (Levy 1965; Levy, Kunitz, and Everett 1969). Whether one kills one's wife because one is drunk or drinks in order to kill one's wife is still an unanswered question.

Not only has drinking become more frequent, but as discussed in chapter 6, drinking styles have been changing, especially in areas where both alcohol and wage labor are more readily available. We still do not know what causes people to drink more, beyond knowing that it is increasingly easy to do so. We have noted that traditional restraints and styles of drinking are being eroded as more Navajos enter the wage-work economy and as the pastoral economy, in which survival depended on cooperation between kinspeople, has declined. But with the disappearance of restraints, what is the impetus to drink that has been released? Is it anomie, the sense of frustration and despair that results from interacting with the dominant society?

Adapting to the surrounding society for Navajos involves behaving like the non-Indians with whom they come into contact. Navajos returning from military service after World War II and the Korean War demanded the right to drink as their comrades in arms did. They had learned a completely different style of drinking as well as different ideas about alcohol use. It is likely that some of the changes taking place are the result of emulating the drinking behaviors of those Anglos with whom Navajos interact the most.

By now our readers may be forgiven for thinking that we have been trying to convince them that Navajos need not be concerned about alcohol abuse. Quite the contrary, our intent has been to show that the way data are presented tends to obscure more than elucidate the nature and causes of a problem. More particularly, we are concerned with the effects of the common practice of comparing Indian mortality rates to those of the nation on how Indians conceive of their use of alcohol and on their efforts to devise and participate in prevention and treatment programs.

We have argued that rural Navajos manifest much the same rates of several conditions widely thought to be indicators of social pathology as the neighboring rural Anglo population. These are important data. First, they suggest that there are very different regional cultures among Anglo Americans. Second, they suggest that the most relevant comparisons of Indian rates may not be to some composite national rate but to neighboring populations that share a common region and that are likely to be the people whose behavior shapes what Indians learn about the dominant culture.

It is easy to see why non-Indian investigators are content to make comparisons with national figures. Health professionals justify budget requests for Indian programs by demonstrating how far Indians lag behind the general population. Many social scientists find confirmation for their conviction that Indians continue to suffer at the hands of the dominant society. Most observers, whether health professionals or academics, come from the American middle class and have had their experience of alcohol shaped by the drinking culture of that predominantly urban segment of the population. When they observe drinking practices that are very different from their own, the comparisons they make are almost always negative. Moreover, the causes of what is perceived as deviant drinking are assumed to be the ones the observer has been brought up to accept—addiction, a character flaw, an attempt to deaden the pain of despair or a sense of failure, even an inherited defect. It is also easier to accept negative social labeling because people like to hear about the frailties of others, and norms tend to be highlighted more by infraction than by conformity.

Most Navajos surveyed by May and Smith (1988) have come to believe the commonly held lay Anglo explanation for Indian drinking, namely, that Indians have a physiological susceptibility to intoxication not shared by non-Indians. They also seem to share Anglos' belief that Indian alcohol use and abuse are widely prevalent despite there being fewer Navajo adults who drink than adults in the general population. The new "medicalized" definitions of alcoholism and offenders—as a disease as opposed to a crime, and the offender as a victim rather than a culprit— are also being accepted by Navajo paraprofessionals, who are coming to view their own people as "sick" (Kunitz and Levy 1974; Levy and Kunitz 1973). Thus, as Navajos adapt to the world around them, they inadvertently internalize negative Anglo views and thereby suffer lowered self-esteem.

Just how these perceptions have distorted Indians' understanding of the world around them was brought home to us when we had occasion to attend an opening of the annual Navajo arts and crafts show at the Museum of Northern Arizona in Flagstaff in the company of a young Navajo friend. As we approached the museum, a well-dressed, very intoxicated Anglo woman came staggering down the steps toward us. Our friend became agitated and implored us to seek medical attention for this woman, whom she took to be seriously ill. She believed that only Indians abused alcohol and that Anglos were eminently sober and well adjusted.

At the same time that these changes in perception are taking place, an increasing number of Indians are coming to the conclusion that only the community can eliminate alcohol abuse (Rhoades et al. 1988). Since 1985, the Indian Health Service has also encouraged the development of prevention programs in Indian communities and schools. For such programs to be successful, however, communities must maintain their energy and enthusiasm. This is possible only if the community has a positive self-image. But by consistently presenting the higher prevalence of alcoholism and alcohol-related pathologies among American Indians, we foster the image of the Indian as sick and of Indian communities as disintegrated. Yet the failure of community-based prevention programs is almost guaranteed if the only way to fund them is to demonstrate that Indians are sicker than Anglo-Americans.

We do not wish to be understood as arguing that Navajos and other Indians do not have difficulties with alcohol that deserve both prevention and treatment services. What we have contended, rather, is that those difficulties may usefully be seen in the context of the regional cultures in which they are embedded instead of in contrast to some homogeneous and nonexistent national culture to which everyone and no one belongs. Viewed in this way, the environmental contribution to the increased risk of death becomes more evident, the role of alcohol assumes more realistic proportions, and negative images of self and community may be rethought.

Alcohol Treatment and the Bureaucratization of Tradition

When we began this research in 1966, mental health and alcohol treatment programs were just being started. Two alcohol treatment programs had been established for a year or two on the eastern side of the reservation. None existed on the western side until an overworked internist in Tuba City, desperate to reduce the toll exacted by alcohol abuse, began the program we studied. Without any support, the services offered were minimal: a drying-out period in the hospital, loading with Antabuse, a wine challenge to demonstrate the effect of Antabuse, and then discharge with a standing order for Antabuse from the hospital pharmacy. Under existing conditions, this was all that could be done. Antabuse was still relatively new, and great hope was held out that it would provide a simple and effective way to get people to stop drinking excessively. There were no formal treatment programs with trained staff readily available. And there were many acute medical and surgical conditions absorbing the time of the hospital staff.

All that began to change within a short period, primarily as the Great Society programs of the 1960s made an increasingly large impact on Indian reservations throughout the country. In this chapter we describe some of the changes in alcohol programs that have occurred since our first study. We suggest that the growth and bureaucratization of alcohol treatment programs

192

exemplify much larger processes at work in Indian affairs; that in fact this is a new sort of pan-Indianism, not millennarian nor reformist at the personal level but accommodative institutionally. It is pan-Indian because both the actors and much of the treatment ideology—if not practice—are increasingly Indian. But because it is a development created by the relation between Indian tribes and the federal government, it is heavily bureaucratized. Hence, we have thought of this process as the bureaucratization of tradition. The growth of such bureaucratized programs is not inevitable but involves a special kind of politics —politics that seem to be characteristic of numerically insignificant, economically weak, and geographically scattered indigenous minority groups in liberal democracies—what has been called Fourth World politics. In the absence of economic and political power, such politics are heavily dependent upon non-native constituencies for both legal and symbolic support. We discuss the notion of Fourth World politics in more detail below.

Finally, we return to a description of the evolution of treatment and prevention programs in the community where we worked. We describe both how such programs grew and changed in response to changes in policy and funding and the diversity that now exists. We suggest but cannot demonstrate that widespread discussion of, and concern with, alcohol abuse may have had a beneficial effect in the community.

THE EVOLUTION OF TREATMENT

Most of the Indian alcohol treatment programs of the late 1960s were supported by the Office of Equal Opportunity. In the early 1970s they were transferred to the National Institute of Alcohol Abuse and Alcoholism (NIAAA) as a result of passage of PL 91–616, the Comprehensive Alcohol Abuse Treatment, Prevention, Rehabilitation Act of 1970. In the mid-1970s, under the terms of the Indian Health Care Improvement Act (PL 94–437), support passed from NIAAA to the Indian Health Service. Thirty-six programs were transferred to IHS in 1978. By 1983 these programs had proliferated to 158 community-based programs and by 1990 to 328. The authorized funding increased equally rapidly: from $3.8 million in 1978 to $20.2 million in 1983 and $24.8 million in 1987 (IHS 1987, 22). The expansion involved not simply more programs but a shift in focus to include women, young people, halfway houses, and much more prevention (Rhoades et al. 1988). These changes were mandated by the Anti-Drug Abuse Act of 1986 (PL 99–570) and by amendments known as the Omnibus Drug Act (PL 100–690) some time later.

The first programs were supported by the Office of Economic Opportunity, where the ideology was one of community participation and control, the employment of indigenous people as paraprofessionals, and the creation of jobs in labor-surplus communities. Elsewhere we have written at length of the consequences of this ideology, and we summarize some of that here (Kunitz and Levy 1974; Levy and Kunitz 1981).

There were several reasons for advocating the employment of local people as health workers, not simply in Indian communities but in urban ghettos as well. One was the belief that only those who knew the community could truly understand the problems and how to solve them. This was generalized to mean that only recovering alcoholics and drug addicts could understand alcoholics and drug addicts and how to deal with them, a view consistent with the philosophy of Alcoholics Anonymous.

A second reason was that it was generally believed that alcohol abuse by Indians was the result of economic deprivation, social disruption, and acculturation. The infusion of money for treatment programs in which community members played an important role was meant to help create economically viable communities and to help give people pride in themselves and their culture. Moreover, if alienation from traditional culture was one of the root causes of alcohol abuse, then having traditional healing rituals as part of the treatment system would help instill both knowledge and pride, restore harmony between the alcoholic and his community, and reduce alienation and the enormous costs exacted by alcohol abuse.*

A third reason was that paraprofessional jobs could be an alternative pathway to more professional occupations. They provided a vehicle for achieving social mobility. Even if mobility did not result, at least unemployment would have been reduced. Indeed, employment was one of the major, if often covert, goals of such programs. Underlying much of this attempt at decentralization and paraprofessionalization was a healthy skepticism about the knowledge and practical expertise of professional providers of services, from teachers to social workers to psychiatrists. In the alcohol treatment field an additional factor was the dearth of available professionals (IOM 1990). The result was that paraprofessional counselors emerged rapidly as the major providers of care, nationwide as well as on Indian reservations.

Many of these reasons underlay those parts of the Indian Health Care Improvement Act that dealt with alcohol abuse. The Senate Committee on Interior and Insular Affairs explained the alcohol treatment sections of the Act and the transfer from NIAAA to IHS as follows:

> With the funding authorized for alcoholism treatment and control, programs would be established and implemented to increase public understanding and awareness of the problems of alcoholism, change communities' attitudes, support rehabilitation sources, develop preventive programs for Indian youth, and design education and training programs in the field of Indian alcoholism. Projects would be designed to provide residential care, individual counseling, job placement, referral services, group therapy, Indian AA groups, recreation and self-government. The essential aspect of these projects would be the integration of Indian cultural patterns into the rehabilitative and learning processes. This would be accomplished, in

* In recent years *cultural oppression, cultural depression,* and *cultural bereavement* have all been used to explain alcohol abuse by Indians. See, e.g., J. Kauffman, Testimony before the Senate Select Committee on Indian Affairs, 7 July 1988. Reprinted in *Healing Hearts,* August 1988, 6–8.

part, by hiring Indian staff, working through individual tribal entities, and emphasizing the Indian's image of himself. (Committee on Interior and Insular Affairs 1974, 87)

In practice, many of these programs met with difficulties. A survey of nine treatment programs on the Navajo reservation in the late 1970s "documented the major problems common to many Indian alcoholism projects."

These programs were found to be characterized by: (1) inadequate funding; (2) extremely poor pay and no career ladder for counselors and other employees; (3) counselors with little or no professional training; (4) counseling generally limited to individual, adult clients with little emphasis on family and community; (5) isolation from professional and community input; (6) neglect of the Indian spiritual aspects of life; (7) little follow-up; (8) a need for diversified staff and treatments; and (9) no guiding theoretical or ideological perspective. In this survey, 73% of all Indian community leaders rated the programs as inadequate and many specifically mentioned a lack of outreach and youth services. (May 1986, 190)

A subsequent nationwide survey of twelve programs came to similar conclusions, which were not very different from criticisms leveled at non-Indian programs (IOM 1990). Partly in response, funding agencies—whether governmental or private— have begun to enforce standards of training and care. It was, for instance, the goal of the Navajo Tribal Action Plan on alcohol and substance abuse to have 90 percent of the counselors in tribal programs "get and retain state certification" (Navajo Tribe 1987, 54). At the same time, the ideology of community control and the importance of indigenous workers persisted.

How to reconcile the use of native treatments and "Indian cultural patterns" with the insistence upon increasing standards of professional training and state certification is not immediately obvious. One way has been to argue that treatment regimens should be tailored to the individual needs of patients. This required a way of assessing those needs and matching them to various therapeutic methods. Indeed, just as "matching" between clients and treatment programs has been advocated nationally (IOM 1990), so has it been advocated for Indian clients and various treatment programs. One example, developed by Sidney Stone-Brown and Rufus Charger, is described by Joan Weibel-Orlando (1987, 275–79).

> Four main elements of world view are assessed in Stone-Brown's model: spiritual/religious, social/recreation, training/educational, familial/self. Each of these elements is rated along four levels or generations that range from highly traditional to highly contemporary. Discrepancies in generational levels across the four world view elements are considered noteworthy. The treatment paradigm is based on the assumption that self-actualization is maximized by attaining equilibrium of the four world view elements. That is to say, self-actualized individuals tend to fall in the same generational level on all four world view elements. Disequilibrium of any of the four elements produces preactualization conflicts that need to be resolved through therapy. Through the use of the world view assessment protocol, apparent preactualization conflicts are identified and treatment is individualized to address the individual's particular conflicts.
>
> . . . Using an amended version of the Native Self-Actualization protocol, it may be possible to match clients according to their life experiences, attitudes, and world views with the most appropriate alcoholism intervention strategy.

Similarly, the Navajo Tribal Action Plan on alcohol and substance abuse described currently available diagnostic and treatment services as follows:

> Services for chronic alcohol abusers emphasize counseling services in agency offices. These approaches are conventional, but in some cases take cognizance of the unique nature of the Navajo culture and personality. The client-counselor relationship serves as the core of programs designed to break the cycle of alcoholic behavior. Family therapy seems well suited to the traditional Navajo values, as does the use of traditional practitioners and the Native American Church. Research into demonstration projects attempting cost effective innovations in

treatment are badly needed, especially those which utilize traditional approaches and unique cultural components. (Navajo Tribe 1987, 20)

To our knowledge, no outcome studies have been done of such attempts to match Indian clients to different traditional and nontraditional treatments, and we therefore have no opinion on the efficacy of such efforts (for example, Weibel-Orlando 1989). More important for our present purposes is what such efforts suggest about the accommodation that is beginning to be made between the requirements for bureaucratic organization of federally funded agencies on the one hand and traditional healing methods on the other.

THE BUREAUCRATIZATION OF TRADITION

Since the nineteenth century social scientists have tried to capture and understand the changes that took place as societies were transformed by colonialism, industrialism, and urbanization. Several paired concepts were coined: gemeinschaft and gesellschaft; folk and urban; traditional and legal-rational authority; mechanical and organic solidarity; and particularism and universalism.

One of the most perplexing changes that occurred is in the way kin-based societies have adapted to, been transformed by, and in turn transformed the bureaucratic institutions imposed upon them by colonial powers. For example, Lloyd Fallers (1965, 238) has pointed out how traditional authority structures in Busoga, Uganda, differ from those of the civil service bureaucracy imported by the English. In the traditional system, "A person was under the authority of the members of his own lineage or the person who was his own patron. Such criteria governing social relations I have called, following Talcott Parsons, 'particularistic.' In the civil service bureaucracy, on the other hand, authority is situational. It is a property of an office, not a person, and its validity depends upon general rules governing the office, not upon the person who holds it."

In contrasting the univocal communication that characterizes modern American society with the ambiguity of expression that characterizes Amhara society, Donald Levine (1985, 35) has written:

> Role specificity of an extreme degree has developed in the United States since the middle of the nineteenth century, as a result of extensive occupational specialization and the rationalization of activities in most spheres of life. Job descriptions have come to enumerate in unambiguous terms the duties and facilities appropriate to each office. This simply accentuates a pattern common to all industrialized societies, which rely on a methodical division of the integrated activities of continuously operating offices, on clearly defined spheres of competence, and on a precise enumeration of official responsibilities and prerogatives.
>
> Amhara social organization, by contrast, exhibits a great deal of functional diffuseness. Kinship, political, and religious roles carry multiple functions. The boundaries of responsibilities and prerogatives associated with them are not clearly defined, and there is considerable overlapping among roles. This pattern of diffuseness encourages the vagueness of ambiguity in communication.

In contrast to the Busoga and Amhara, the descriptions of the development of political structures among the Navajo paint a somewhat different picture. For example, Mary Shepardson (1963, 117) observed that traditional Navajo social organization provided the "freedom to develop a new political system."

> Freedom from within the society is inherent in the flexibility of traditional Navajo social structure and authority patterns. This means that there are no individuals or corporate groups with vested interests of great strength and power to be superseded or displaced. No family or clan group inherits super-ordinate authority. Leadership roles are achieved, not ascribed. No fixed power structure accompanies the ceremo-

nial system. No secret societies, no all-pervading theocratic government, hinder the growth of a secular authority. Population increases and new, complicated economic problems cannot be handled with the old informal structures; the new system is needed because it is geared to new problems. The transition from an informal, nonauthoritarian, diffuse, face-to-face system of traditional government to a modern, formal system is difficult. Old family patterns of cooperation, informal controls, witchcraft accusations, distrust of fixed rules, and delegation of authority act to slow up the rate of institutionalization, but they do not block the development.

Aubrey Williams, too, has observed that when Navajos have not been forced, they have adopted many features of Anglo-American political structure "with a minimum amount of opposition and conflict" (1970, 63). But as Shepardson pointed out, the establishment of a tribal government has not been without difficulties. Institutionalization has been successful, however, not simply because Navajo social organization and culture facilitated it, but because the evolving structure of the reservation economy has made it virtually inevitable.

Indian reservations have much in common with so-called MIRAB states. MIRAB is an acronym applied to Pacific Island microstates and refers to their economic structure, which is based upon *mi*gration, the *r*emittance of the migrants' wages home, *a*id from donor nations, and work in government *b*ureaucracies as the most stable and most common form of wage work in the community. In MIRAB economies, aid is often given for development projects but is generally used to support existing government agencies. The situation is somewhat different on Indian reservations, where government agencies are supported directly by the federal government or the tribe, primarily for the purpose of providing services. This is the case on the Navajo reservation where two-thirds of the employed population works in one or another government bureaucracy devoted to health, education, or welfare.

What Indian reservations and MIRAB states have in common is the overwhelming significance of government agencies as the major employers and source of stable cash incomes. Thus the contrast between the primarily welfare-subsistence economy and the highly structured government bureaucracy is particularly stark. There are few intermediating institutions. Moreover, as a result of changes in the subsistence economy, the penetration of a cash economy, the expansion of education, and the activities of Christian missionaries, the indigenous society and culture in such communities have undergone dramatic change. On the Navajo reservation, for instance, the traditional religious and healing system has changed substantially. The number of singers who know full ceremonies has declined even as the population has grown, and many sings have become extinct. Moreover, adequate private resources scarcely exist to pay for the major ceremonies that still do exist. In an attempt to preserve much of their culture, many Navajos have turned to tribal or federal government bureaucracies as a major source of funds to subsidize the training of traditional healers and to pay them for their services because the welfare-subsistence economy can no longer do it.

These agencies have been willing to provide support for such activities as training traditional Navajo healers (see, for example, *New York Times,* 6 May 1972). But one must be prepared to deal with a bureaucracy: one must do it in terms that the bureaucracy is equipped to understand: this means shaping the treatment system to conform to the requirements of the funding agency. Thus, on the Navajo reservation, "The major provider of alcoholism services . . . is the NAP (Navajo Alcohol Program), which is located in the Behavioral Health Department of the Navajo Nation Division of Health Improvement Services (DHIS)" (Navajo Tribe 1987, 27). This program was established in 1965 and supported first by the Office of Navajo Economic Opportunity, then by the National Institute on Alcohol Abuse and Alcoholism, and then by contract funds through the Indian

Health Service to the Navajo Tribe under the terms of the Indian Health Care Improvement Act.[†] The contract with the Indian Health Service requires "the institution of a uniform reporting system for alcoholism programs . . . presently in use in the Navajo Area. Extensive staff training in the use of this system has been necessary" (Navajo Tribe 1987, 30). The provision of services, including traditional healing services, to clients of the alcohol program must be reported to the Indian Health Service using code list 13, "client service codes." The list is given below to illustrate the bureaucratization in which traditional healing rituals are becoming enmeshed.

01 Traditional Group Counseling: Group counseling led by a Medicine Person, Pipe Carrier, Shaman, Elder, or other traditional person who deals with Indian culture, traditions, values, and other issues in a traditional manner

02 Traditional Medicine: Healing ceremonies or activities performed by a Medicine Person, Pipe Carrier, Shaman, or Elder for the benefit of a client

03 Sweat Lodge: Participation in Sweat Lodge Ceremonies

04 Native American Treatment: Participation in Native American Church ceremonies (Peyote Church) led by a Road Man, who has been recommended by a local NAC chapter, and conducted primarily for the purpose of treating persons with alcohol and drug problems. This code should not be used for those Native American Church services conducted for general prayer service, birthdays, or other purposes.

05 Cultural Discussions/Activities: General cultural discussion groups or activities such as bead work, drumming, singing, dancing, crafts, and so forth

06 Initial Contact, Placement, and Assessment: Completion of forms 1, 2, 3, and 11, or that process of initial contact

07 Individual Counseling: Formal (scheduled) or informal (unscheduled) one-to-one session

---

[†]By 1990 there were thirteen community-based treatment programs (one accredited) with fifty-one counselors (twenty-four accredited) (Burns 1991, 80).

08 Family Counseling: Counseling family members either with or without the client present

09 Group Counseling: Counseling in groups

10 Spiritual Counseling: Counseling performed by clergy, lay person, or traditional spiritual person who addresses the spiritual aspects of alcoholism or drug abuse recovery

11 Client Alcohol Education: Client participation in alcohol education classes. (Does not include DWI sessions required by state law or court order.)

12 General Client Education: Educational activities such as GED classes or Adult Basic Education

13 Self-Help Skills Training: Classes pertaining to nutrition, budgeting, resume preparation, parenting, etc.

14 Occupational Therapy: Activities related to career counseling, aptitude testing, job training, etc.

15 Recreational Therapy: Activities related to exercise programs, organized sports, camping, hiking, etc.

16 Preventive Activities: Participation in activities which have as their primary purpose the prevention of substance abuse. These include education, alternatives to substance abuse, discussions, clubs, etc.

17 Crisis Intervention: Activities related to first aid, detoxification, emergency medical treatment, suicide intervention, and family abuse, neglect, or violence

18 Outreach: Activities which have as their primary purpose the motivation of potential clients to enter treatment

19 Follow Up/Aftercare, Contact: Services provided to a client after discharge from outpatient status. This includes time spent in completing the Follow-Up Status Report.

20 Follow Up/Aftercare, No Contact: Time spent attempting to provide services after discharge from outpatient status but no direct contact with client was made

21 Criminal Justice: Services provided with or on the client's behalf dealing with a judge, officer of the court, prosecutor, attorney, parole, or probation officer. Direct services, such as group or individual counseling, which incarcerated are recorded under other service codes

22 DWI Sessions: Alcohol Education sessions mandated by state law or court order

23 Antabuse Therapy: Monitored Antabuse provided by the program

24 Participation in Medical Treatment Process: Medical services sponsored or paid by the program

25 Assistance Services: Assistance to client in arranging or obtaining services outside the program, such as welfare, jobs, medical treatment, church services, etc. Most time spent in making referrals is recorded in this category and should be specified and coded (from code list 5, page 44) in block 5 on the Service Report 9.

26 Collateral Consultation: Discussions pertaining to a client with persons who have a personal relation with the client (i.e., employer, teacher, friend, etc.)

27 Case Consultation: Discussions pertaining to a client with persons who have a professional relation with the client (i.e., caseworker, doctor, mental health worker, other staff members, etc.)

28 Referral to A.A.: Services assisting a client in getting to meetings, obtaining a sponsor, etc. Time spent in A.A. meetings can be recorded.

29 Adult Day Care: Usually treatment provided on an 8–5 basis in a halfway house or other structured treatment program

30 Child Care (other than residential child care): Usually day care or babysitting while parent is in outpatient treatment

31 Youth Treatment: For youth outpatient treatment components. Also may use regular service codes (i.e., individual counseling).

32 Travel with or for Client: Client transportation or travel in behalf of the client (that is, travel to see the client, travel to meet for case consultation, etc.)

33 Support Sessions: Sessions held on an informal basis, of a general nature, not related to an established treatment plan. (Example: the outpatient client who stops by for a visit and cup of coffee.)

NOTE
Service codes record only those services directly provided, sponsored, or paid by the program. Other services provided to the client by other agencies or individuals not directly

associated with the program are recorded as referrals in section 5 of the Services Report.

Another example comes from the schedule of activities at one residential treatment center. Two days a week sessions on spirituality are conducted; one evening a week after the open AA meeting there is a sweat lodge; and one morning a week, after meditation there is another sweat lodge (for men); other activities at the same time include doing chores, work activities, and so on.

On the Navajo reservation, the Department of Behavioral Health, part of the tribal government's Division of Health, is developing a "Navajo Nation Mobile Treatment Unit [MTU]," which "will provide traditional treatment utilizing therapists and traditional healers in a mobile environment. Therapists and healers will travel throughout the reservation, providing services to clients and families who might not otherwise have access to such services. This treatment is targeted for Navajo Nation citizens suffering from substance abuse and related social problems." The leaflet describing the project goes on:

PRINCIPLES OF THE PROJECT
1. Empowerment of the Navajo People
2. Towards Hozho: Using Culture as the Solution
3. Creating Traditional Settings for Healing
4. Developing Long Term Social Solutions for Substance Abuse

GOALS
1. To disseminate education and prevention information
2. To use Navajo traditional techniques for curing alcohol and substance abuse
3. To empower Navajo individuals, families, and communities
4. To foster interagency coordination
5. To establish a referral system for people in need
6. To identify necessary legislative action
7. To initiate staff training and professional development
8. To contribute to data gathering, research and evaluation

The description concludes: "Clients will consult with traditional diagnostician, counselors, therapists and other relevant MTU project staff to determine the type of ceremonies to be conducted and choose the singer/healer to perform the ceremonies. One singer/healer specializing in healing modules will travel with the MTU project. He will assist as necessary when clients choose other singer/healers."

The development of the Mobile Treatment Unit is but one element of a much more ambitious effort to establish a Navajo nation recovery center. The proposed program is to base "its treatment plans, principles, goals and objectives on Navajo traditional religion, healing methods and teachings. Additionally the use of the Navajo language is necessary to convey specific prayers, songs and teachings. As such the Navajo language needs to be revived and used to communicate spirituality, philosophy and teachings to deter alcohol abuse." It is also proposed that there will be "a strong evaluation component. The evaluation will measure all relevant variables, such as effectiveness of treatment modules, treatment population descriptions, staff ratings, etc."

The proposed teaching modules cover various aspects of Navajo religion and values. For example, module 5, "Understanding Your Role in Life," describes "the teachings of Talking God, Changing Woman, Corn Pollen Boy, and Corn Beetle Girl regarding the importance of Navajo." The objectives are: "1. To gain an understanding of how it is our role in life to have love, faith, hope, preparation and plans; 2. to teach patients how cultural laws and beliefs shape their lives and behavior; 3. to encourage patients to make positive changes in their lives."

The proposed healing modules include ceremonies to cure a variety of problems. Module 3, "Led by Talking God," for example, is "a ceremony to cure craziness, wildness, disorientation, hallucination, intoxication, restlessness, roaming." It lasts four hours and costs $150, plus a buckskin and basket. The objectives listed are: "1. To cure the patient of symptoms listed above; 2. to instill in the patient a sense of well-being, and freedom from the symptoms listed above; 3. to promote an appreciation for Navajo heritage and identity."

The Religious and Spiritual Assessment is done to determine religious preference, the extent of appreciation for Navajo religion and its practice, fluency in the Navajo language, and a sense of spirituality. There is a form for the traditional healer's diagnosis and the ceremonies needed, and there are numerous evaluation forms for the patients to fill out.

The point of describing this material in such detail is to give a sense of the way traditional healing practices are being integrated into the bureaucratic requirements of formal organizations. They are just several of many techniques in the therapeutic armamentarium that are being made routine. To conform to the bureaucratic requirements of sponsoring agencies, whether private or governmental, all the methods that characterize such organizations must be followed—an entirely understandable adaptation for Indians to make. On the other hand, we are impressed that the programs are being shaped by bureaucratic needs. Traditional healing methods have now become merely remnants of a larger context in which they were an integral part of widely shared religious values. This is analogous to the situation we have described elsewhere in respect of the shift from a fully functioning traditional system of religious healing to a folk system that will function "more as an expression of ethnic independence and pride than as a system of healing or a coherent religion" (Levy 1983, 120).

Moreover, it is not clear that traditional methods are being used to any significant extent in the treatment programs. In table 9.1 we provide the numbers of clients receiving various indigenous treatments over a six-year period. The data are far from perfect but do suggest that few clients participated in traditional healing rituals of any sort. We do not know why: whether clients did not request such services, treatment programs did not provide them readily, or both.

Our follow-up interviews suggest that, except for the Native American (peyote) Church, indigenous rituals are not widely used for the treatment of alcohol use and that some clients resent having the rituals imposed on them in the treatment setting. Indeed, among the self-defined problem drinkers in our study (including both the hospital and community samples), the primary means of stopping was, according to the respondents themselves, first, a formal treatment program (invariably paid for by the Indian Health Service or located in an Indian Health Service facility); second, doing it on one's own; third, stopping with family support; and fourth, the Native American Church. No one mentioned traditional Navajo religion. Among non-problem drinkers who stopped, doing it on one's own was the primary way, followed by the Native American Church. Again, the traditional Navajo religion was not invoked by any of the respondents. Seven people, however, had used various traditional religious ceremonies (or parts of them) at some time in

Table 9.1 Use of Traditional Healing Methods in Alcohol Treatment
Programs on the Navajo Reservation, Fiscal Years 1985–1990

Type of Service	Number of Clients					
	1985	1986	1987	1988	1989	1990
Traditional group counseling	32	27	49	16	22	19
Traditional medicine	6	6	7	3	7	6
Sweat lodge	10	5	19	12	12	24
Native American treatment (peyote)	11	5	3	3	16	3
Cultural discussion	228	143	226	147	131	59
Total clients receiving traditional therapy	287	186	304	181	188	111
Total clients	1,294	1,047	2,111	1,820	1,767	1,565
Proportion receiving traditional therapy (%)*	22	18	14	10	11	7

Source: Annual reports of the Navajo Alcohol Program, Behavioral Health Department, Division of Health Improvement Services, Navajo Nation, Window Rock, Arizona

* Clients may have received more than one mode of traditional therapy, thus reducing the total number receiving traditional therapy by an unknown amount.

the five years before the interview to help them to stop using alcohol.

To the extent that traditional rituals are used, however, they are becoming part of a folk system that has both pan-Indian and local manifestations. We have mentioned several of the local manifestations on the Navajo reservation. For pan-Indian manifestations, it has been suggested that the clearest expression is to be found in the widespread use of sweat lodges, especially in treatment programs catering to more than one tribe.‡ This is perhaps only the most recent example of the pan-Indian movements that have arisen over the past two centuries, often as a means of dealing with the ravages of alcohol abuse. They have been classified as either millennarian or accommodative (see, for example, Hall 1986), depending on whether they espouse a belief in the disappearance of Europeans and a return to a precontact way of life, or a belief in constructively adapting to the inevitable presence of Europeans. Clearly, the kind of pan-Indian ideology at work in the programs and proposals we have

---

†Most frequently used of traditional healing methods is the Sweat Lodge, largely because in one form or another it was widely used in many precontact Indian societies. Hall (1986), who has done a survey of the use of the Sweat Lodge in Indian alcohol treatment programs, has commented that.

> as a pan-Indian symbol the sweat lodge is effective because its original distribution was wide and because it makes both a physically and culturally powerful impression; it possesses a disarming simplicity. As an example of the extent to which the sweat lodge has become a symbol of Indian religion and identity, the Native American Rights Fund reports that most states that have Indian prisoners have sweat lodges available for Indian inmates, and recommends it for all. According to many Indian people, participation in the sweat is a symbol of a person's affirmation of Indian identity. (Hall 1986, 171)

A recent publication of the Robert Wood Johnson Foundation, the source of more private foundation support to health-related research and programs than any other private foundation in the United States, devotes considerable space to Native American treatment center which is the recipient of much of its support and which includes as a major treatment modality sweat lodges. See *Advances*, the national newsletter of the Robert Wood Johnson Foundation (vol. 4, no. 3 [fall 1991]): "Native Americans Use Ancient Tribal Customs to Help Heal Modern Health Problems."

been describing is of an accommodative nature and not simply the reflection of a common oppositional culture. It is as well a reflection of the incorporation of Indians into the institutions of the larger society.

But like Aboriginal Australians and Canadian Indians, American Indians make up a very small and scattered minority in a vast nation, and the question with which they all must grapple is how to make that larger society listen and respond to their claims for justice. Intertribal unity and an emergent pan-indigenous self-consciousness may be necessary but are certainly not sufficient. Lawsuits brought by Indian tribes on their own behalf are one way of pressing claims. The capture or mobilization of public opinion is another.

Great amounts have been written on the diffusion of innovations, both among individuals and among formal organizations. One of the points that emerges over and over in these studies is that innovations are not likely to be adopted unless they are compatible with the values of individuals, acting either for themselves or for organizations. Clearly, to make these traditional innovations acceptable, they must be packaged in ways that make them seem workable in a bureaucratized setting. But why should federal bureaucrats be willing even to consider such innovations, when a generation or more ago such a thing would have been unthinkable? We have already noted that the growth of paraprofessionalism was one of the ways the introduction of traditional healing was legitimated in treatment programs. Beyond those political developments were major changes in American culture, particularly the emergence of New Age ideas.

FOURTH WORLD POLITICS
IN THE NEW AGE

Fourth World is a term that was coined by Canadian Indian leader George Manuel (Manuel and Poslums 1974) to describe those native peoples overwhelmed by European immigrants and now a minority in their own lands. One of the questions with which all such peoples must deal is how to mobilize public opinion in support of their claims (Dyck 1985). Over the past two or three decades the ecology and holistic health movements have been among the vehicles to do this used by American Indians.

Though it has a long history in Western and Oriental thought, holistic health has gained increasing currency in the West since the 1960s and is integral to what is considered New Age thought. It is based on several assumptions, of which the most crucial for our purposes are:

> Each person is a microcosm of the macrocosm. To understand the individual one must understand the forces and elements of the cosmos. Each person reflects the social environment as well. Thus, personal health and social fulfillment connect intimately. Sickness is a blow to individual and social freedom.
>
> Each individual is a unique blend of physical, social, and spiritual forces. Generalization, characteristic of cosmopolitan medicine, is inappropriate.
>
> Illness is a lesson. It is a sign that the person is not being used properly. Illness will be either a prelude to a new life way, if the lesson is learned, or it will be repeated.
>
> Physical, emotional, mental, and spiritual realities are inseparably linked. They are interconnected. The most powerful therapies act on the "weak," high-level spiritual sphere. (English-Lueck 1990, 18)

That each person reflects the forces of the natural and social world means that she or he cannot be considered in isolation from the environment and that discord in the environment is reflected in disorder in the individual.

The uniqueness of each individual's forces means that the healer's task requires knowledge of the particular individual, not abstract knowledge of a disease that is everywhere the same. This is very similar to the professional knowledge that is said to have characterized nineteenth-century allopathic physicians (Warner 1986) and stands in stark contrast to the professional knowledge that characterizes twentieth-century physicians.

That illness is a lesson implies that healers are teachers as much as they are curers. For they teach their patients the lessons implicit in each illness, lessons having to do with how one lives, how one relates to others, and so on.

That the various spheres are intimately bound to one another and that the spiritual sphere is crucially important means that only those cures that work on the spirit can be truly long-lasting. "Holistic health practitioners explicitly seek to achieve harmony on spiritual, social, and personal levels by changing behavior and engaging the natural defenses of the system. Holistic healers actively attempt to reintroduce spirituality and empathic sharing into the client/healer relationship. Educating clients to accept responsibility for their own health care and the prevention of disharmony are the paramount goals" (English-Lueck 1990, 20).

It is not our purpose here to explore why these ideas have gained such currency in the late twentieth century. Michael Harner (1990), an anthropologist who has made a career teaching people how to become shamans, draws upon material from Indian and other tribal peoples. He attributes the widespread interest in shamanism to several causes, including the search for personally known truth, now that the Age of Faith is behind us; the ease with which shamanistic methods can be learned and thus their suitability for busy people; the emergence of the holistic health movement ("Many of the New Age practices in the holistic health field represent the rediscovery, through recent experimentation, of methods once widely known in tribal and folk practice"); and the emergence of "spiritual ecology"— "Shamanism provides something largely lacking in the anthropocentric 'great' religions: reverence for, and spiritual communication with, the other beings of the Earth and with the Planet itself" (Harner 1990, xi–xiii). What we do wish to point out are some of the ways these New Age ideas in the larger culture draw upon Native American themes and, conversely, the way Native Americans draw upon these notions from the larger

society to legitimate their activities at both the individual and
the institutional level.

Indian Traditions in the New Age

One of the most frequent ways Indian religious rituals and
beliefs are drawn upon is for self-help and to achieve peace of
mind. We have already cited Harner's work. Less well known
but drawing just as explicitly upon Native American sources is
the work of Thomas Mails (1988), a Lutheran minister whose
book, *Secret Native American Pathways: A Guide to Inner
Peace,* provides easily followed rituals to eliminate stress, experience a vision quest, call back the dead, and so on.

The transformative impact of Indian religions and rituals on
a non-Indian is described in considerable autobiographical detail
by Carl Hammerschlag (1988), a psychiatrist who has worked
for many years in the Indian Health Service. He writes that his
Indian patients and friends have taught him how to be a healer.
"I am a better healer now. I have learned that the patient doesn't
need a scientist who simply carries out instructions from the
laboratory manual. Patients don't want to be cases—they want
to be healed. They want to participate in their own wellness or
their own death. Patients are the principal agents in their lives,
and as much as they want to be well, they want peace and
understanding. To find such a healing peace they need to feel
that a connection exists between themselves and the healer and
between themselves and something larger than self or science"
(p. 137).

Thus at both a personal and professional level, a knowledge
of Indian religion is said to promote an alternative way of
understanding oneself, one's world, and illness and healing. This
way of understanding is distinct from the way of knowing that
has dominated this century. But beyond the personal level, Indian religious values have been used by non-Indians at a political
level as well. For example, an Indian prophetic tradition is said
to predict the end of the world as we know it if Euro-Americans

do not adhere to more ecologically sound ways of living. The situation of the Hopi Indians in northeastern Arizona, who have resisted coal mining on their land and invoked their responsibility to protect all life, is cited most frequently (such as Peterson 1990). The intimate connection with holistic health is made explicitly in *The New Holistic Health Handbook* (Bliss 1985). "All creation on this Earth contains a spirit, a life force. This includes rocks, plants, hills, trees, sky and animals. The Mother Earth is a living, sensitive, breathing organism. The forces of all creation are dynamically interwoven into a harmonious whole. Physical and mental illness occurs when this balance is upset. The purpose of all healing ceremonies is to preserve or restore personal and universal harmony" (Newhouse and Amodeo 1985, 48).

Not only have non-Indians used Indian religious teachings for their own purposes, but Indians have used the availability of a receptive audience for their purposes too. Some of these purposes have been largely personal, others have been institutional. A number of Indians have gained prominence as healers and prophets among non-Indians. Generally their teachings are pan-Indian in origin rather than from a specific tribe. For example, in the foreword to a book by Medicine Grizzlybear Lake, Rolling Thunder—who designates himself an Intertribal Medicine Man—writes: "Bobby [aka Medicine Grizzlybear] was taught and trained by over sixteen different Elderly Medicine Men and Women and traditional ceremonial leaders from different tribes" (Lake 1991, ix). Medicine Grizzlybear Lake (1990, 1) himself has written, "The traditional Native healer is an endangered species now. But there is an opportunity for modern Native and Western people to share in the knowledge of past Native healers and the few remaining ones who are with us in the New Age." Several other Indian or part-Indian women and men have started interracial communities, associations, or private foundations to spread their particular version of traditional Indian beliefs: the Bear Tribe Medicine Society (Sun Bear, Wabun, and Weinstock

1987), the Meta Tantay Foundation, and the Four Directions Foundation being among them (Newhouse and Amodeo 1985, 52).

There is an entrepreneurial and self-promotional flavor to many of these activities that has not gone uncriticized by other Indians. Indeed, "the New Age's appropriation of Native American spirituality [is viewed] as cultural imperialism; whereas the older Euro-American invaders stole the land, the new invaders are trying to steal the religion of native peoples" (Melton 1991, 336; see also *Navajo Times*, 20 May 1993, and *Native American Smoke Signals*, May 1993). The American Indian Movement (AIM) has been particularly critical of this development. Ideas of Native American spirituality, however, have had uses at an institutional level as well. For example, an Indian professional therapist, John Redtail Freesoul, "conducts sweat ceremonies in different New Mexico prisons for various Native Americans incarcerated there" (Heinerman 1989, 72). He is quoted as saying: "'It's the epitome of group therapy. I didn't plan to use the sweat in therapy. I was using it in my personal life and sharing it with friends. After I saw the value, I took it to my clients. If I'd lost my temper, shot someone, and got five years, I'd need the sweat lodge more than ever. It would be the only way to go inside myself and see why I did it. And speaking practically, the sweat can assure sobriety in people who have used alcohol or drugs for years because they cannot enter unless they've been drug free for at least 48 hours. The key to the sweat ceremony is personal accountability and responsibility to God for one's own behavior. Your behavior can spark behavior in me and it is the same with the spirit world" (ibid., 73–74).

Indian spiritual values are also invoked to justify organizational behavior that most practitioners, Native American or not, would regard as perfectly sensible. For example, an editorial in a newsletter from the American Indian Health Care Association states:

The Native American view of wellness (not health) invariably is a holistic one. Regardless of tribal affiliation, Indian people believe that being well includes being well physically, mentally, and spiritually. In the Navajo view, there is no separation between spirituality/religion and physical well-being/medicine. The medicine wheel of the Plains Indians reflects the inter-connectedness of the emotional, physical and spiritual well-being. The circle is used by many Indian tribes to symbolize the inter-connectedness of life; there is no beginning and no end and it includes all elements of the environment. The symbolism of the circle is evident throughout Indian culture. PowWow dances are performed in a circle; many Indian healing ceremonies are performed in a circle; Indian prayers are said in a circle.

Modern Western medicine compartmentalizes wellness and health care. If a Native American living in a large city today becomes un-well—sick, emotionally disturbed, or lacking in spiritual guidance—he or she is referred to a physician, mental health counselor, or religious leader. The specialization of medicine requires even further compartmentalizing—by specific diseases, mental illnesses and age groups. Part of the stresses of urban living can be traced to the necessity to belong to both systems, in the modern medical system and the traditional belief system. Feelings of alienation, or not really belonging in either system, contribute to depression and hopelessness.

If urban Indian health care services are to approximate a more holistic approach while retaining the modern Western medical model, the overall view of inter-connectedness must be applied in daily clinic activities. When a client seeks alcohol abuse counseling, that client should also be referred to the AIDS Educator in order to discuss how alcohol inhibits good judgment regarding unprotected sexual activity or experimenting with IV drugs. Similar internal referral patterns should exist for patients who seek medical treatment for other sexually transmitted diseases. Since current alcohol abuse and/or incidence of other sexually transmitted disease seem to be strongly

associated with HIV infection risk, these types of internal referral patterns make sense for the total care of the patient.
(AIDSBRIEFS 1991, 1–2)

Traditional Indian values have also been invoked in discussions of holistic health care to emphasize the importance of
individual responsibility for health. For example, an Indian
speaker at a conference on diabetes in Indian communities is
quoted as saying, "People choose whether or not they will be
healthy or ill. When a person chooses to be ill, it can be a
learning experience. Medicine people know this and will not
take your learning experience away. Medicine people exhibit
unconditional love and take people through the process of thinking about themselves, said Monetathchi. 'Medicine men have
been underground for years because the world hasn't been ready.
Now medicine people have been told to talk a little bit more'"
(NIHB 1980, 9).

And of course, the attempt to establish and formalize alcohol
treatment programs based upon "traditional teachings and healing methods" is another important example of how Native
American ideas of healing have achieved bureaucratic legitimacy
as a result of the receptivity of the larger culture to ideas of
holistic health. The authors of the Navajo Tribal Action Plan
on alcohol and substance abuse wrote that:

> the problem of alcohol/substance abuse cannot be dealt with
> separately by isolated programs. Health care resources must
> be mobilized to respond to the holistic nature of the problem
> and solutions only through a similarly holistic programmatic
> perspective, and programmatic integration. Programs will
> emerge from local, regional and nation-wide initiatives. Their
> proper integration and support is possible only through the
> legal and ethical exercise of Navajo Tribal sovereignty and
> self-determination. The coordinating effort of the Tribe, as the
> central sovereign entity for addressing the multiplex problem
> of alcohol/substance abuse, is also the only means by which

Navajo and Euro-American health care can work to mutual benefit.

As the chief base of unity in Navajo life is the family, the family and all its members must be an integral part of all prevention, treatment, intervention, and educational endeavors. It is only with their involvement that the holistic perspective of the problems and its possible solutions can be maintained. (Navajo Tribe 1987, 4–5)

The traditional cultural values that Indians invoke, especially those having to do with holism, bear an uncanny resemblance to New Age ideas as well as to alternative traditions within orthodox medicine. This is not simply because New Age ideas and psychosomatic medicine reflect Indian cultural beliefs, but because many Indians, like many non-Indian Americans, have absorbed these ideas as part of the ambient cultural atmosphere. More specifically, some contemporary Indians working in health and social service bureaucracies have accepted as an accurate rendering of their traditional culture the picture painted by non-Indian New Age savants and psychosomaticists. For example, a Navajo woman described the substance abuse treatment program for which she worked as using "cultural therapy . . . We use the biopsychosocial model." This model of health and disease has long been promulgated by George Engel (1977), professor emeritus of psychiatry and medicine at the University of Rochester. It does not draw its inspiration from any Native American religious tradition, but in the thinking of our informant it has been assimilated in an understanding of Navajo religion. More than that, it has become a way of describing and explaining the healing characteristics of cultural therapy.

Another Navajo, a man also responsible for administering an alcohol treatment program, described the traditional Navajo view of each human being as a circle divided into quarters, representing the physical body, the emotions, the mind, and the spirit, all surrounded by another circle representing the family and society. This is precisely one of the assumptions on which

New Age thought is based and, we would argue, represents a diffusion into Navajo culture of formulations of personality organization that were not there previously.

These illustrations are meant to suggest that there has been mutual influence—Indian on Euro-American culture as well as of Euro-American on Indian culture—and that some Indians are reinterpreting their traditions in light of the Euro-American understanding of those traditions, as well as in the light of western notions of health and disease that have achieved a respectable, even if minority, place in the academy.

Considering all the rhetoric, it is interesting that the evidence from individual Navajo respondents and treatment programs indicates that traditional healing methods are not widely used in treating alcohol abuse. (The major exception has been membership in the Native American Church.) We think there are probably several reasons. First, our own fieldwork with ceremonialists suggests that alcoholism was not one of the problems they were called on to treat. Second, even if the traditional system is appropriate, it is simply not salient to many young adult Navajos. Third, even when it is salient, it is expensive and beyond the means of many individuals. Fourth, many sings especially those thought to be good for the treatment of mental problems[5]—have become extinct, many older ceremonialists have died without professional issue, and an increasing proportion of those who remain know only parts of major ceremonies. Both supply and demand have decreased.

If the reality is that traditional methods are not widely used to treat the problem of alcohol abuse, why expend the effort to institutionalize them? Many of those who are seeking to institutionalize them within the health and education bureaucracies are seeking to preserve them in the only way that seems possible:

[5]For example, Coyote Way, Frenzy Witchcraft Way, Beadway. The nine night Mountaintop Way, though not extinct, is expensive and is rarely performed today.

by ensuring financial support for training and access to ritual. The paradox is, as we have suggested, that the very attempt at preservation inevitably involves change. It is our impression that from a fully integrated healing system a system of folk medicine composed of parts of the older structure is emerging.

In addition to preservation the most important considerations are the rhetorical and symbolic functions that are so important in all politics, including especially Fourth World politics. The assertion of the importance of traditional healing not only reinforces ethnic pride but helps to legitimate claims to control the institutionalized treatment system itself. For to the extent that the system can be said to depend on indigenous local knowledge rather than professional (and presumably universal) knowledge, local people—not cosmopolitan professionals—can claim the special expertise necessary to staff and manage it. It is no accident that such claims are made particularly in the areas of mental health and substance abuse, not surgery or internal medicine, for the claims to universally valid knowledge have been asserted more successfully in the latter than in the former domains.

Further, the importation of various non-Indian notions of holism, health, and disease into a version of Navajo culture represents an important attempt by many serious and thoughtful people to recover, preserve, and use a tradition that has been largely lost to them. In the process, they are undoubtedly creating something new and quite different from what Navajos a generation or more ago would have understood to be the core of Navajo culture. There is nothing surprising or offensive in this. It is a process in which all peoples engage.

Thus, there are several reasons that Navajos should wish to integrate a version of traditional culture into the bureaucratized health care system. It is not so obvious, as we have already noted, why bureaucracies would be open to this sort of change when not so long ago such attempts would have been dismissed out of hand. We have said that part of the answer has to do

with changes in American culture. Another part of the explanation is organizational. There is reason to think that complex,
loosely integrated organizations are more likely to be open to
innovation than other organizations (Greer 1977, 517). Such
organizations usually have a diverse group of employees, and
there may be relative autonomy in various parts of the organization to institute innovations that do not have a significant
impact on other units. The various agencies on the Navajo
reservation form such a loosely integrated system, and it is
therefore of little consequence to some units if others wish to
innovate by making traditional modes of treatment available to
their clients. If alcohol treatment programs provide sweat lodges
for their clients, the surgeons will not care. Thus, although there
is a bureaucratic imperative that requires the regularization and
standardization of treatment forms, the structure of the bureaucracy may make it more or less open to such innovations as
those we have described.

That traditional healing methods have been integrated into
the formal treatment system has meant that they are dealt with
just as any other therapeutic modality, quite separate from the
religious-healing system that originally gave them meaning. That
government bureaucracies have responded at all is undoubtedly
because they are embedded in a liberal democracy in which
multiculturalism has become a positive value, in which bureaucracies serving Indians are becoming increasingly Indianized,
and in which ideas having to do with alternative healing have
gained widespread legitimacy.

CONCLUSION

We have described some of the latent functions of alcohol treatment programs: employment, empowerment, the preservation
of important religious knowledge, and a sense of cultural identity. It is not clear in what ways these functions are related to

the single manifest function of such programs: reducing alcohol abuse in the population. The mortality data described in chapter 4 indicate that something is having an influence on drinking behavior, since deaths due to alcoholic cirrhosis and motor vehicle accidents have declined substantially from the 1970s to the late 1980s. We think that community-based prevention and treatment programs have played an important role, but just how important, it is impossible to determine. We briefly describe several programs that have developed in recent years in Tuba City to indicate how such programs may influence behavior and, ultimately, mortality and morbidity patterns.**

One of the most thoroughgoing changes has been in treatment programs. We said at the beginning of the chapter that the first program was established by an internist in the mid-1960s and that it consisted of hospital admission, a drying-out period, a test dose of Antabuse and a wine challenge, and then discharge with a prescription for more Antabuse from the hospital pharmacy. There was no further counseling or support provided. Inevitably misunderstandings about the use of the medication arose. We said in chapter 6 that some of the members of the Medicine family believed that several of their relatives had died as a result of taking Antabuse rather than from the excessive use of alcohol. Other people believed that Antabuse would act like an antibiotic and eliminate their need for alcohol.

By the early 1970s the programs in Tuba City and in other communities across the reservation had begun to change, providing counseling rather than simply handing out Antabuse "like aspirin," as one counselor characterized the early years of treatment programs. Limited training was available at the University of Utah, but according to one graduate, the view taught seemed to emphasize "blaming the victim," and there was little taught about the effects of alcohol abuse on the psychology of the

---

**The following examples were provided by Tracy Andrews and are quoted from an unpublished report.

abuser or his or her family. The counseling that was then available from the treatment programs emphasized work with middle-aged men: detoxification, rehabilitation, vocational counseling, and job training. There were also the beginnings of community education, which ultimately opened the door to prevention programs.

Beginning in the late 1970s, partly as a result of the Indian Health Care Improvement Act, a wider focus developed: on the families of alcohol abusers; on women, who were beginning to be perceived as drinking more abusively than they had in the past; and on adolescents. Much of this focus involved prevention as well as treatment.

Funding has been fitful, and there has been and continues to be great staff turnover. Nonetheless, in Tuba City and other reservation communities a range of programs and activities is now available. These include a tribally run but IHS- and state-funded Alcohol Recovery Center, which provides outpatient counseling and aftercare for people who have returned from residential treatment programs (there was none in Tuba City at the time of our study), as well as community education and outreach.

The local schools are also developing prevention, education, and support programs not available to previous generations of Navajo children. It will be recalled that Medicine's daughter Julia said her grandparents never spoke with her about alcohol, even though many family members were drinking abusively. She thought that they did not want her to know about alcohol and pointed out that in the traditional Navajo way, the elderly did not discuss problems with children. There has been a growing concern that information about the potential dangers of alcohol use must be made available to children early, to help them understand what they sometimes experience in their own family and to help them make choices about their own drinking behavior. In the local high school and grade schools, programs aim at encouraging peer-group support for not using alcohol and other drugs and for creating opportunities for children to share their experiences and questions.

Another local program focused on education about and prevention of fetal alcohol syndrome and fetal alcohol effect was begun in 1988 and is now a model within the Indian Health Service. These diagnoses were unknown only fifteen years ago, and the education of health care professionals has been only a few steps ahead of the education of the public. The Tuba City program attempts to convince women who seek help to cross the boundaries of their social networks to accept institutionally based support. Like other alcohol treatment programs on the reservation, the FAS programs aim at involving a wide network of healthy relatives to form a support system for the pregnant mother who needs to stop drinking. The reality is often that the pregnant woman must break away from friends and family members who would encourage her to continue drinking, or at best are noncommittal about her continued drinking. The FAS program staff attempt to provide consistent and dependable support, but erratic and inadequate funding policies often undermine their efforts.

Yet another local effort occurred in October 1990, while this study was in progress. A voluntary association in Tuba City organized a week-long series of events focused on substance-use education and prevention programs with the theme "My Choice—Drug Free." One of the highlights was the second annual "Hands across Tuba City," which involved schools, community groups, and interested participants in forming a human chain along the town's main streets. A videotape of this event from the previous year drew considerable interest at a national substance-abuse conference. Other activities included training for school faculty in substance-abuse prevention, a parent-community substance-abuse prevention workshop, and a "run for sobriety," in which all generations, from preschoolers to the elderly, were invited to participate in a relay race through the town. The group that took on the responsibility of planning and organizing the week's activities calls itself the "Networking Adolescent Caregivers."

All these programs are very different indeed from the first program established at the same time as our original study in 1966. At that time young adult and middle-aged men made up most of the patients, and treatment was essentially based upon a medical model of alcohol abuse. The limited resources available at the time made this orientation inevitable, regardless of the treatment philosophy or preferences of the program's founder. Much has changed over the past twenty-five years. In the programs we have described, as well as others in Tuba City and across the Navajo and other reservations, attempts are being made to speak about topics generally not discussed in the past; to deal with both sexes and all ages; to emphasize prevention as well as cure; and to create alternative sources of support for people wishing to cease or avoid abusing alcohol and other substances. We do not know how many of the latent functions of these programs have been achieved—employment, empowerment, and cultural and religious preservation. We do think there is reason to believe that the manifest functions are being achieved.

10

Conclusions

The older men in the original study, especially those in the more traditional sample, were able to stop or severely curtail their drinking by the time they were middle-aged, despite the fact that they were indistinguishable from alcoholics in several measures, including the incidence of withdrawal symptoms. This pattern of heavy binge drinking, which we called the traditional Navajo style, was still found in 1990, predominantly among Plateau men but also among men in the Hospital group who came from other rural areas.

In addition to this traditional style, however, there was a deviant and more debilitating form of unrestrained drinking. Solitary drinking as opposed to drinking in groups with kinsmen was considered by Navajos to be a sign of a problem drinker, and this criterion identified those most at risk for negative outcomes more successfully than a diagnosis of alcohol dependence using DSM-III-R criteria.

Eighty percent of male social drinkers were abstinent in 1990, regardless of study group, and only 6 percent, all in the Hospital group, had died of causes that were probably alcohol-related. Abstinence was most often found among Plateau men (93 percent) versus men from Tuba City (87 percent) or the Hospital group (61 percent).*

*This rate of remission in the treatment group is about the same as rates

226

Solitary drinkers were less likely to have attained abstinence and more likely to have died from alcohol-related causes. There were only two solitary drinkers from the Plateau, one of whom was abstinent by the time of the follow-up, the other was drinking in a controlled manner. The picture was less encouraging in Tuba City, where only 27 percent of the men were abstinent and an equal portion had died from alcohol-related causes. It did not come as a surprise that the largest portion (38 percent) of alcohol-related deaths occurred in the Hospital group. Less expected, however, was that an equal proportion of Hospital men were abstinent in 1990. None of the solitary drinkers in the Tuba City and Hospital groups who were still drinking in 1990 was doing so in a controlled manner.

Solitary drinkers also had a lifetime history of depression more often than social drinkers, and although most men—regardless of style—felt that drinking had been a problem at some time in their lives, solitary drinkers were more likely to feel it was still a problem in 1990.

What is significant about these findings is the high portion of high-risk men who were able to become abstinent over a period of twenty-five years. It is also worth noting that the deaths of two social drinkers were probably alcohol-related. Clearly there is no inevitable progression, no natural history of a disease process revealed by these findings. Even when we can describe different Navajo drinking careers, great variability remains, much of it probably attributable to circumstances occurring over the course of a life and not predictable at the outset (Finney and Moos 1992).

Yet the drinking histories of this group are in many ways typical of what is found among alcohol-dependent drinkers in the general population, where rates of spontaneous remission appear to increase markedly after age sixty. Among the Navajos, abstinence appears to be attained somewhat earlier, by the

reported in other treatment groups followed for almost as long (Finney and Moos 1991, table 1).

fourth or fifth decades. An earlier age of onset of drinking for men than for women is also found among non-Indian drinkers. Other differences between men and women are also distinct in both populations. Nationally, alcohol-dependent women are more likely to have a history of mood disorders than men are, and spontaneous remission is less frequent. Similarly, Navajo women with severe alcohol problems are more likely to have acute personal or psychological problems than Navajo men.

These findings raised a number of questions. Was the high rate of remission among the social drinkers a result of cultural values and the fact that, until recently, alcohol has been less available in the rural areas of the reservation? Was the emergence of solitary, unrestrained drinking due to the convergence of high-risk drinkers in such transitional communities as Tuba City, the breakdown of kin-based social networks and cultural values, or to the greater availability of alcohol? We have found evidence to support all three interpretations.

Many of the men who were solitary drinkers started their drinking away from the reservation, either in the military service or while working as laborers, and rural Navajos in the eastern, more wage labor–dependent counties of the reservation had mortality rates from cirrhosis, accidents, homicide, and suicide comparable to those of the rural Anglos in the region. Both learning and environmental factors appear to be involved in fostering this form of drinking. At the same time, however, there is tenuous evidence that some of the men who died from alcohol-related causes had antisocial personalities. If this is ultimately shown to be the case, it would go far to explain why some families have been decimated by alcohol abuse over several generations and would agree with recent research findings in non-Indian populations.

Overall, Navajo drinking is far more heterogeneous than we suspected. Historically, the drinking style learned from Anglos during the nineteenth century persisted as long as it did because of the isolation of the reservation from the surrounding Anglo populations. Gradually, however, as more and more Navajos acquired experience away from the reservation, new styles of drinking were learned. Owing to the large regional differences across the reservation—some areas having greater access to wage labor than others—the development of different drinking styles has been anything but uniform. Improved transportation as well as an increased involvement in a cash-based economy have steadily made alcohol more available. (Still, we have no evidence that solitary drinking was unknown among rural Navajos who had access to alcohol, a topic to which we return below.)

Before stock reduction in the 1930s, the Plateau families were among the wealthiest in the area. As such, they are not representative of the entire rural population. Other studies have shown that poorer families adapted to the changing economy in various ways, some adapting successfully to the off-reservation wage economy, others resisting education on the reserva tion. It is certain that other styles of drinking must also be taken into account. In 1966, the Navajo long-term residents of Flagstaff appeared to have adopted a style of drinking found among the employed working class of western urban areas. Yet Flagstaff also displayed drinking styles that were far less restrained; cowboy bars, for example, hosted drinkers who tended to violence as often as in bars catering to reservation Navajos. In sum, Navajos were increasingly exposed to several drinking subcultures.

We have seen that the rural Anglo populations of the Southwest have high mortality rates from cirrhosis, accidents, homicide, and suicide, and we have surmised that many Navajo men in transitional reservation communities have learned how to drink from these "neighbors" at work and in bordertown bars. Similarly, lower urban mortality rates reflect changes in Southwestern city life as the region's population grows, augmented by considerable immigration from the urbanized East. Those very few Navajos who attended college and obtained white-collar or professional employment away from the reservation drank like the Anglos with whom they socialized. One Tuba City woman, now living in Phoenix, had before-dinner cocktails with friends, and two college-educated daughters of Plateau parents married non-Navajos, lived in large cities, and did not drink at all.

The heterogeneity of Navajo drinking styles should help put to rest the idea that the high rate of alcohol abuse among certain Indian populations is biologically based. It does not, however, allow us to say with any certainty whether or not any particular style is biologically based. It has been argued from studies in non-Indian populations that the excessive self-destructive drinking of some young men, along with an associated diagnosis of antisocial personality disorder, has a large biological component (Cadoret et al. 1985; Gilligan, Reich, and Cloninger 1987; McGue, Pickens, and Sivkus 1992). Our data do not deal with this aspect of etiology—although there is evidence that such individuals appear in our study population—nor do they deal directly with the issue of biologically explained family clusters of excessive alcohol use. In the case of the Medicine family, for example, we are not able to reject the hypothesis that the devastation we have described is due to a genetically determined propensity to drink to excess. There are two points to be made, however. First, alcohol dependence and abuse by women has not been shown to be inherited, and the high concordance of such behaviors between dizygotic male and female twins has been said to support the overwhelming explanatory significance of the environment in these cases (McGue, Pickens, and Sivkus 1992).[†] Which is to say, in instances where brothers and sisters are alcohol abusers, it is much more likely that the family or larger social context explains the phenomenon than that a com-

———

[†]A recent study claims that much alcohol abuse among women is also inherited (Kendler et al. 1993). Clearly the issue is still unresolved.

mon genetic inheritance does. Second, in the case of the Medicine family, we have argued that it was the community environment of the second generation that resulted in their abusive drinking, not alcohol abuse by their parents (whether learned or inherited). This is a more parsimonious explanation than one that invokes biological mechanisms that have not yet been shown to exist.

The importance we have placed on the context in which alcohol use is learned is of a piece with what others have observed about the use of a variety of substances. MacAndrew and Edgerton (1969) have made a similar argument using ethnohistorical data from North America. Norman Zinberg (1984) showed that the controlled use of substances like marijuana, opiates, and LSD was largely dependent on the setting in which use was learned and in which it occurred thereafter. Maggie Brady (1992) has shown that the prevalence of petrol sniffing by Australian Aboriginal youngsters is best explained by the type of community in which they live.

Clearly, as Zinberg argues, the pharmacological effects of different substances are important, but how one responds to and learns to understand those effects is not simply a matter of an individual's psychological set or biological inheritance, but is to a great extent a matter of the setting in which exposure occurs and in which use is learned and pursued. Indeed, his notion of drug, psychological set, and setting is identical to the public health notion of the importance of agent, host, and environment in explaining various diseases. We have argued that the setting, or environment, is key in the explanation of the patterns of alcohol use we have observed, even while recognizing that individual set (or host characteristics) may turn out to be especially important in the explanation of one type of excessive alcohol use.

Our results are in agreement with many but not all of the generalizations from the literature on the cross-cultural studies of alcohol use. Mac Marshall (1979, 451–55) has summarized several of them:‡ "When members of a society have had sufficient time to develop a widely shared set of beliefs and values pertaining to drinking and drunkenness, the consequences of alcohol consumption are not usually disruptive for most persons in that society. On the other hand, where beverage alcohol has been introduced within the past century and such a set of beliefs and values has not developed completely, social—and sometimes physiological—problems with ethanol commonly result."

The evidence from the South Tuba sample as well as from the Medicine family suggests that rapid exposure to easily accessible alcohol can indeed have catastrophic effects. But the experience of the Plateau group suggests that exposure in the context of a cohesive and extensive social network in which access is limited and use constrained by preexisting norms and obligations does not necessarily have the same devastating effects.

> Where opportunities for group or community recreation are few and alcoholic beverages are available, alcohol consumption will become a major form of recreational activity in a community ("the boredom rule").

Again the data from South Tuba support this generalization. Although we have not emphasized it in previous chapters, many people, especially young men, explain their drinking by saying there is nothing else to do. In addition to the absence of recreational opportunities, however, high rates of unemployment also contribute to boredom and to time hanging heavy on people's hands.

> Typically, alcoholic beverages are used more by males than by females and more by young adults than by preadolescents or older persons. Hence in any society the major consumers of

---

‡He has suggested several other generalizations in addition to those we quote, but our study does not address all of them.

beverage alcohol are most likely to be young men between their mid-teens and their mid-thirties.

Our results are entirely consistent with this observation. Though it is so common as to seem self-evident, the reason is not obvious. One part of the explanation is undoubtedly that women metabolize alcohol differently than men. Lower average weights, a higher proportion of body fat, and a lower proportion of fluid relative to body weight among women than men means that it takes less alcohol on average to make women drunk. Another part of the explanation has to do with the high probability that a certain proportion of young male drinkers is biologically likely to consume large amounts of alcohol (McGue, Pickens, and Sivkus 1992). Moreover, in all societies, young men engage more in risk-taking behavior than other age-sex groups. Presumably this too is biologically based. Alcohol use may simply be part of that constellation of behaviors,

Peoples who lacked alcoholic beverages aboriginally borrowed styles of drunken comportment along with the beverages from those who introduced them to "demon rum."

Once again our data are consistent with this generalization. Yet there is also good evidence that the receiving culture is not simply a tabula rasa, but may be more or less susceptible to both alcoholic beverages and the style of drinking of those who introduced them to it. In our first study, we suggested that the way Hopi Indians used alcoholic beverages was very different from the way Navajos did (Levy and Kunitz 1974). It appears that the flamboyant style of drinking so common on the frontier resonated more thoroughly with Navajo than with Hopi values. We suggested that this was the result of the varying patterns of social control that characterized these societies. Hopis, as agricultural, village-dwelling people, were more likely to exert strong controls over the behavior of individuals, whereas Navajos were more likely to value individual autonomy and thus were less likely to intervene in alcohol use even when it became socially disruptive.

> Solitary, addictive, pathological drinking behavior does not occur to any significant extent in small-scale, traditional, pre-industrial societies; such behavior appears to be a concomitant of complex, modern, industrialized societies.

Our data on Hopi alcohol use are cited by Marshall as the one exception to this generalization, but everything that we and others have learned about the Navajo conception of alcoholism suggests that solitary drinking is regarded as deviant and has been for some time. Although Navajos are indeed embedded in a complex, modern, industrialized society, they themselves cannot be described in those terms, certainly they could not a generation or more ago. Moreover, solitary, addictive, pathological drinking is statistically rare even in complex societies. One has to look even more closely to find it in small-scale societies. When we first reported such behaviors among Hopis, we were accused of falsifying the data, for it flew in the face of what everyone knew to be the truth about Hopi behavior. We suspect that something similar is true in many other small-scale, traditional societies: such behavior may be either hidden and therefore unobserved or observed but so infrequent in absolute numbers as to be dismissed as insignificant.

These generalizations, even with the caveats we have registered, all emphasize the importance of alcohol use as an inextricably social and cultural phenomenon. This was not the emphasis of the prevention and treatment programs for Indians when they were initiated in the 1960s. At that time alcohol abuse was treated as a problem that characterized individuals, mostly men. Many of the developments in the Navajo treatment programs that occurred since that time appear to pay more attention to drinking behavior as a social and cultural phenomenon that must be understood and influenced in its social context. By so doing they may be addressing some of our findings.

For example, though even now far fewer women than men drink (see table 4.7), a higher portion of women who drink suffer untoward outcomes. This seemed to be true among our respondents, though the number of women who consumed alcohol was very small. We suspect that it is true of younger women as well, though we do not have data to demonstrate it. Because women start drinking at a later age, often owing to the influence of their husbands, there are few risk factors that early screening can identify. Treatment programs have, however, begun to pay more attention to the needs of women drinkers. By emphasizing family-oriented therapy, wives may now be educated before the onset of abuse. The Indian Health Service program for the identification of women at risk for giving birth to children with fetal alcohol syndrome and fetal alcohol effect is an important recognition of these problems. The fact that the most serious women abusers in our study also had severe personality or real-world problems suggests that mental health workers should work closely with alcohol counselors, referring clients to one another as needed.

A second example: virtually all the participants in the study demonstrated an almost complete lack of knowledge about the physiological effects of drinking, and many in Tuba City knew little about Antabuse despite having been in the Antabuse program. This is not to say that Navajos ever thought of drinking as a good thing. Intoxication was known to lead to accidents and "crazy" behavior. Drunkenness, in fact, was always considered antithetical to Navajo concepts of health and well-being. Nevertheless, attitudes were ambivalent, and the state of intoxication appears to have resonated with less explicit Navajo values involving supernatural power. There was divided opinion among ceremonialists, for example—some believing that alcohol enhanced their abilities, others holding the opposite. The educational programs that have been started in the schools address this issue directly.

To take a third example, we have observed that where the

social fabric was strong and where religious congregations such as the Native American Church created new community bonds, alcohol abuse was either prevented at the start or recovery from abusive drinking was enhanced. Conversely, in Tuba City, where community values governing the use of alcohol were absent, drinking proceeded unrestrained. Community-based prevention and treatment programs are thus an encouraging development.

The importance of community support as exemplified by the Native American Church may also help to explain why traditional Navajo religious ceremonies are not widely used for treating alcohol abuse and why there seems to be a redefinition of what traditional practices involve. Even though traditional ceremonies drew together a wide network of kin, they were one-time affairs aimed at restoring an individual's health. When the ceremony was over, the guests dispersed. Membership in the Native American Church and other religious bodies is different. An ongoing relation with a community of fellow-believers is created: it meets frequently, persists over time, and often involves day-to-day interactions outside the formal religious meetings. It works to separate individuals from their previous social network in a way that a one-time ceremony cannot.

It is perhaps for this reason that traditional religious practices are being redefined. Informants (not the subjects of this study) talk of bringing family members with them to participate in a consultation with a traditional healer, something that was not usual in the past. They talk about reconstituting a sense of community through their religious practices. We can only speculate that we are seeing a redefinition of traditional religion based in part on New Age interpretations of traditional Indian religious values and in part in response to an awareness that many problems that confront Navajos require continuous support for their resolution or management.

We may also speculate that certain cultures may have religious systems that are better preadapted to deal with chronic behavioral problems than others. Where treatment is focused on the individual and does not involve sustained contact between the patient and a supportive network, the system may not be as well suited to coping with such problems as in a culture where religious societies persist through time and at least have the potential to control their members' behavior and support their recovery.

These observations and the fact that few in the treatment programs opted for the available traditional therapies of the sweat lodge, sings, or counseling by a ceremonial singer suggest that considerable thought should be given to the guiding philosophy of these programs. Nonetheless, the emphasis on self-help, self-pride, and expanding consciousness made by the holistic, New Age philosophy of healing adopted by the Navajo programs is encouraging. The belief that aboriginal religion and values are superior to those of modern medicine, however, may be counterproductive. The notion that Indian drinkers are somehow qualitatively different from their non-Indian counterparts and require Indian therapies seems similar to the idea that only an alcoholic can treat another alcoholic. Such notions may serve only to accentuate the already existing divisions separating Indians from surrounding populations. It may, indeed, work to deprive Navajos and other Indian peoples of whatever theoretical and practical advances in treatment are made in the future.[5] The treatment programs with which we are familiar are eclectic and offer clients options. Thus, as a practical rather than rhetorical matter, these risks may be small.

Despite encouraging developments, however, it is also clear that there has been little progress in assessing the magnitude or even the nature of the problem. Virtually all Navajo men have drinking histories that by the most commonly used criteria would class them as alcohol abusers, and 74 percent of men over age twenty-one were drinking at the time of our first in-

[5]A similar observation has been made by Maggie Brady (1991) about treatment programs for Australian Aborigines.

terview. If all were to be labeled alcoholic, it would be impossible for even well-funded programs to accommodate them. It may be profitable for treatment programs to screen potential clients first by drinking style: traditional-style social drinkers would be given a lower priority than solitary drinkers. Efforts should be made either in the programs themselves or through funded research to discover other risk factors that are manifested before the onset of drinking—that is, during adolescence. If males with conduct disorder in childhood, say, are found to be at high risk to develop severe sequelae of alcohol abuse and dependence in adulthood, efforts should be made to identify them through prevention programs in schools.

The shift of emphasis among Navajo prevention and treatment programs away from the conception of alcoholism as a disease is congruent with the findings of this study, which lead us to conclude that we are not dealing with a single disease process so much as with the undesirable consequences of excessive alcohol consumption. According to Peter Conrad and Joseph Schneider (1985, 105–6): "The most likely alternative paradigm would seem to focus on the concept of 'problems' caused by or associated with drinking. In this approach, sick alcoholics become 'problem drinkers' whose patterns of drinking behavior are documented carefully in longitudinal or epidemiological studies. The problems approach . . . is less etiological and correctional than the disease paradigm. No underlying disease entity or mechanism is assumed to account for the drinking behavior under study. Causes . . . are inferred cautiously from empirically established relationships."

This redefinition of alcoholism as a problem rather than a disease places it in the rapidly expanding domain that includes a wide variety of behaviors with undesirable medical outcomes—poor eating habits that lead to obesity or high cholesterol, or such addictive behaviors as gambling and smoking. But the choice of labels for undesirable behavior matters only if the labeling helps in deciding how to prevent, change, or eliminate the behavior. We have suggested that describing the ways Navajos drink as a disease reduces confidence and discourages a sense of competence by implying that the behavior is involuntary. But insofar as the so-called problems paradigm eschews a concern with etiology and considers heavy drinking as an independent variable that causes problems, but not a dependent variable whose causes are to be understood, it limits the possibilities of intelligently designed prevention programs.

The argument about whether heavy drinking is a disease is far from trivial. The outcome has implications for health insurance coverage, the legal system, and the labeling and lives of people who drink a lot. Our view is, however, that there is no intrinsic characteristic that makes heavy alcohol consumption— or for that matter any other condition—a disease or some other sort of phenomenon. In any society such decisions are matters of consensus or, especially in a pluralist society such as ours, dissension. However heavy drinking is defined—whether as sin, disease, or problem—it can be studied naturalistically. It makes little difference what labels are applied so long as no common cause or uniform treatment is implied. The very ambiguity of the situation demands that we reject the notion that Navajo, or indeed all Indian, drinking is a single phenomenon ascribable to one or a few identifiable causes calling for a specific type of treatment.

Appendix A

A Retrospective Diagnosis of Psychoactive Substance Dependence according to DSM-III-R Criteria

The diagnosis of *psychoactive substance* (including alcohol) *dependence* requires:

A. That the patient meet at least three of the following criteria:
1. The substance is often taken in larger amounts or over a longer period than the person intended.
2. A persistent desire, or one or more unsuccessful efforts, to cut down or control substance use.
3. A great deal of time spent in activities necessary to get the substance, taking the substance, or recovering from its effects.
4. Frequent intoxication—or withdrawal symptoms in avoiding intoxication—when expected to fulfill major role obligations at work, school, or home (for example, does not go to work because hung over, goes to school or work high, intoxicated while taking care of his or her children), or when substance use is physically hazardous (such as: drives when intoxicated).
5. Important social, occupational, or recreational activities are given up or reduced because of substance use.
6. Substance use is continued despite a knowledge of having a persistent or recurrent social, psychological, or physical problem that is caused or exacerbated by the use of the substance.
7. Marked tolerance: a need for markedly increased

241

amounts of the substance (that is, at least a 50 percent increase) in order to achieve intoxication or a desired effect, or markedly diminished effect with continued use of the same amount.

8. Characteristic withdrawal symptoms.
9. The substance is often taken to relieve or avoid withdrawal symptoms.

B. Some symptoms of the disturbance have persisted for at least one month or have occurred repeatedly over a longer period.

Criteria for severity of *psychoactive substance dependence:*

Mild: Few, if any, symptoms in excess of those required to make the diagnosis, and the symptoms result in no more than mild impairment in occupational functioning in usual social activities or relations with others.

Moderate: Symptoms or functional impairment between *mild* and *severe.*

Severe: Many symptoms in excess of those required to make the diagnosis, and those symptoms markedly interfering with occupational functioning or with usual social activities or relations with others.

In partial remission: In the past six months, some use of the substance and some symptoms of dependence.

In full remission: In the past six months, either no use of the substance or use of the substance with no symptoms of dependence.

From the original records from 1966, we were unable to define the level of severity, but we did have enough data to determine whether people who were consuming alcohol at that time met at least three of the criteria. The information we used was as follows:

1. An item on the *preoccupation with alcohol scale* stated: "Once I start drinking it is difficult for me to stop before I get completely intoxicated." We used this to deter-

mine whether the respondent met the first criterion for alcohol dependence.

2. We had no consistent data for the second criterion: a persistent desire to cut down or control substance abuse or one or more unsuccessful efforts to do so.

3. Similarly, we had no consistent data for criterion 3, the amount of time spent getting, consuming, or recovering from alcohol use.

4. For criterion 4, dealing with the ability to fulfill role obligations and with the use of alcohol in physically hazardous ways, we had police records on driving while intoxicated, as well as a scale of *troubles due to drinking*.

5. For criterion 5, whether the individual had given up or reduced important activities, we had no consistent information.

6. For criterion 6, that the individual had continued substance despite being aware of problems, the items on the *troubles due to drinking* scale were again useful, as well as questions having to do with hematemesis, melena, and other medical consequences of alcohol use. In addition, the medical record often contained information on hospital and clinic visits for alcohol-related trauma.

7. Increased tolerance: an item on the *preoccupation scale* stated, "Alcohol has less effect on me than it used to." Paradoxically, many Navajos claimed that the longer they used alcohol, the less it took to get them drunk.

8. Characteristic withdrawal symptoms: a series of questions on the original interview asked about the presence or absence of typical withdrawal symptoms.

9. We had no consistent information on whether alcohol was taken to relieve or avoid withdrawal symptoms. One item on the *preoccupation scale*, "I take a drink the first thing when I get up in the morning," could be interpreted as addressing this issue, but we were suffi-

ciently uncertain of that interpretation that we did not use it.

Thus, we did not have consistent information on several important criteria, but enough information was available to conclude that all but one of the hospital sample people met the criteria for alcohol dependence, and that eleven of sixteen people who were currently using alcohol at the time of our first study also met the same criteria.

Appendix B
Alcohol Follow-up Questionnaire

Name: _____

1. Informant number _____
2. Community of residence _____
3. How long have you lived in this camp? _____
4. In this community? _____
5. Camp composition* _____
6. Number of own children in camp _____
7. Wage work currently? Yes _____ ; No _____
8. If yes: Employer _____ ; # months worked ____;
   Position _____ ; approximate annual salary _____
9. Unearned income (circle each source): social security; pension; ADC;† unemployment tribal welfare; other
10. Religious preference (circle all that apply): Traditional;

Note. A separate but similar "proxy" questionnaire was answered by at least two relatives of those informants who had died. The questions referred to the time immediately before the informant's death.

*From the camp composition sheet that lists each household and its members by name, sex, age, and relation to the head of the camp, code whether camp is matrilocal, patrilocal, mixed matrilocal and patrilocal, or other.

†Aid to Dependent Children

245

Native American Church; Catholic; LDC;[‡] Protestant
(give denomination) ————————————————————;
other (describe) ————————————————————

11. Have you had a sing within the past year? (circle one)
    Yes   No   Unknown

12. How many? _____

13. Which ones? (give reasons for each) _____

14. How many days did it (or they) last? _____

15. Did you have any sings two years ago? (circle one)
    Yes   No   Unknown

16. How many? _____

17. Which ones? (give reasons for each) _____

18. How many days did it (or they) last? _____

19. Did you have any sings three years ago? (circle one)
    Yes   No   Unknown

20. How many? _____

21. Which ones? (give reasons for each) _____

22. How many days did it (or they) last? _____

23. Did you have any sings four years ago? (circle one)
    Yes   No   Unknown

24. How many? _____

25. Which ones? (give reasons for each) _____

26. How many days did it (or they) last? _____

27. Did you have any sings five years ago? (circle one)
    Yes   No   Unknown

28. How many? _____

29. Which ones? (give reasons for each) _____

30. How many days did it (or they) last? _____

31. Have you been a patient at a peyote meeting this year?
    Yes   No   Unknown

32. Two years ago?   Yes   No   Unknown

33. Three years ago?   Yes   No   Unknown

‡Latter-day Saints (Mormon)

34. Four years ago?	Yes	No	Unknown
35. Five years ago?	Yes	No	Unknown

MOBILITY

36. I get around as easily as ever: (circle one)
   Yes   No   Unknown

	Check if affirmative	Score	Check if proxy answer[S]
37. I get around only within my house (or hogan or trailer).	_____	086	_____
38. I am staying in bed more.	_____	081	_____
39. I am staying in bed most of the time.	_____	109	_____
40. I stay at home most of the time.	_____	066	_____
41. I do not go to the trading post.	_____	048	_____
42. I stay away from home only for brief periods.	_____	054	_____
43. I do not get around in the dark or in unlighted places without someone's help.	_____	072	_____

BODY CARE AND MOVEMENT

	Yes	Occas.	No	Score	Proxy (if yes)
44. I make difficult moves with help, for example, getting into or out of cars or pick-ups.	___	___	___	084	_____

[S]Occasionally a relative present at the interview may provide the information.

45. I do not move in or out of bed or chairs by myself but am moved by a person or mechanical aid. ___ ___ ___ 121 ___

46. I stand only for short periods. ___ ___ ___ 072 ___

47. I do not maintain balance. ___ ___ ___ 098 ___

48. I move my hands or fingers with some limitation/difficulty. ___ ___ ___ 064 ___

49. I stand up only with someone's help. ___ ___ ___ 100 ___

50. I kneel, stoop, or bend down only by holding on to something. ___ ___ ___ 064 ___

51. I am in a restricted position all the time. ___ ___ ___ 125 ___

52. I am very clumsy in body movements. ___ ___ ___ 058 ___

53. I get in and out of bed or chairs by grasping something for support or using a cane or walker. ___ ___ ___ 082 ___

54. I stay lying down most of the time. ___ ___ ___ 113 ___

55. I change position frequently. ___ ___ ___ 030 ___

56. I hold on to something to move myself in bed. ___ ___ ___ 086 ___

57. I do not bathe myself completely but require assistance when bathing. ___ ___ ___ 089 ___

58. I do not bathe myself at all but am bathed by someone else.	___	___	___	115	___
59. I use a bedpan with assistance.	___	___	___	114	___
60. I have trouble getting on shoes, socks, or stockings.	___	___	___	057	___
61. I do not have control of my bladder.	___	___	___	124	___
62. I do not fasten my clothing, for example, I require help with buttons, zippers, shoelaces.	___	___	___	074	___
63. I spend most of the time partly undressed or in pajamas.	___	___	___	074	___
64. I do not have control of my bowels.	___	___	___	128	___
65. I dress myself, but do so very slowly.	___	___	___	043	___
66. I get dressed only with someone's help.	___	___	___	088	___

DEPRESSION BEHAVIORS (If the answer to any of these items is yes, ask the supplemental questions at the end of the scale. Remind the informant that these questions refer to the present and to the past couple of years.)

	Past month		Past year	
67. Have you had periods of at least 2 weeks during which you felt depressed and did not care about anything anymore?	Yes	No	Yes	No
68. Have there been times when you felt that you were not a good person, that you were useless and a burden to others?	Yes	No	Yes	No

69. Was there a time when you did
    not want to eat?   Yes   No   Yes   No

70. Did you ever lose a lot of weight
    when you were not trying to?   Yes   No   Yes   No

71. Have there been times when you
    had trouble going to sleep, stay-
    ing asleep, or waking too easily? Yes   No   Yes   No

72. Have there been times when you
    felt tired all the time?   Yes   No   Yes   No

73. Have there been times when you
    had to be moving all the time—
    that is, you couldn't sit still and
    had to get up and walk?   Yes   No   Yes   No

74. Has there been a time when you
    felt that life was not worth liv-
    ing and that you wanted to die? Yes   No   Yes   No

75. Have you ever thought of killing
    yourself?   Yes   No   Yes   No

76. Have you ever tried to kill your-
    self?   Yes   No   Yes   No

FOR EACH OF THE PRECEDING QUESTIONS RELATED TO
DEPRESSION, WHERE AN AFFIRMATIVE ANSWER IS
GIVEN, ASK THE FOLLOWING QUESTIONS:

77. Duration of episode?

78. When did it happen?

79. Surrounding circumstances, for example, those associated
    with an illness, loss of a loved one, etc.

80. Was there a history of similar episodes? And if so, when they started.

81. Were any of the depression questions answered by anyone other than the informant?

Yes   No

82. If yes, who was it? _____

83. Which questions? _____

PATTERNS OF ALCOHOL USE

84. How would you describe your own use of alcohol? (circle one)
Lifelong abstainer; currently an abstainer; currently drinking; other (describe)

85. For how long have you been drinking in this manner? _____

86. Could you describe a typical time within the past year when you drank? (when, where, with whom, why, how much)

_____ _____

_____ _____

_____ _____

_____ _____

DEFINITION OF ALCOHOL (Check statement[s] only if currently drinking.)

87. Alcoholic beverages make a so-
cial gathering more enjoyable.   Yes   No   ?**

88. Alcoholic beverages make me
feel more satisfied with myself.   Yes   No   ?

89. Alcoholic beverages help me
overcome shyness.   Yes   No   ?

90. Alcoholic beverages help me
to get along better with other
people.   Yes   No   ?

**Don't know.

91. Alcoholic beverages make me
    less self-conscious.   Yes   No   ?
92. Alcoholic beverages make me
    more carefree.   Yes   No   ?
93. Alcoholic beverages give me
    pleasure.   Yes   No   ?
94. A drink sometimes makes me
    feel better.   Yes   No   ?

QUANTITY-FREQUENCY

95. How much do you tend to drink at a sitting?
    1–5 glasses of beer
    1–3 bottles of beer
    1–2 drinks of liquor
    1–3 glasses of wine

    6–9 glasses of beer
    4–6 bottles of beer
    3–4 drinks of liquor
    4–5 glasses of wine

    10 or more glasses of beer
    7 or more bottles of beer
    5 or more drinks of liquor
    6 or more glasses of wine

    Other
    (Describe) ——————————————————————————
96. How often do you drink?
    At most once a month
    More than once a month
    Two to four times a month
    More than once a week

PREOCCUPATION WITH ALCOHOL.   Which statement
would you make about yourself?

97. I stay intoxicated for several
    days at a time.   Yes   No   ?
98. I worry about not being able to
    get a drink when I need one. Yes   No   ?

99. I sneak drinks when no one is
looking.   Yes   No   ?

100. Once I start drinking it is difficult for me to stop before I get
completely intoxicated.   Yes   No   ?

101. I get intoxicated on work-days.   Yes   No   ?

102. I take a drink the first thing
when I get up in the morning.   Yes   No   ?

103. I awaken the next day not
being able to remember some of
the things I had done while I
was drinking.   Yes   No   ?

104. I neglect my regular meals when
I am drinking.   Yes   No   ?

105. I don't nurse my drinks. I toss
them down pretty fast.   Yes   No   ?

106. I drink for the effect of alcohol
(with little attention to the type
of beverage or brand name).   Yes   No   ?

107. Liquor has less effect on me
than it used to.   Yes   No   ?

TROUBLE DUE TO DRINKING. These questions apply to the
previous two years.

108. Has an employer ever fired you
or threatened to fire you if you
did not cut down or quit drinking?   Yes   No   ?

109. Has your spouse or other relative ever complained that you
spend too much money for alcohol?   Yes   No   ?

110. Has your spouse ever threatened to leave you if you did not
do something about your drinking?   Yes   No   ?

111. Have you ever been picked up
by the police for intoxication or
other charges involving alcohol?   Yes   No   ?

112. Has a physician ever told you
that drinking was injuring your
health?   Yes   No   ?

MEDICAL.   These questions refer to the past two years.

113. After you have been drinking,
are you shaky and nervous?   Yes   No   ?

114. After you have been drinking,
have you ever heard voices
when no one is around?   Yes   No   ?

115. After you have been drinking,
have you ever seen strange
things that you couldn't explain, like small animals crawl-
ing on the walls?   Yes   No   ?

NOTE: If the answer to either question 114 or 115 is yes, please
describe the incidents below. What did you see, hear, etc.? How
long after drinking? How long had the drinking episode gone on?

116. Has alcohol ever been a problem for you? (If the answer to
116 is no, skip to 120)   Yes   No

117. If yes, at what age did it become a problem?   _____

118. Is alcohol still a problem?   Yes   No

119. If not, why and how did it stop being a problem?

120. If you used to drink but don't anymore, why did you stop
drinking?

LIFE HISTORY QUESTIONS

121. Wage work/occupational history/geographic mobility

122. Changing family: loss of spouse or child, deaths, marriages

123. Treatment forms: Alcoholics Anonymous, Antabuse, tribal programs, etc.

124. Serious health problems: hospitalizations (if so, where? when? what for?)

125. Do you continue to have health problems related to alcohol even after having stopped drinking?

126. Did you attend sings, NAC meetings, or have other religious experiences that occurred more than five years ago and were related to alcohol use?

127. History of alcohol use (changing styles of drinking, related events, periods of abstinence)

128. Do you think people here on the reservation use alcohol differently than when we first did this survey over twenty years ago?

Abbreviations

ADAMHA	Alcohol, Drug, and Mental Health Administration
AIM	American Indian Movement
CDC	Centers for Disease Control
CES-D	Center for Epidemiological Studies-Depression
DHIS	[Navajo Nation] Division of Health Improvement Services
DIS-D	Diagnostic Interview Schedule for Depression
DSM	*Diagnostic and Statistical Manual for Psychiatric Disorders*
DWI	driving while intoxicated
ECA	Epidemiologic Catchment Area
FAE	fetal alcohol effect
FAS	fetal alcohol syndrome
GED	graduate equivalency diploma
HIV	human immunodeficiency virus
ICDA	International Classification of Diseases Adapted
IHS	Indian Health Service
IOM	Institute of Medicine
MIRAB	*mi*gration, *r*emittance, *a*id, and *b*ureaucracies
MMFQ	Milbrook Memorial Fund Quarterly
MTU	mobile treatment unit
NAC	Native American Church
NAIHS	Navajo Area Indian Health Service
NAP	Navajo Alcohol Program

NIAAA	National Institute on Alcohol Abuse and Alcoholism
NIHB	National Indian Health Board
NIMH	National Institute of Mental Health
PHS	Public Health Service
SIP	Sickness Impact Profile

References

Aberle, D. F. 1966. *The Peyote Religion among the Navajo.* Chicago: Aldine.

———. 1973. "Navajo." In D. M. Schneider and K. Gough, eds., *Matrilineal Kinship.* Berkeley: University of California Press.

Adams, W. Y. 1963. *Shonto: A Study of the Role of the Trader in a Modern Navajo Community.* Smithsonian Institution, Bureau of American Ethnology, Bulletin 188. Washington, D.C.: U.S. Government Printing Office.

AIDSBRIEFS. 1991. "Holistic care for Native Americans." St. Paul, Minn.: American Indian Health Care Association.

American Psychiatric Association. 1987. *Diagnostic and Statistical Manual of Mental Disorders (Third Edition, Revised), DSM-III-R.* Washington, D.C.: American Psychiatric Association.

Arizona Department of Economic Security. 1990. *Arizona Statistics 2: Annual Planning Information, 1990–1991.* Phoenix: Arizona Department of Economic Security, Research Administration.

Arizona Department of Transportation. 1979–81. *Arizona Traffic Accident Summary.* Phoenix.

Babor, T. F., and Z. S. Dolinsky. 1988. "Alcoholic typologies: Historical evolution and empirical evaluation of some common classification schemes." In L. R. M. Rose and J. Barrett, eds., *Alcoholism: Origins and Outcome.* New York: Raven Press.

Bailey, G., and R. G. Bailey. 1986. *A History of the Navajos:*

The Reservation Years. Santa Fe: School of American Research Press.

Bailey, L. R. 1964. *The Long Walk: A History of the Navajo Wars, 1846–68.* Los Angeles: Westernlore Press.

Baker, S. P., R. A. Whitfield, and B. O'Neill. 1987. "Geographic variations in mortality from motor vehicle crashes." *New England Journal of Medicine* 316:1384–87.

Beckman, L. J., and H. Amaro. 1986. "Personal and social difficulties faced by women and men entering treatment." *Journal of Studies on Alcohol* 47:135–45.

Bliss, S., ed. 1985. *The New Holistic Health Handbook: Living Well in the New Age.* Lexington, Mass.: Stephen Greene Press.

Blue, M. 1988. *The Witch Purge of 1878: Oral and Documentary History in the Early Navajo Reservation Years.* Tsaile, Ariz.: Navajo Community College Press.

Boffetta, P., and L. Garfinkel. 1990. "Alcohol drinking and mortality among men enrolled in an American Cancer Society prospective study." *Epidemiology* 1:342–48.

Brady, M. 1991. "Barriers to effective interventions in Aboriginal substance abuse." Paper presented at the annual conference of the Public Health Association of Australia, Alice Springs, 29 Sept.–2 Oct.

————. 1992. *Heavy Metal: The Social Meaning of Petrol Sniffing in Australia.* Canberra: Aboriginal Studies Press.

Braiker, H. B. 1984. "Therapeutic issues in the treatment of alcoholic women." In S. Wilsnack and L. J. Beckman, eds., *Alcohol Problems of Women: Consequences and Interventions.* New York: Guilford.

Brown, D. N. 1965. "A Study of Heavy Drinking at Taos Pueblo." Tucson: University of Arizona, Department of Anthropology. Mimeo.

Brown, R. C., B. S. Gurunanjappa, R. J. Hawk, and D. Bitsuie. 1970. "The epidemiology of accidents among the Navajo Indians." *Public Health Reports* 85:881–88.

Brugge, D. M. 1983. "Navajo history and prehistory to 1850." In A. Ortiz, ed., *Handbook of North American Indians, 10, Southwest.* Washington, D.C.: Smithsonian Institution.

Burns, T. 1991. "Excerpts from the program review of the Alcoholism and Substance Abuse Programs Branch." *IHS Primary Care Provider* 16:80–82.

Cadoret, R. J., T. W. O'Gorman, E. Troughton, and E. Heywood. 1985. "Alcoholism and antisocial personality: Interrelationships, genetic and environmental factors." *Archives of General Psychiatry* 42:161–67.

Callaway, D. G., J. E. Levy, and E. B. Henderson. 1976. *The Effects of Power Production and Strip Mining on Local Navajo Populations.* Lake Powell Research Project Bulletin no. 22. Los Angeles: University of California, Institute of Geophysics and Planetary Physics.

Carter, K. C. 1977. "The germ theory, beriberi, and the deficiency theory of disease." *Medical History* 21:119–36.

————. 1985. "Koch's postulates in relation to the work of Jacob Henle and Edwin Klebs." *Medical History* 29:353–69.

Cassileth, B. R., E. J. Lusk, D. Guerry, A. D. Blake, W. P. Walsh, L. Kascius, and D. J. Shultz. 1991. "Survival and quality of life among patients receiving unproven as compared with conventional cancer therapy." *New England Journal of Medicine* 324:1180–85.

Chronkite, R. C., and Moos, R. H. 1980. "Determinants of the posttreatment functioning of alcoholic patients: A conceptual framework." *Journal of Consulting and Clinical Psychology* 48:305–16.

Cloninger, C. R., K. O. Christiansen, T. Reich, and I. I. Gottesman. 1978. "Implications of sex differences in the prevalences of antisocial personality, alcoholism, and criminality for familial transmission." *Archives of General Psychiatry* 35:941–51.

Committee on Interior and Insular Affairs. 1974. *Report of the Committee on Interior and Insular Affairs, United States Senate, together with Additional Views to Accompany S. 2938 (Indian Health Care Improvement Act.* Washington, D.C.: U.S. Government Printing Office.

Conrad, P., and J. W. Schneider. 1985. *Deviance and Medicalization: From Badness to Sickness.* Columbus: Merrill.

Cotton, N. S. 1979. "The familial incidence of alcoholism: A review." *Journal of Studies on Alcohol* 40:89–116.

Crane, L. 1915. Narrative section of the *Annual Report for the Moqui Indian Reservation.* U.S. Department of the Interior, Indian Service. Photocopy.

Crookshank, F. G. 1926. Introduction to *An Introduction to the History of Medicine,* ed. C. G. Cumston. New York: Alfred A. Knopf.

de Gennaro, N. 1990. *Arizona statistical abstract: A 1990 data handbook*. University of Arizona, Division of Economic and Business Research.

Devor, E. J., and C. R. Cloninger. 1989. "Genetics of alcoholism." *Annual Review of Genetics* 23:19–36.

Dozier, E. P. 1966. "Problem drinking among American Indians: The role of socio-cultural deprivation." *Quarterly Journal of Studies on Alcohol* 27:72–87.

Drew, L. R. H. 1968. "Alcoholism as a self-limiting disease." *Quarterly Journal of Studies on Alcohol* 29:956–67.

Driver, H. E. 1969. *Indians of North America*. 2d rev. ed., Chicago: University of Chicago Press.

Dyck, N., ed. 1985. *Indigenous Peoples and the Nation-State: Fourth World Politics in Canada, Australia, and Norway*. Social and Economic Papers, no. 14. St. John's Newfoundland, Canada: Memorial University of Newfoundland, Institute of Social and Economic Research.

Dyk, W. 1947. *A Navajo Autobiography*. Viking Fund Publications in Anthropology, no. 8.

Edwards, G. 1984. "Drinking in longitudinal perspective: Career and natural history." *British Journal of Addiction* 75:175–83.

Engel, G. L. 1977. "The need for a new medical model: A challenge for biomedicine." *Science* 196:129–36.

English-Lueck, J. A. 1990. *Health in the New Age: A Study in California Holistic Practices*. Albuquerque: University of New Mexico Press.

Ensel, W. M. 1982. "The role of age in the relationship of gender and marital status to depression." *Journal of Nervous and Mental Disease* 170:536–43.

Fallers, L. A. 1965. *Bantu Bureaucracy: A Century of Political Evolution among the Basoga of Uganda*. Chicago: University of Chicago Press.

Fe Caces, M., F. S. Stinson, and S. D. Elliott. 1991. *County Alcohol Problem Indicators, 1979–1985*. U.S. Alcohol Epidemiologic Data Reference Manual, vol. 3, 3d ed. Rockville, Md.: National Institute on Alcohol Abuse and Alcoholism.

Feighner, J. P., E. Robins, S. B. Guze, R. A. Woodruff, G. Winokur, R. Munoz. 1972. "Diagnostic criteria for use in psychiatric research." *Archives of General Psychiatry* 26:57–63.

Ferguson, F. N. 1968. "Navaho drinking: Some tentative hypotheses." *Human Organization* 27:156–67.

——. 1970. "A treatment program for Navaho alcoholics: Results after four years." *Quarterly Journal of Studies on Alcohol* 31:898–919.

Field, P. B. 1962. "A new cross-cultural study of drunkenness." In D. J. Pittman and C. R. Snyder, eds., *Society, Culture, and Drinking Patterns*. New York: Wiley.

Fillmore, K. M. 1988. *Alcohol Use across the Life Course: A Critical Review of Seventy Years of International Longitudinal Research*. Toronto: Addiction Research Foundation.

Fingarette, H. 1988. *Heavy Drinking: The Myth of Alcoholism as a Disease*. Berkeley: University of California Press.

Finney, J. W., and R. H. Moos. 1991. "The long-term course of treated alcoholism: I, Mortality, relapse and remissions rates and comparisons with community controls." *Journal of Studies on Alcohol* 52:44–54.

——. 1992. "The long-term course of treated alcoholism: II, Predictors and correlates of ten-year functioning and mortality." *Journal of Studies on Alcohol* 53:142–53.

Franciscan Fathers. 1910. *Ethnological Dictionary of the Navaho Language*. St. Michaels, Ariz.: Franciscan Fathers.

Gilligan, S. B., T. Reich, and C. R. Cloninger. 1987. "Etiologic heterogeneity in alcoholism." *Genetic Epidemiology* 4:395–414.

Goffman, E. 1961. "The moral career of the mental patient." In E. Goffman, *Asylums: Essays on the Social Situation of Mental Patients and Other Inmates*. Garden City, N.Y.: Anchor Books.

Gordon, R. J. 1987. *Arizona Rural Health Provider Atlas*. University of Arizona, Department of Family and Community Medicine.

Grant, B. F., T. S. Zobeck, and R. P. Pickering. 1990. *Liver Cirrhosis Mortality in the United States, 1973–1987*. Surveillance report no. 15. Rockville, Md.: U.S. Department of Health and Human Services, National Institute of Alcohol Abuse and Alcoholism, Division of Biometry and Epidemiology, Alcohol Epidemiologic Data System, PHS, ADAMHA.

Graves, T. D. 1970. "The personal adjustment of Navajo Indian migrants to Denver, Colorado." *American Anthropologist* 72:35–54.

Greenberg, E. R., C. G. Chute, T. Stukel, J. A. Baron, D. H. Freeman, J. Yates, and R. Korson. 1988. "Social and economic factors in the choice of lung cancer treatment." *New England Journal of Medicine* 318:612–17.

Greer, A. L. 1977. "Advances in the study of diffusion of innovation in health care organizations." *MMFQ/Health and Society* 55:505–32.

Gregg, J. [1845] 1954. *Commerce of the Prairies*. M. L. Moorehead, ed. Norman: University of Oklahoma Press.

Hackney, S. 1969. "Southern Violence." In H. G. Graham and T. R. Gurr, eds., *Violence in America: Historical and Comparative Perspectives, A Report to the National Commission on the Causes and Prevention of Violence, June 1969*. New York: Signet Books, New American Library.

Hall, R. L. 1986. "Alcohol treatment in American Indian populations: An indigenous treatment modality compared with traditional approaches." *Annals of the New York Academy of Sciences* 472:168–78.

Hammerschlag, C. A. 1988. *The Dancing Healers: A Doctor's Journey of Healing with Native Americans*. San Francisco: Harper and Row.

Harner, M. 1990. *The Way of the Shaman*. San Francisco: Harper and Row.

Heath, D. B. 1958. "Drinking patterns of the Bolivian Camba." *Quarterly Journal of Studies on Alcohol* 19:491–508.

Heinerman, J. 1989. *Spiritual Wisdom of the Native Americans*. San Rafael, Calif.: Cassandra Press.

Helzer, J. E., and T. R. Pryzbeck. 1988. "The co-occurrence of alcoholism with other psychiatric disorders in the general population and its impact on treatment." *Journal of Studies on Alcohol* 49:219–24.

Helzer, J. E., L. N. Robins, and J. R. Taylor. 1985. "The extent of long-term moderate drinking among alcoholics discharged from medical and psychiatric treatment facilities." *New England Journal of Medicine* 312:1678–82.

Henderson, E. B. 1985. "Status and Social Change among the Western Navajo." Ph.D. diss., University of Arizona, Department of Anthropology, Tucson.

Hesselbrock, V. M. 1986. "Family history of psychopathology in alcoholics: A review and issues." In R. E. Meyer, ed., *Psychopathology and Addictive Disorders*. New York: Guilford.

Hill, T. W. 1974. "From hell-raiser to family man." In J. Spradley and D. McCurdy, eds., *Conformity and Conflict: Readings in Cultural Anthropology,* 2d ed. Boston: Little, Brown.

Horton, D. 1943. "The function of alcohol in primitive societies." *Quarterly Journal of Studies on Alcohol* 4:199–320.

Indian Health Service (IHS). 1970. *1968 Indian Vital Statistics: Navajo Area.* Tucson: U.S. Department of Health, Education, and Welfare, Health Program Systems Center, Indian Health Service.

———. 1971. *Indian Health Trends and Services, 1970 Edition.* PHS Publication 2092. Washington, D.C.: U.S. Department of Health, Education and Welfare, Office of of Program Planning and Evaluation, Program Analysis and Statistics Branch, Indian Health Service.

———. 1975. *Navajo Area Mortality Report, Fiscal Year 1974.* Window Rock, Ariz.: Navajo Area Indian Health Service, Office of Program Planning and Evaluation.

———. 1987. *IHS Alcoholism/Substance Abuse Prevention Initiative.* Rockville, Md.: U.S. Department of Health and Human Services, Public Health Service, Health Resources and Services Administration, IHS, Office of Health Programs, Alcoholism/Substance Abuse Program Branch.

Institute of Medicine (IOM). 1990. *Broadening the Base of Treatment for Alcohol Problems.* Washington, D.C.: National Academy of Sciences Press.

Jessor, R., T. D. Graves, R. C. Hanson, and S. L. Jessor. 1968. *Society, Personality, and Deviant Behavior: A Study of a Tri-ethnic Community.* New York: Holt, Rinehart, and Winston.

Jorgensen, J. G. 1980. *Western Indians: Comparative Environments, Languages, and Cultures of 172 Western American Tribes.* San Francisco: W. H. Freeman.

Katz, P. S., and P. A. May. 1979. *Motor Vehicle Accidents on the Navajo Reservation, 1973–1975.* Window Rock, Ariz.: Navajo Health Authority.

Kendell, R. E. 1989. "Clinical validity." *Psychological Medicine* 19:45–55.

Kendler, K. S., A. C. Heath, M. C. Neale, R. C. Kessler, and L. J. Eaves. 1993. "A population-based twin study of alcoholism in women." *Journal of the American Medical Association* 268:1877–82.

Kivlahan, D. R., R. D. Walker, D. M. Donovan, and H. D. Mischkel. 1985. "Detoxification recidivism among urban American Indian alcoholics." *American Journal of Psychiatry* 142:1467–70.

Kluckhohn, C. [1944] 1962. *Navaho Witchcraft.* Boston: Beacon.

Kluckhohn, C., and D. C. Leighton. 1946. *The Navaho.* Cambridge: Harvard University Press.

Kunitz, S. J. 1983. *Disease Change and the Role of Medicine: The Navajo Experience.* Berkeley: University of California Press.

———. 1987. "Explanations and ideologies of mortality patterns." *Population and Development Review* 13:379–408.

———. 1988. "Hookworm and pellagra: Exemplary diseases in the new South." *Journal of Health and Behavior* 29:139–48.

Kunitz, S. J., and J. E. Levy. 1974. "Changing ideas of alcohol use among Navajo Indians." *Quarterly Journal of Studies on Alcohol* 35:243–59.

———. 1991. *Navajo Aging: From Family to Institutional Support.* Tucson: University of Arizona Press.

Kunitz, S. J., J. E. Levy, and M. Everett. 1969. "Alcoholic cirrhosis among the Navaho." *Quarterly Journal of Studies on Alcohol* 30:672–85.

Kunitz, S. J., J. E. Levy, C. L. Odoroff, and J. Bollinger. 1971. "The epidemiology of alcoholic cirrhosis in two Southwestern Indian tribes." *Quarterly Journal of Studies on Alcohol* 32:706–20.

La Barre, W. 1964. *The Peyote Cult.* New enl. ed. Hamden, Conn.: Shoe String Press.

Lake, Medicine Grizzlybear. 1991. *Native Healer: Initiation into an Ancient Art.* Wheaton, Ill.: Quest Books, Theosophical Publishing House.

Lanternari, V. 1963. *The Religions of the Oppressed: A Study of Modern Messianic Cults.* Trans. Lisa Sergio. New York: Alfred A. Knopf.

Lemert, E. M. 1956. "Alcoholism and the sociocultural situation." *Quarterly Journal of Studies on Alcohol* 17:306–17.

Lender, M. E., and J. K. Martin. 1987. *Drinking in America: A History.* New York: Free Press.

Levine, D. N. 1985. *The Flight from Ambiguity: Essays in Social and Cultural Theory.* Chicago: University of Chicago Press.

Levy, J. E. 1965. "Navajo suicide." *Human Organization* 24:308–18.

———. 1983. "Traditional Navajo health beliefs and practices." In

S. J. Kunitz, *Disease Change and the Role of Medicine*. Berkeley: University of California Press.

———. 1992. "Comments on May's alcohol policy considerations for Indian reservations and bordertown communities." *Journal of the National Center for American Indian and Alaska Native Mental Health Research* 4:95–100.

Levy, J. E., E. B. Henderson, and T. J. Andrew. 1989. "The effects of regional variation and temporal change on matrilineal elements of Navajo social organization." *Journal of Anthropological Research* 45:351–77.

Levy, J. E., and S. J. Kunitz. 1971. "Indian reservations, anomie, and social pathologies." *Southwestern Journal of Anthropology* 27:97–128.

———. 1973. "Indian drinking: Problems of data collection and interpretation." In *Proceedings of the First Annual Alcoholism Conference of the National Institute on Alcohol Abuse and Alcoholism*. Washington, D.C.: U.S. Public Health Service, U.S. Government Printing Office.

———. 1974. *Indian Drinking: Navajo Practices and Anglo-American Theories*. New York: Wiley.

———. 1981. "Economic and political factors inhibiting the use of basic research findings in Indian alcoholism programs." *Journal of Studies on Alcohol* 9 (supp.): 60–72

Levy, J. E., S. J. Kunitz, and M. Everett. 1969. "Navajo criminal homicide." *Southwestern Journal of Anthropology* 25:124–52

Levy, J. E., S. J. Kunitz, and E. B. Henderson. 1987. "Hopi deviance in historical and epidemiological perspective." In Joseph Jorgensen and Leland Donald, eds., *Themes in Ethnology and Culture History: Essays in Honor of David F. Aberle*. Berkeley: Folklore Institute.

Levy, J. E., R. Neutra, and D. Parker. 1987. *Hand Trembling, Frenzy Witchcraft, and Moth Madness: A Study of Navajo Seizure Disorders*. Tucson: University of Arizona Press.

Longabaugh, R. 1988. "Longitudinal outcome studies." In R. M. Rose and J. E. Barrett, eds., *Alcoholism: Origins and Outcome*. New York: Raven Press.

MacAndrew, C., and R. B. Edgerton. 1969. *Drunken Comportment: A Social Explanation*. Chicago: Aldine.

McDonald, F. 1988. "Prologue." In Grady McWhiney, *Cracker Cul-*

ture: Celtic Ways in the Old South. Tuscaloosa: University of Alabama Press.

MacGregor, G. 1946. *Warriors without Weapons.* Chicago: University of Chicago Press.

McGue, M., R. W. Pickens, and D. X. Sivkis. 1992. "Sex and age effects on the inheritance of alcohol problems: A twin study." *Journal of Abnormal Psychology* 101:3–17.

McNitt, F. 1962. *The Indian Traders.* Norman: University of Oklahoma Press.

McWhiney, G. 1988. *Cracker Culture: Celtic Ways in the Old South.* Tuscaloosa: University of Alabama Press.

Madsen, W., and C. Madsen. 1969. "The cultural structure of Mexican drinking." *Quarterly Journal of Studies on Alcohol* 30:701–18.

Mails, T. E. 1988. *Secret Native American Pathways: A Guide to Inner Peace.* Tulsa: Council Oak Books.

Manual, G., and M. Poslums. 1974. *The Fourth World: An Indian Reality.* New York: Free Press.

Marjot, D. H. 1970. "The length of the drinking bout preceding alcohol withdrawal states." *British Journal of Addiction* 64:307–14.

Marshall, M., ed. 1979. *Beliefs, Behaviors, and Alcoholic Beverages: A Cross-Cultural Survey.* Ann Arbor: University of Michigan Press.

Maulitz, R. C. 1979. "'Physician versus bacteriologist': The ideology of science in clinical medicine." In M. J. Vogel and C. E. Rosenberg, eds., *The Therapeutic Revolution.* Philadelphia: University of Pennsylvania Press.

May, P. A. 1986. "Alcohol and drug misuse prevention programs for American Indians: Needs and opportunities." *Journal of Studies on Alcohol* 47:187–95.

———. 1992. "Alcohol policy considerations for Indian reservations and bordertown communities." *Journal of the National Center for American Indian and Alaska Native Mental Health Research* 4:5–63.

May, P. A., K. J. Hymbaugh, J. M. Aase, and J. M. Samet. 1983. "Epidemiology of fetal alcohol syndrome among American Indians of the Southwest." *Social Biology* 30:374–87.

May, P. A., and M. B. Smith. 1988. "Some Navajo Indian opinions about alcohol abuse and prohibition: A survey and recommendations for policy." *Journal of Studies on Alcohol* 49:324–34.

Melton, J. G. 1991. *New Age Almanac.* Detroit: Visible Ink Press.

Merikangas, K. R. 1990. "The genetic epidemiology of alcoholism." *Psychological Medicine* 20:11–22.

Merton, R. K. 1968. *Social Theory and Social Structure.* New York: Free Press.

Mills, C. W. 1959. *The Sociological Imagination.* Oxford: Oxford University Press.

National Center for Health Statistics. 1959–88. *Vital Statistics of the United States, 1959–1988.* Vol. 2, *Mortality.* Hyattsville, Md.: U.S. Department of Health and Human Services.

———. 1970. *Motor Vehicle Accident Deaths in the United States, 1950–1967.* Vital and Health Statistics, series 20, no. 9. Rockville, Md.

National Indian Health Book (NIHB). 1980. "Indian nurses conference examines problems of diabetes holistic health care, and changing role of nurses in Indian communities." *NIHB Health Reporter* 2.8–10.

National Institute on Alcohol Abuse and Alcoholism (NIAAA). 1985. *Alcoholism. An Inherited Disease.* Rockville, Md.: U.S. Department of Health and Human Services, Public Health Service, Alcohol, Drug Abuse, and Mental Health Association.

Navajo Area Indian Health Service (NAIHS). 1988. *Area Profile.* Window Rock, Ariz.: U.S. Department of Health and Human Services, Office of Program Planning and Development.

———. 1989. *1986 Natality-Mortality Report.* Window Rock, Ariz.: U.S. Department of Health and Human Services, Office of Program Planning and Development.

———. 1990. *Health Statistics Report: Alcohol-Related Mortality/ Morbidity and Violence.* Window Rock, Ariz.: U.S. Public Health Service, Office of Program Planning and Development.

Navajo Tribe. 1987. *Tribal Action Plan: Developed in Response to the Omnibus Drug Act of 1986, P.L. 99–570.* Window Rock, Ariz.: Navajo Nation.

Navajo Year Book. 1958. *The Navajo Yearbook: Report No. 7.* Ed. Robert W. Young. Window Rock, Ariz.: Navajo Agency.

Newhouse, S. R., and J. Amodeo. 1985. "Native American healing." In S. Bliss, ed., *The New Holistic Health Handbook*. Lexington, Mass.: Stephen Greene Press.

Peele, S. 1986. "The implications and limitations of genetic models of alcoholism and other addictions." *Journal of Studies on Alcohol* 47:63–73.

Peterson, S. 1990. *Native American Prophecies: Examining the History, Wisdom and Startling Predictions of Visionary Native Americans*. New York: Paragon House.

Phelps Stokes Fund. 1939. *The Navajo Indian Problem*. New York.

Polich, J. M., D. J. Armor, and H. B. Braiker. 1981. *The Course of Alcoholism: Four Years after Treatment*. New York: Wiley.

Redfield, R. 1955. *The Little Community: Viewpoints for the Study of a Human Whole*. Chicago: University of Chicago Press.

Rhoades, E. R., R. D. Mason, P. Eddy, E. M. Smith, and T. R. Burns. 1988. "The Indian Health Service approach to alcoholism among American Indians and Alaska natives." *Public Health Reports* 103:621–27.

Robins, L. N., J. E. Helzer, J. Croughan, and K. Ratcliff. 1981. "The National Institute of Mental Health diagnostic interview schedule: Its history, characteristics and validity." *Archives of General Psychiatry* 38:381–89.

Robins, L. N., J. E. Helzer, J. Croughan, J. B. W. Williams, and R. L. Spitzer. 1981. "NIMH diagnostic interview schedule: Version III." Bethesda: National Institute of Mental Health.

Room, R. 1983. "Sociology and the disease concept of alcoholism." In *Research Advances in Alcohol and Drug Problems*, vol. 7. New York: Plenum.

Rorabaugh, W. J. 1979. *The Alcoholic Republic: An American Tradition*. Oxford: Oxford University Press.

Rosenberg, C. E. 1979. "The therapeutic revolution: Medicine, meaning, and social change in nineteenth-century America." In M. J. Vogel and C. E. Rosenberg, eds., *The Therapeutic Revolution*. Philadelphia: University of Pennsylvania Press.

Savard, R. J. 1968. "Effects of disulfiram therapy on relationships within the Navajo drinking group." *Quarterly Journal of Studies on Alcohol* 29:909–16.

Searles, J. S. 1988. "The role of genetics in the pathogenesis of alcoholism." *Journal of Abnormal Psychology* 97:153–67.

Shepardson, M. 1963. *Navajo Ways in Government: A Study in Political Process.* American Anthropological Association, Memoir 96. Menasha, Wisconsin.

Shore, J. H. 1975. "American Indian suicide: Fact and fancy." *Psychiatry* 38:86–91.

Simmons, O. G. 1962. "Ambivalence and the learning of drinking behavior in a Peruvian community." In D. J. Pittman and C. R. Snyder, eds., *Society, Culture, and Drinking Patterns.* New York: Wiley.

Slotkin, J. S. 1956. *The Peyote Religion: A Study in Indian-White Relations.* Glencoe, Ill.: Free Press.

Spicer, E. H. 1962. *Cycles of Conquest.* Tucson: University of Arizona Press.

Sun Bear, Wabun, and B. Weinstock. 1987. *The Path of Power.* New York: Prentice Hall.

Tabakoff, B., and P. L. Hoffman. 1988. "Genetics and biological markers of risk for alcoholism." *Public Health Reports* 103:690–98.

Topper, M. D. 1985. "Navajo 'Alcoholism': Drinking, Alcohol Abuse, and Treatment in a Changing Cultural Environment." In L. A. Bennett and G. M. Ames, eds., *The American Experience with Alcohol: Contrasting Cultural Perspectives.* New York: Plenum.

Topper, M. D., and J. Curtis. 1987. "Extended family therapy: A clinical approach to the treatment of synergistic dual anomic depression among Navajo agency-town adolescents." *Journal of Community Psychology* 15:334–48.

U.S. Census Bureau. 1973. *Statistical Abstract of the United States: 1973.* 94th ed. Washington, D.C.

———. *Census of the Population, 1960–1990.* Vol. 1, *Characteristics of the Population.* Washington, D.C.

Underhill, R. 1956. *The Navajos.* Norman: University of Oklahoma Press.

Vaillant, G. E. 1983. *The Natural History of Alcoholism: Causes, Patterns, and Paths to Recovery.* Cambridge: Harvard University Press.

———. 1988. "Some differential effects of genes and environment on alcoholism." In R. M. Rose and J. Barrett, eds., *Alcoholism: Origins and Outcome.* New York: Raven.

Valley National Bank of Arizona. 1984. *Arizona Statistical Review.* Phoenix.

VanValkenburgh, R. 1948. "Navajo Naat'aani." *Kiva* 13:14–23.

Warner, J. H. 1986. *The Therapeutic Perspective: Medical Practice, Knowledge, and Identity in America 1820–1885.* Cambridge: Harvard University Press.

Weibel-Orlando, J. 1987. "Culture-specific treatment modalities: Assessing client-to-treatment fit in Indian alcoholism programs." *Treatment and Prevention of Alcohol Problems: A Resource Manual.* New York: Academic.

————. 1989. "Hooked on healing: Anthropologists, alcohol and intervention." *Human Organization* 48:148–55.

Westermeyer, J. 1989. "Nontreatment factors affecting treatment outcome in substance abuse." *American Journal of Drug and Alcohol Abuse* 15:13–29.

Westermeyer, J., and E. Peake. 1983. "A ten-year follow-up of alcoholic Native Americans in Minnesota." *American Journal of Psychiatry* 140:189–94.

Westermeyer, J., and J. Neider. 1986. "Cultural affiliation among American Indian alcoholics: Correlations and change over a ten year period." *Annals of the New York Academy of Science* 472:179–88.

Williams, A. W., Jr. 1970. *Navajo Political Process.* Washington, D.C.: Smithsonian Institution Press.

Williams, G. D., F. S. Stinson, S. D. Brooks, and J. Noble. 1991. *Apparent Per Capita Alcohol Consumption: National, State and Regional Trends, 1977–1988.* Rockville, Md.: U.S. Department of Health and Human Services, PHS, ADAMHA, National Institute on Alcohol Abuse and Alcoholism, Division of Biometry and Epidemiology, Alcohol Epidemiologic Data System.

Wilson, L. G., and J. H. Shore. 1975. "Evaluation of a regional Indian alcohol program." *American Journal of Psychiatry* 132:255–58.

Wolfe, S., and M. Victor. 1970. "The physiological basis of the alcohol withdrawal syndrome." Paper presented at the Symposium on Recent Advances in Studies on Alcoholism. Sponsored by the National Center for Prevention and Control of Alcoholism, National Institutes of Mental Health, Washington, D.C., 25–27 June 1970.

World Almanac. 1989. *The World Almanac and Book of Facts, 1990.* New York: Pharos Books.

Wyman, L., and C. Kluckhohn. 1938. *Navajo Classification of Their Song Ceremonials.* American Anthropological Association Memoir 50.

Wyman, L. C., and B. B Thorne. 1945. "Notes on Navajo suicide." *American Anthropologist* 47:278–88.

Young, Robert W., and William Morgan. 1980. *The Navajo Language: A Grammar and Colloquial Dictionary.* Albuquerque: University of New Mexico Press.

Zinberg, N. E. 1984. *Drug, Set, and Setting: The Basis for Controlled Intoxicant Use.* New Haven: Yale University Press.

Zobeck, T. S., S. D. Elliott, B. F. Grant, and D. Bertolucci. 1991. *Trends in Alcohol-Related Fatal Traffic Crashes, United States: 1977–1988.* Surveillance report no. 17. Rockville, Md.: U.S. Department of Health and Human Services, PHS, ADAMHA, National Institute on Alcohol Abuse and Alcoholism, Division of Biometry and Epidemiology, Alcohol Epidemiologic Data System.

Zung, W. W. 1965. "A self rating depression scale." *Archives of General Psychiatry* 12:63–70.

Index

Aberle, David F., 23, 27
Aborigines, 2, 231
abstinence from alcohol, 8, 29, 102, 125–26; survival patterns and, 75, 77, 80, 81; reasons for, 110–14; groups compared, 226–27, 228
accidents, 51, 185 86, 228 See also motor vehicle accidents
acculturation, 5, 21, 137, 194; impact of, 66–68, 181, 188–91
agave wine, 12
agencies for alcohol problems, 201–2, 205
agency towns, 9
age of drinkers, 29, 34, 48–49, 53, 55–57, 180; survival patterns, 75, 76–77, 78–83, 86, 94
alcoholism: anxiety hypothesis and, 22; biological causes of, 30, 33, 34–35, 230; as disease, 32, 40, 114, 125–26, 238–39; inherited, 34–35, 166–67, 190; psychiatric causes of, 37–39, 42–43; redefined, 238–39
American Indian Movement (AIM), 215

Amhara society, 199
Anglo mortality data, 177, 178, 180, 182, 185, 186, 229–30
anomie theory, 21, 22
Antabuse, 4, 85, 235; use of, 44–45, 75–77, 165–66, 222
Apache Indians, 12, 13, 14, 52n
Arizona, 173, 178. See also mortality rates (regional)
Armor, D. J., 43
arrests, 8, 20, 85, 86
availability of alcohol, 5–6, 6, 176, 128, 129, 134, 137, 228

barter economy, 20
beer, 12
binge drinking, 16, 17, 20–21, 22–23, 100, 126
Black, Robert, 19
black Americans, 35–36
boarding school experience, 66
bootlegging, 18, 19, 142, 145, 153, 164, 165
bordertown group, 4–5
Brady, Maggie, 231
Braiker, H. B., 43
brandy, 13, 14

Brugge, David, 13
Busoga people, 198, 199

Calhoun, James S., 15
"career" model, 39–42
cash economy, 20
cause and course, 29, 30, 31, 32
ceremonies, 114–17, 120, 131–32.
   See also religious values; traditional healing; treatment programs
Charger, Rufus, 197
Christianity, 28, 112, 113, 116
cirrhosis, 6, 47, 63, 86, 228; among
   Hopis, 41–42, 137; mortality rates
   for, 51–54; regions compared,
   175, 176, 179–81, 182
classification of drinkers, 36–39, 44
community control ideology, 7, 196,
   222
community influence, 125–29, 191,
   231, 232, 236; nature of, 9; and
   kin group erosion, 130–33; adaptations in, 134–38
Conrad, Peter, 238
controlled drinking, 8, 29, 43
Cox model, 72, 73, 74
Coyote in myth, 114
Crookshank, F. G., 30
culture: preservation of, 194–95,
   221. See also sociocultural
   factors

Definition of Alcohol scales, 104
depression, 8–9, 86–87, 88, 89, 95;
   among men, 106–8; among
   women, 118, 126; groups compared, 227, 228; questionnaire for,
   249–51
Depression (1930–40), 19–20
deviance theory, 21–22
"deviant" behavior, 8

diagnosis of alcohol dependence,
   109–10
diagnostic adequacy, 50
diseases related to alcohol, 62. See
   also cirrhosis
dislocation of Navajos, 23
dram drinking, 16–17
Drew, Leslie, 43
drinking careers: characteristics of,
   99–103
"drinking ethic," 12
drinking styles, 1–2, 3; new, 180–81,
   188–89, 229
Drunken Comportment (MacAndrew
   and Edgerton), 20
"drunken Indian" image, 169–70
Durkheim, Emile, 21

economic change. See livestock reduction; wage labor
Edgerton, Robert B., 20, 22,
   231
education, 10, 11, 102, 103, 116,
   135, 223–24
Edwards, Griffith, 39
employment, 221
empowerment, 194–95, 221
Enemy Way, 18
Engel, George, 218
environmental factors, 167, 176,
   185–86, 188, 228, 231
epilepsy, 41, 124
ethnic pride, 220, 221
Europeans, 1–2, 3, 12

Fallers, Lloyd, 198
family participation, 166, 235
family responsibilities, 111
family study, 139, 164–67; first generation drinkers, 140–46; daughters, 146–51; sons, 151–59; third

generation, 159–63; fourth generation, 163–64
Feighner, J. P., 38, 39
Ferguson, Frances, 44
fetal alcohol syndrome, 65, 163–64, 166, 224, 235
Field, Peter, 22
Fillmore, Kaye, 34
Fisher's Exact Test, 86, 89
Flagstaff, Ariz., 3, 4, 9, 64, 65, 70, 75
Fourth World politics, 193, 210–11, 220
Franciscan Fathers, 18
Freesoul, John Redtail, 215
fur companies, 172
Fustel de Coulanges, Numa-Denys, 21

Ganado Mucho, 24
germ theory, 32, 37
Goffman, Erving, 40
Goldberger, Joseph, 33
Graves, Theodore, 22

Hackney, S., 170
Hall, R. L., 209n
Hammerschlag, Carl, 213
Harner, Michael, 212
healing ritual, 113, 194–95, 201. See also traditional healing
health, 111–12
Henderson, Eric, 127, 135
homicide, 6, 47, 137; data for, 58–61, 62, 63; case study, 89–91; regions compared, 171, 176; groups compared, 186–87, 188, 228
Hopi Indians, 19, 136, 137, 214, 233, 234; cirrhosis among, 41, 42, 52
Horton, Donald, 22

hospital group, 70, 74, 75, 77, 82, 88
house parties, 66, 101

incest, 124, 125
Indian Health Service (IHS), 49, 59, 191, 195
individual responsibility, 217
innovation, 21
isolation drinking. See solitary drinking

Jefferson, Thomas, 170
Jessor, Richard, 22
job responsibility, 111

Katz, P. S., 57, 182
kin groups, 3–4, 70, 100, 137–38, 165, 188, 228; erosion of, 129–33
Kivlahan, Daniel, 45
Kluckhohn, Clyde, 21, 24
Koch, Robert, 32

Lake, Medicine Grizzlybear, 214
lawsuits, 210
least traditional communities, 3–4
legislation regarding alcohol abuse, 193–94, 223
Leighton, Dorothea, 21
Levine, Donald, 199
Levy, Jerrold, 41
livestock reduction, 3–4, 26–27, 229; effects of, 128, 129, 131, 133–34
locals as health workers, 194, 196
Longabaugh, Richard, 44
longitudinal alcohol studies, 29–31; in nonclinical populations, 31–36; in clinical populations, 36–39, 43–46; models, 39–42

MacAndrew, Craig, 20, 22, 231
McDonald, Forrest, 170
McWhiney, Grady, 170
Mails, Thomas, 213
Maine, Henry, 21
maize beer, 18
Mann-Whitney U-test, 82, 83, 86
Manuel, George, 210–11
Manuelito, 24–25
Marshall, Mac, 232, 234
Marx, Karl, 21
May, P. A., 57, 64, 182, 190
medical facilities, 7, 173, 175,
  183–84
men drinkers, 34, 101; drinking sta-
  tus, 103–6; self-perception of,
  108–10; abstinence in, 110–14;
  ceremonial treatment for, 114–17.
  See also depression; family study
mental illness, 113
Merton, Robert, 21
mesquite wine, 12
Mexicans, 14, 15
MIRAB states, 200–201
"Moral Career of the Mental Patient,
  The" (Goffman), 40
Morgan, Louis Henry, 21
mortality rates (general), 43, 47–50,
  66–68; ecological correlations,
  61–63; and patterns of alcohol
  use, 64–65; sexes compared, 76–
  77, 84; non-alcoholic-related, 93–
  94. *See also* cirrhosis; homicide;
  motor vehicle accidents; suicide;
  survival patterns
mortality rates (regional): factors
  in, 168–69; North and South,
  170–72; regions compared,
  173–75; counties compared,
  177–79; change of perception of,
  189–91

motor vehicle accidents, 6–7, 47, 63,
  93; mortality rates for, 54–57; regions compared, 173, 175, 176,
  181–86

National Institute on Alcohol Abuse
  and Alcoholism (NIAAA), 193, 194,
  195
Native American Church (NAC), 28,
  114, 236; value of, 110, 111,
  208–9; ethical code of, 112–13
"natural history" model, 39–42
Navajo drinking, 2–6; early history
  of, 12–17; in twentieth century,
  19–28; types of, 66–67
Navajo language, 206
Navajo Nation Mobile Treatment
  Unit, 205–7
Navajo Police Department, 49, 59
Navajo Tribal Action Plan, 196, 197,
  217
Neider, J., 45
New Age: ideas, 210–12, 236, 237;
  Indian tradition and, 213–21; soci-
  eties, 214–15
New Deal, 20
New Holistic Health Handbook, The
  (Bliss), 214
New Mexico, 173, 178. *See also*
  mortality rates (regional)

Papago Indians, 12
paraprofessionalization, 195, 210
Parsons, Talcott, 198
pastoral economy. *See* livestock reduction
Peake, E., 45
peer pressure, 120–21
peyote religion, 27–28, 112–13, 115,
  120, 147, 148, 158. *See also*
  Native American Church

Phelps Stokes Fund, 20
Pima Indians, 12
Plateau group, 3–4, 9, 103–4; mortality data for, 64, 65; survival patterns, 69–70, 74. *See also* community influence
population statistics, 48–49, 50, 178–79
posttreatment phenomena, 44
predictive validity, 38–39, 43
Preoccupation with Alcohol scales, 99, 104, 242–43, 252–53
Prohibition, 19–20
psychoactive substance dependency, 241–44
public opinion, 210, 211
Pueblo groups, 13, 14, 15

Quantity-Frequency measure, 95

reasons for drinking, 190; theories regarding, 20–25; drinkers' views of, 25–28
reasons to stop drinking, 255
rebellion, 71
recovery rates, 103
recreational opportunities, 232–33
religious values, 13, 110, 111–13, 201, 206, 207, 236–37
remission of drinking, 34, 43, 126, 228
reservation society, 71. *See also* kin groups; Plateau group; South Tuba group
residence: effects of, 102–3, 120
retreatism, 21, 24, 26
Riordan, Timothy, 25
ritualism, 21
River Yuma Indians, 12

road improvement, 6–7, 20, 129, 179, 182, 229
Robert Wood Johnson Foundation, 209*n*
Rolling Thunder, 214
Rorabaugh, William, 17
rural populations, 177, 178, 189–90, 229–30

Savard, Robert, 44
Schneider, Joseph, 238
Secret Native American Pathways (Mails), 213
self-help, 237
self-image, 191, 237
self-perception of drinkers, 108, 120–21
sex-specific data, 48–49, 53, 66; in accidents, 55–57; survival patterns in, 74–75, 78–83, 85–86, 97–98. *See also* men drinkers; women drinkers
sexual abuse, 126
Shepardson, Mary, 199, 200
Shore, J. H., 45, 169
Shoshone-Bannock Indians, 169
sings, 219, 237. *See also* traditional healing; treatment programs
Sioux aggression, 21–22
slave trade, 14
Smith, M. B., 64, 190
smoking, 35
sober societies, 22
social disorganization, 21
social drinking, 8–9, 103, 107, 226, 227, 228
social support for programs, 166
social systems, 199–202
sociocultural factors, 39, 45–46, 120–21, 194, 234–35; in

sociocultural factors (continued)
responses to drinking, 40–42; and
types of drinking, 66–67
solitary drinking, 8–9, 11, 66, 101;
depression and, 107–8; women
and, 117, 118, 119; groups compared, 226, 227, 228, 234
South Tuba group, 136–38; mortality data for, 64, 65; survival patterns in, 70, 74, 75, 88. *See also*
family study
Spanish in Southwest, 13, 14
"spiritual ecology," 212–13
"Squaw dances," 18
Stone-Brown, Sidney, 197
styles of drinking, 100–103
suicide, 6, 47, 89; data for, 58–61,
62, 63; case study, 91–93; factors
in, 107–8, 169; groups compared,
137, 186–87, 188, 228; regions
compared, 169, 171, 173, 176
survival patterns, 69–71; analysis
methods for, 72–74; factors in,
87–89, 95–98. *See also individual
groups*
sweat lodge, 205, 209*n*, 215, 237

"Taos lightning," 15
telephones, 184
Tönnies, Ferdinand, 21
Topper, Martin, 66, 67, 68, 113
trading forts, 14, 15
traditional communities, 3–4. *See
also* Plateau group
traditional healing: bureaucratization
of, 198–201, 206–10; "code list"
for, 202–5
transitional communities, 3–4. *See
also* South Tuba group
treatment programs, 10, 238; effects
of, 43–44, 45; ceremonial treat-

ment, 114–17; development of,
192–98; innovations in, 223–25
troubles due to drinking scale, 243,
253
Tuba City. *See* South Tuba group
types of drinking, 75

Underhill, Ruth, 24, 25
urban populations, 177–78, 179,
189–90

Vaillant, George, 34, 35, 125

wage labor, 129, 133, 134, 188, 229;
effects of, 66, 136, 137
Weber, Max, 21
Weibel-Orlando, Joan, 197
Westermeyer, Joseph, 45
whiskey, 14, 16, 18, 25, 128, 171–72
Williams, Aubrey, 200
Wilson, Lawrence, 45
wine, 12, 13, 14
Winslow, Ariz., 64, 65
witchcraft, 24, 113, 124
withdrawal symptoms, 8–9, 104–6,
118, 119
women drinkers, 18, 34, 65, 144,
230, 233; in clinical sample, 7–9;
sex for alcohol and, 66, 101–2;
survival patterns of, 75, 76, 78,
80, 82, 89, 98; drinking styles of,
117–19; reasons for drinking,
121–22; case studies, 122–25;
empty-nest phenomenon in, 138.
See also family study
World War II, 5, 129, 188

Zinberg, Norman, 231
Zuni Indians, 12, 14–15, 52